MICHAEL DOUGHERTY PRESENTS

KRAMPUS

SHADOW OF SAINT NICHOLAS

LEGENDARY

A **LEGENDARY COMICS** PRODUCTION
PRESENTED BY **MICHAEL DOUGHERTY**

KRAMPUS
SHADOW OF SAINT NICHOLAS

STORIES BY
TODD CASEY & MICHAEL DOUGHERTY & ZACH SHIELDS

WRITTEN BY
ZACH SHIELDS & TODD CASEY

CO-WRITTEN BY
LAURA SHIELDS (STORY II)

I
ART BY
CHRISTIAN DIBARI
COLORS BY
MIKE SPICER

II
ART BY
MAAN HOUSE
COLORS BY
GUY MAJOR

III
ART BY
STUART SAYGER
COLORS BY
GUY MAJOR

IV
ART BY
MICHAEL MONTENAT
COLORS BY
MIKE SPICER

LETTERING BY **A LARGER WORLD STUDIOS**   COVER ART BY **FIONA STAPLES**
BOOK DESIGNED BY **JOHN J. HILL**   EDITED BY **ROBERT NAPTON**

SPECIAL THANKS TO **ALEX GARCIA, BARNABY LEGG, SHIRIT BRADLEY, & BENJAMIN WRIGHT**

LEGENDARY

THOMAS TULL Chairman and Chief Executive Officer
JON JASHNI President and Chief Creative Officer   **MARTY WILLHITE** Chief Operating Officer & General Counsel   **ALEX GARCIA** Executive Vice President, Creative Affairs
EMILY CASTEL Chief Marketing Officer   **JESSICA KANTOR** VP, Business and Legal Affairs   **BARNABY LEGG** VP, Theatrical Marketing
DANIEL FEINBERG VP, Corporate Counsel   **PEARL WIBLE** Director, Digital Content   **MANSI PATEL** VP, Creative Services

LEGENDARY COMICS
BOB SCHRECK Senior Vice President, Editor-in-Chief   **ROBERT NAPTON** Vice President, Editorial Director
DAVID SADOVE Publishing Operations Coordinator   **GREG TUMBARELLO** Editor
Published by **LEGENDARY COMICS** - 2900 West Alameda Ave Suite 1500 Burbank, CA 91505

INTRODUCTION

I've never been a fan of Christmas parties. While I've always loved the holiday itself, the traditional yuletide gathering usually conjured a mix of social anxiety, family obligation, or awkward interactions with drunken co-workers. Christmas parties also paled in comparison to Halloween festivities, drowning us in pre-sold fake cheer dressed up in tacky sweaters, lacking the mischievous fun-loving shadow that we get to unleash every October 31st. In fact, for those of us who love Halloween above all other holidays, the first of November is usually a day of mourning as we watch stores replace bats and witches with reindeer and elves virtually overnight.

Sure, Christmas was fun but something always felt like it was missing. As if the holiday's true origins were being purposely hidden from us, candy-coated in peppermint and gingerbread, drowned in egg nog, and whitewashed by saccharin movies and TV specials. Christmas felt like it was hiding something, and it turns out that just by scratching a little at its glossy surface something darker and more mysterious could be found lurking. Because just like Halloween, Easter, and other holidays we attribute to Judeo-Christian beliefs, it turns out the winter holidays belonged to the pagans long before department stores, and their version of a yuletide gathering was a lot more interesting than your typical Secret Santa gift exchange.

It also turns out Christmas' main mascot was hiding something. Santa Claus had a shadow, a mischievous counterpart who was mostly forgotten over the centuries but has slowly resurfaced to reclaim his proper place next to the jolly fat elf. Sporting cloven hooves, huge horns, a serpentine tongue, and a sack full of naughty children to haul off to the underworld, Krampus was everything that Christmas was missing. A dispenser of punishments instead of gifts, here was a guy who could bring a healthy dose of Halloween-style fear and fun to the party. It was love at first sight.

Bringing Krampus to the big screen was always the main goal, but in order to introduce him to as many as people as possible, my cohorts and I knew we needed to build a nest for him in comic books as well. His mythology and history was too big and too rich to be contained to one movie, and after centuries of waiting in the shadows, it only made sense to give the Christmas Devil his due. My partners, Todd Casey and Zach Shields have thrown together one hell of a Christmas party with a guest list that includes some of the most talented writers and artists working today, including Laura Shields, Christian Dibari (*The Warriors*), Maan House (*Witchblade*), Stuart Sayger (*Bionicle*), Michael Montenat (*Hellraiser*), and the magical Fiona Staples (*Saga*) once again lending her dark arts for our cover. Like a *Krampusnacht* parade full of rampaging heathens, they've embraced the Christmas Devil's mischievous nature and whipped up stories full of drunken mall Santas, sadistic elves, and guilty souls yearning for holiday redemption.

Some of you might be new to Krampus, others may have heard him whispered about over the years. Either way, we hope this collection of stories will only deepen your love of the character and the holiday itself while also giving you something to talk about the next time you find yourself bored at a Christmas party, and maybe even give you pause the next time you hear something on the roof…

Merry Krampus!

Michael Dougherty

September 2015

I

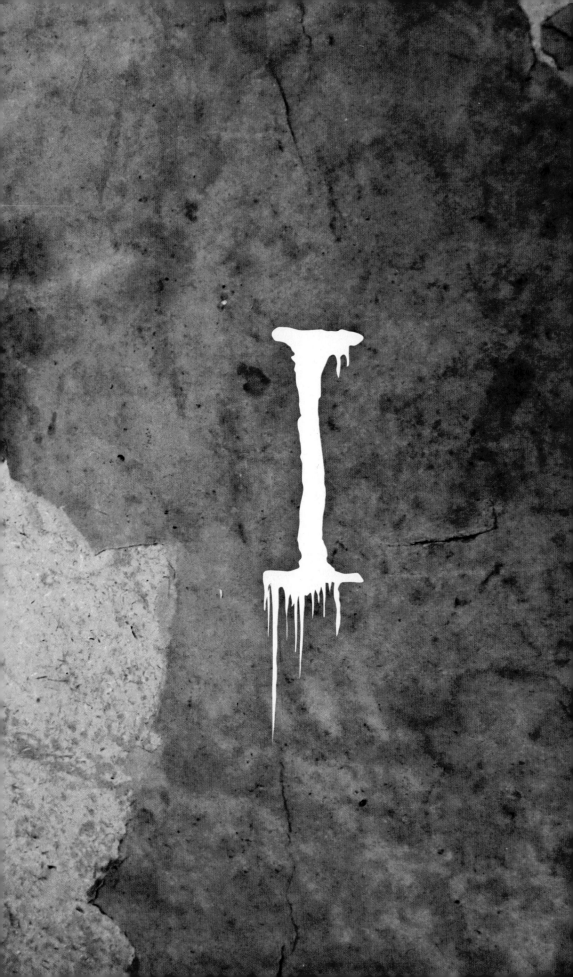

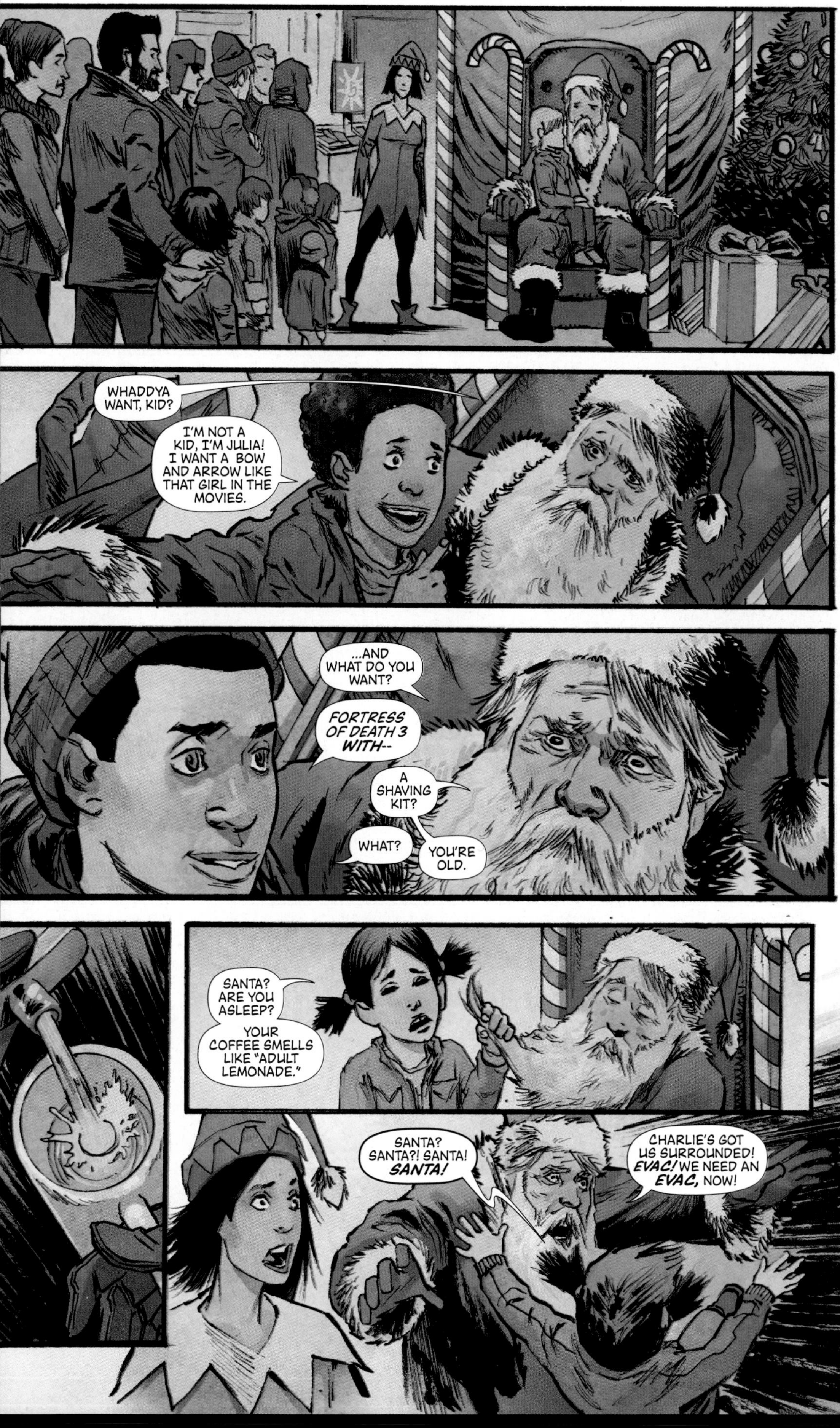
WHADDYA WANT, KID?
I'M NOT A KID, I'M JULIA! I WANT A BOW AND ARROW LIKE THAT GIRL IN THE MOVIES.
...AND WHAT DO YOU WANT?
FORTRESS OF DEATH 3 WITH--
A SHAVING KIT?
WHAT?
YOU'RE OLD.
SANTA? ARE YOU ASLEEP?
YOUR COFFEE SMELLS LIKE "ADULT LEMONADE."
SANTA? SANTA?! SANTA! SANTA!
CHARLIE'S GOT US SURROUNDED! EVAC! WE NEED AN EVAC, NOW!

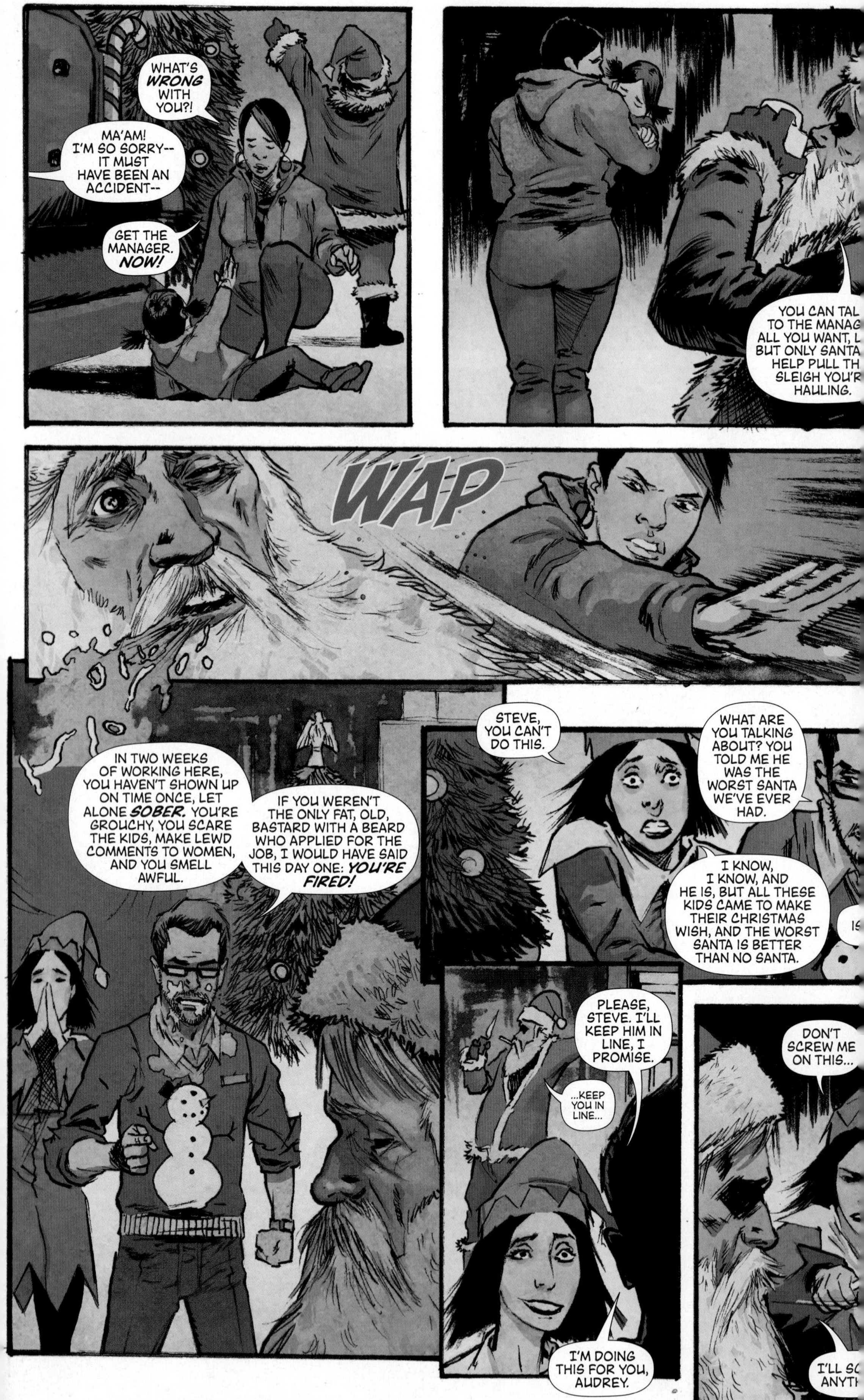
WHAT'S WRONG WITH YOU?!
MA'AM! I'M SO SORRY-- IT MUST HAVE BEEN AN ACCIDENT--
GET THE MANAGER. NOW!
YOU CAN TAL TO THE MANAG ALL YOU WANT, L BUT ONLY SANTA HELP PULL TH SLEIGH YOU'R HAULING.
WAP
IN TWO WEEKS OF WORKING HERE, YOU HAVEN'T SHOWN UP ON TIME ONCE, LET ALONE SOBER. YOU'RE GROUCHY, YOU SCARE THE KIDS, MAKE LEWD COMMENTS TO WOMEN, AND YOU SMELL AWFUL.
IF YOU WEREN'T THE ONLY FAT, OLD, BASTARD WITH A BEARD WHO APPLIED FOR THE JOB, I WOULD HAVE SAID THIS DAY ONE: YOU'RE FIRED!
STEVE, YOU CAN'T DO THIS.
WHAT ARE YOU TALKING ABOUT? YOU TOLD ME HE WAS THE WORST SANTA WE'VE EVER HAD.
I KNOW, I KNOW, AND HE IS, BUT ALL THESE KIDS CAME TO MAKE THEIR CHRISTMAS WISH, AND THE WORST SANTA IS BETTER THAN NO SANTA.
PLEASE, STEVE. I'LL KEEP HIM IN LINE, I PROMISE.
...KEEP YOU IN LINE...
I'M DOING THIS FOR YOU, AUDREY.
DON'T SCREW ME ON THIS...
I'LL SC ANYTH

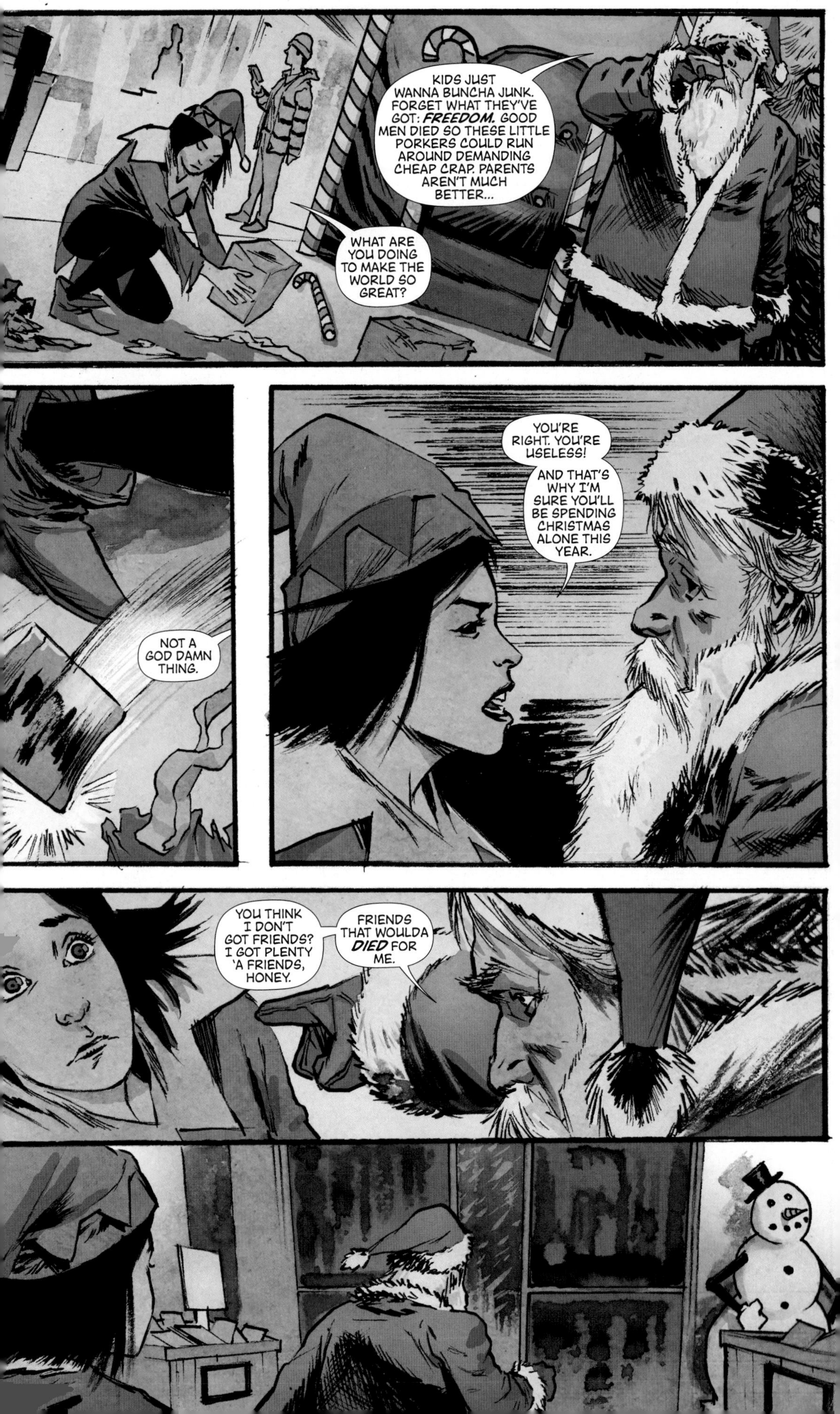
KIDS JUST WANNA BUNCHA JUNK. FORGET WHAT THEY'VE GOT: FREEDOM. GOOD MEN DIED SO THESE LITTLE PORKERS COULD RUN AROUND DEMANDING CHEAP CRAP. PARENTS AREN'T MUCH BETTER...
WHAT ARE YOU DOING TO MAKE THE WORLD SO GREAT?
NOT A GOD DAMN THING.
YOU'RE RIGHT. YOU'RE USELESS!
AND THAT'S WHY I'M SURE YOU'LL BE SPENDING CHRISTMAS ALONE THIS YEAR.
YOU THINK I DON'T GOT FRIENDS? I GOT PLENTY 'A FRIENDS, HONEY.
FRIENDS THAT WOULDA DIED FOR ME.

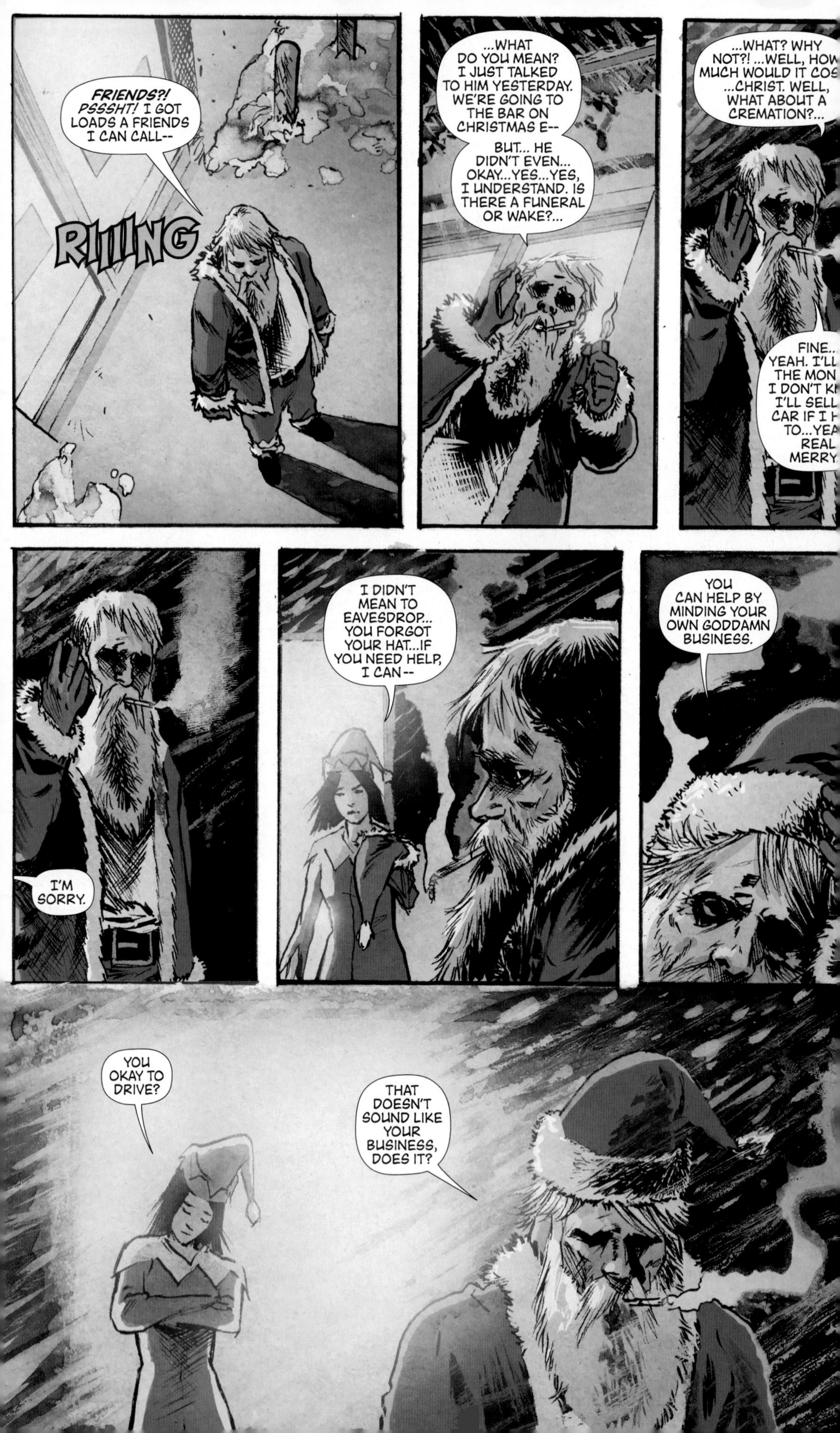

FRIENDS?! PSSSHT! I GOT LOADS A FRIENDS I CAN CALL--
RIIIING
...WHAT DO YOU MEAN? I JUST TALKED TO HIM YESTERDAY. WE'RE GOING TO THE BAR ON CHRISTMAS E--
BUT... HE DIDN'T EVEN... OKAY...YES...YES, I UNDERSTAND. IS THERE A FUNERAL OR WAKE?...
...WHAT? WHY NOT?! ...WELL, HOW MUCH WOULD IT COS ...CHRIST. WELL, WHAT ABOUT A CREMATION?...
FINE... YEAH. I'LL THE MON I DON'T K I'LL SELL CAR IF I TO...YEA REAL MERRY
I'M SORRY.
I DIDN'T MEAN TO EAVESDROP... YOU FORGOT YOUR HAT...IF YOU NEED HELP, I CAN--
YOU CAN HELP BY MINDING YOUR OWN GODDAMN BUSINESS.
YOU OKAY TO DRIVE?
THAT DOESN'T SOUND LIKE YOUR BUSINESS, DOES IT?

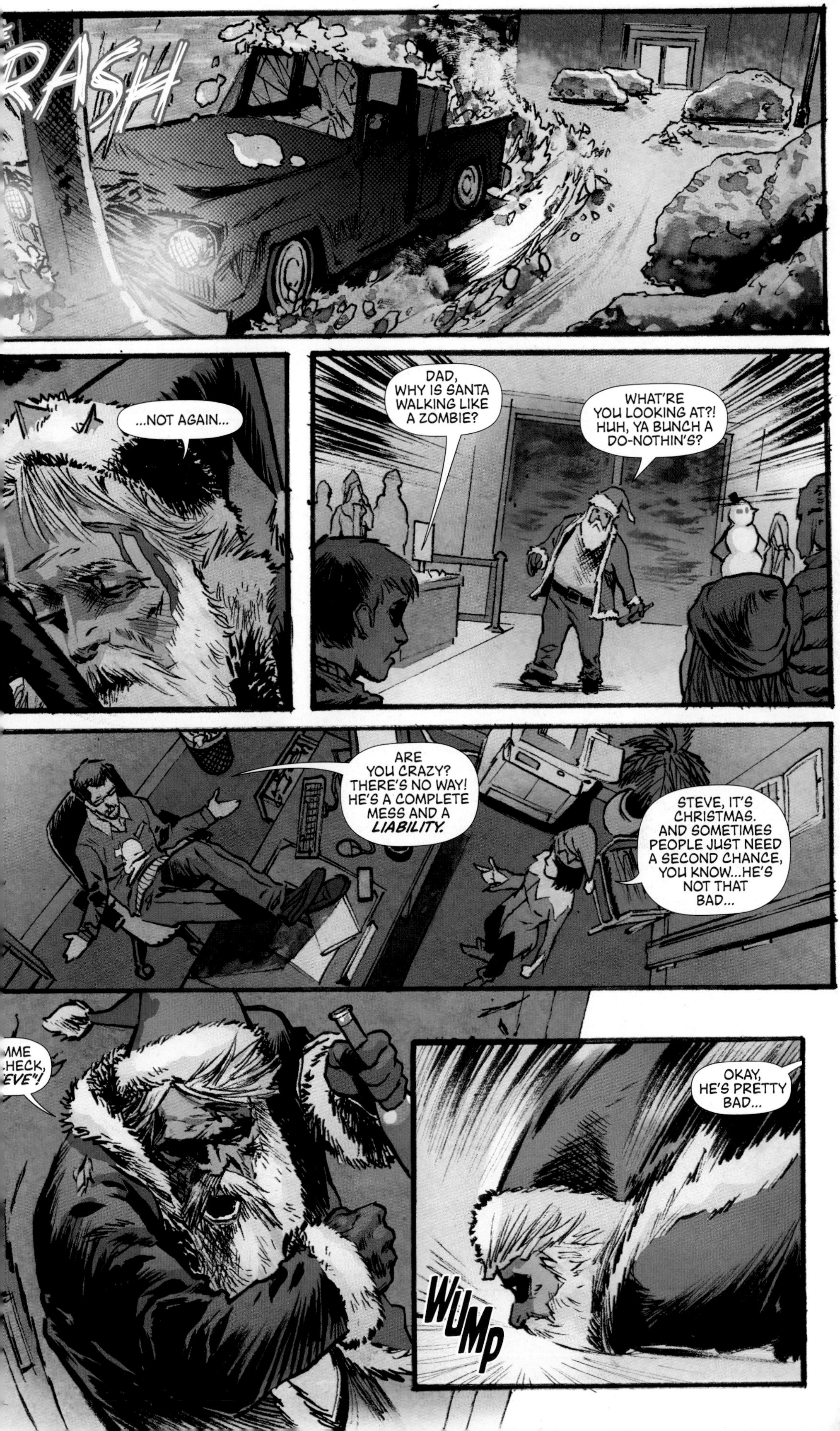
RASH
...NOT AGAIN...
DAD, WHY IS SANTA WALKING LIKE A ZOMBIE?
WHAT'RE YOU LOOKING AT?! HUH, YA BUNCH A DO-NOTHIN'S?
ARE YOU CRAZY? THERE'S NO WAY! HE'S A COMPLETE MESS AND A ***LIABILITY.***
STEVE, IT'S CHRISTMAS. AND SOMETIMES PEOPLE JUST NEED A SECOND CHANCE, YOU KNOW...HE'S NOT THAT BAD...
MME HECK, EVE"!
OKAY, HE'S PRETTY BAD...
WUMP

WHAT THE...?

UUUUUUUUGGHHH

YOU PASSED OUT. AND THEN... WELL, A LOT OF STUFF HAPPENED...

I HOPE I'M NOT PREGNANT.

HA...BUT SERIOUSLY, WE'RE, UH, WE'RE STUCK HERE...SOMETHING CRAZY HAPPENED WITH THE WEATHER AND NOW THERE'S LIKE THIRTY PEOPLE - INCLUDING A FEW KIDS, STUCK IN THE STORE.

"STUCK"? I DON'T THINK SO, SISTER, I GOT A PROMISE TO KEEP.

AREN'T YO FORGETTIN SOMETHIN LIKE HOW YOU KINDA CRASHEI YOUR CAR

BUT EVEN IF YOU HAD A CAR, THE WHOLE CITY IS ON LOCKDOWN. THEY'RE TELLING EVERYONE TO STAY INSIDE BECAUSE THE ROADS ARE TOO DANGEROUS, BUT I THINK THERE'S MORE TO IT. I'VE BEEN HEARING A LOT OF SIRENS.

ANY OTHER GOOD NEWS?

THEY SAID TO EXPECT POWER OUTAGES...

AH, CRAP.

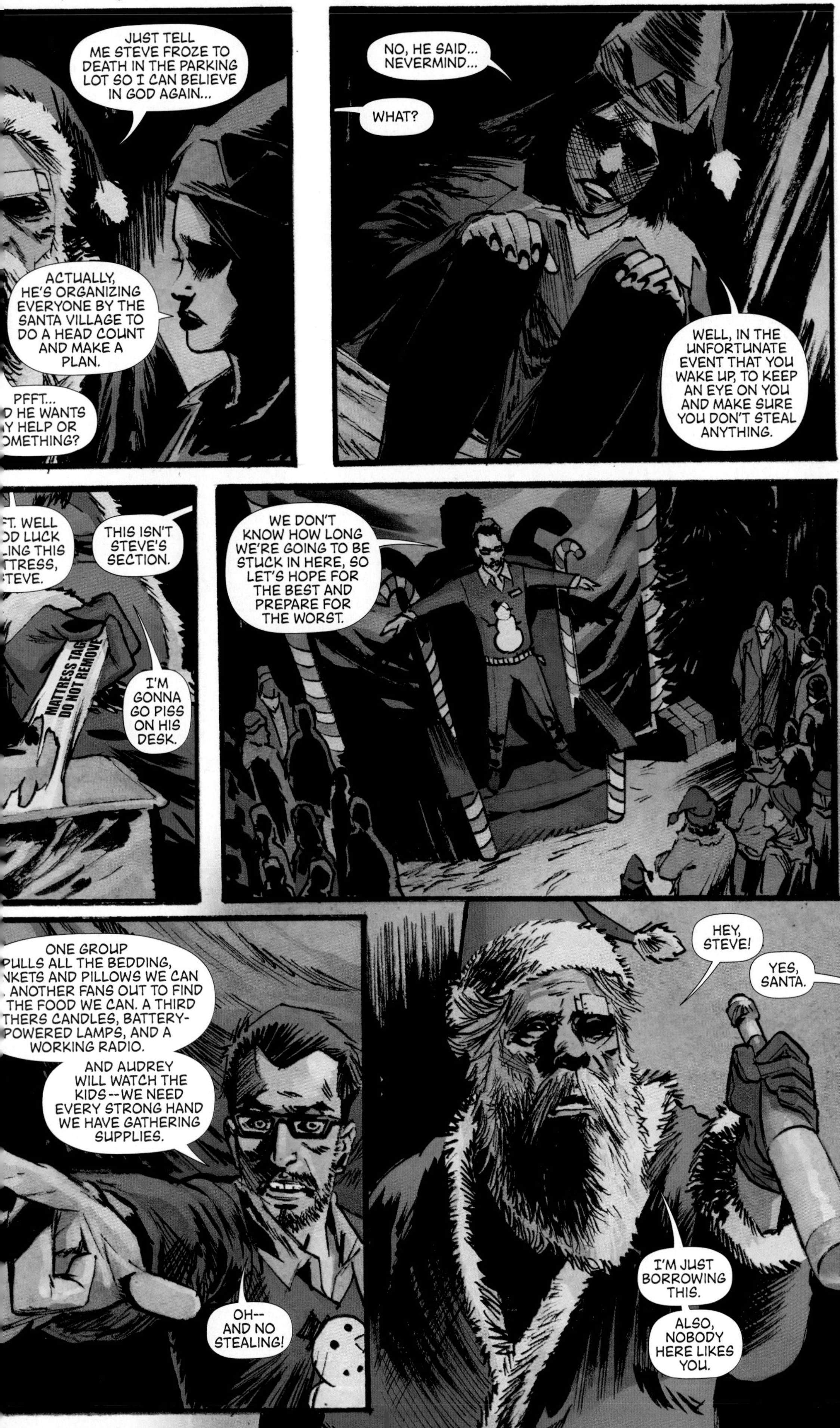
JUST TELL ME STEVE FROZE TO DEATH IN THE PARKING LOT SO I CAN BELIEVE IN GOD AGAIN...
ACTUALLY, HE'S ORGANIZING EVERYONE BY THE SANTA VILLAGE TO DO A HEAD COUNT AND MAKE A PLAN.
PFFT... D HE WANTS Y HELP OR OMETHING?
NO, HE SAID... NEVERMIND...
WHAT?
WELL, IN THE UNFORTUNATE EVENT THAT YOU WAKE UP, TO KEEP AN EYE ON YOU AND MAKE SURE YOU DON'T STEAL ANYTHING.
FT. WELL DD LUCK LING THIS TTRESS, TEVE.
THIS ISN'T STEVE'S SECTION.
MATTRESS TAG DO NOT REMOVE
I'M GONNA GO PISS ON HIS DESK.
WE DON'T KNOW HOW LONG WE'RE GOING TO BE STUCK IN HERE, SO LET'S HOPE FOR THE BEST AND PREPARE FOR THE WORST.
ONE GROUP PULLS ALL THE BEDDING, NKETS AND PILLOWS WE CAN , ANOTHER FANS OUT TO FIND THE FOOD WE CAN. A THIRD THERS CANDLES, BATTERY-POWERED LAMPS, AND A WORKING RADIO.
AND AUDREY WILL WATCH THE KIDS--WE NEED EVERY STRONG HAND WE HAVE GATHERING SUPPLIES.
OH-- AND NO STEALING!
HEY, STEVE!
YES, SANTA.
I'M JUST BORROWING THIS.
ALSO, NOBODY HERE LIKES YOU.

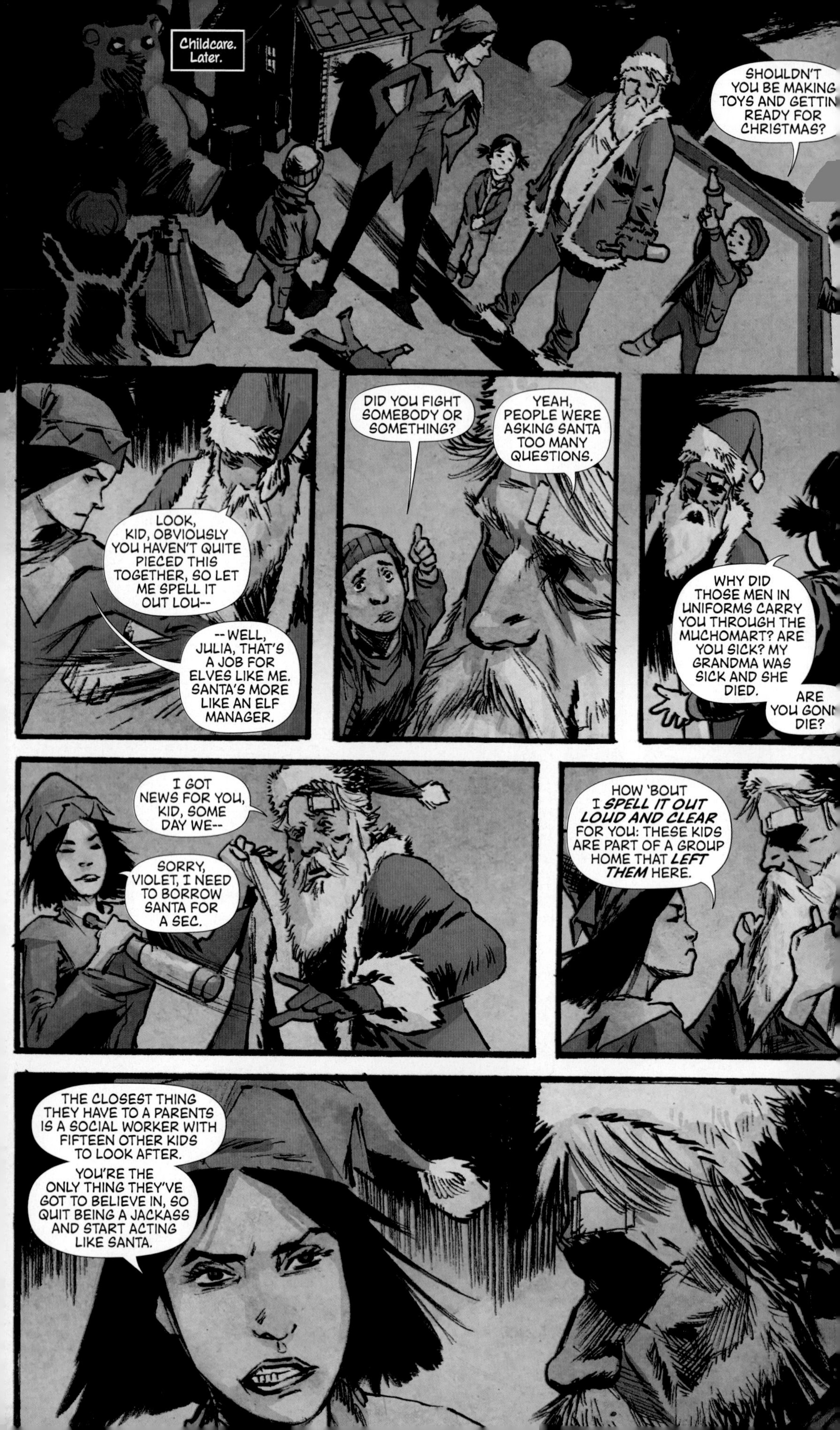
Childcare. Later.
SHOULDN'T YOU BE MAKING TOYS AND GETTIN READY FOR CHRISTMAS?
LOOK, KID, OBVIOUSLY YOU HAVEN'T QUITE PIECED THIS TOGETHER, SO LET ME SPELL IT OUT LOU--
--WELL, JULIA, THAT'S A JOB FOR ELVES LIKE ME. SANTA'S MORE LIKE AN ELF MANAGER.
DID YOU FIGHT SOMEBODY OR SOMETHING?
YEAH, PEOPLE WERE ASKING SANTA TOO MANY QUESTIONS.
WHY DID THOSE MEN IN UNIFORMS CARRY YOU THROUGH THE MUCHOMART? ARE YOU SICK? MY GRANDMA WAS SICK AND SHE DIED.
ARE YOU GONN DIE?
I GOT NEWS FOR YOU, KID, SOME DAY WE--
SORRY, VIOLET, I NEED TO BORROW SANTA FOR A SEC.
HOW 'BOUT I SPELL IT OUT LOUD AND CLEAR FOR YOU: THESE KIDS ARE PART OF A GROUP HOME THAT LEFT THEM HERE.
THE CLOSEST THING THEY HAVE TO A PARENTS IS A SOCIAL WORKER WITH FIFTEEN OTHER KIDS TO LOOK AFTER.
YOU'RE THE ONLY THING THEY'VE GOT TO BELIEVE IN, SO QUIT BEING A JACKASS AND START ACTING LIKE SANTA.

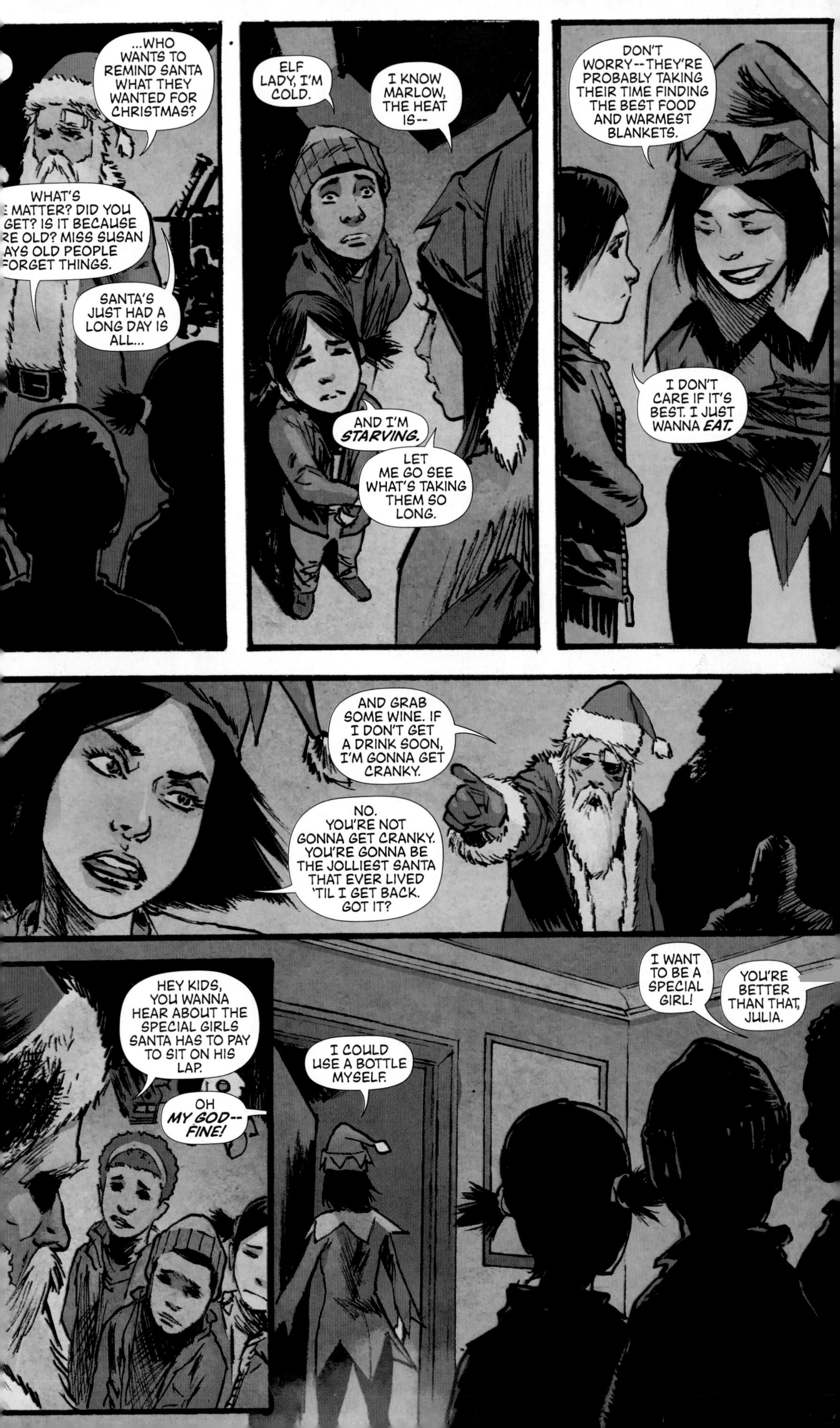
...WHO WANTS TO REMIND SANTA WHAT THEY WANTED FOR CHRISTMAS?
WHAT'S E MATTER? DID YOU GET? IS IT BECAUSE RE OLD? MISS SUSAN AYS OLD PEOPLE FORGET THINGS.
SANTA'S JUST HAD A LONG DAY IS ALL...
ELF LADY, I'M COLD.
I KNOW MARLOW, THE HEAT IS--
AND I'M STARVING.
LET ME GO SEE WHAT'S TAKING THEM SO LONG.
DON'T WORRY--THEY'RE PROBABLY TAKING THEIR TIME FINDING THE BEST FOOD AND WARMEST BLANKETS.
I DON'T CARE IF IT'S BEST. I JUST WANNA EAT.
AND GRAB SOME WINE. IF I DON'T GET A DRINK SOON, I'M GONNA GET CRANKY.
NO. YOU'RE NOT GONNA GET CRANKY. YOU'RE GONNA BE THE JOLLIEST SANTA THAT EVER LIVED 'TIL I GET BACK. GOT IT?
HEY KIDS, YOU WANNA HEAR ABOUT THE SPECIAL GIRLS SANTA HAS TO PAY TO SIT ON HIS LAP.
OH MY GOD-- FINE!
I COULD USE A BOTTLE MYSELF.
I WANT TO BE A SPECIAL GIRL!
YOU'RE BETTER THAN THAT, JULIA.

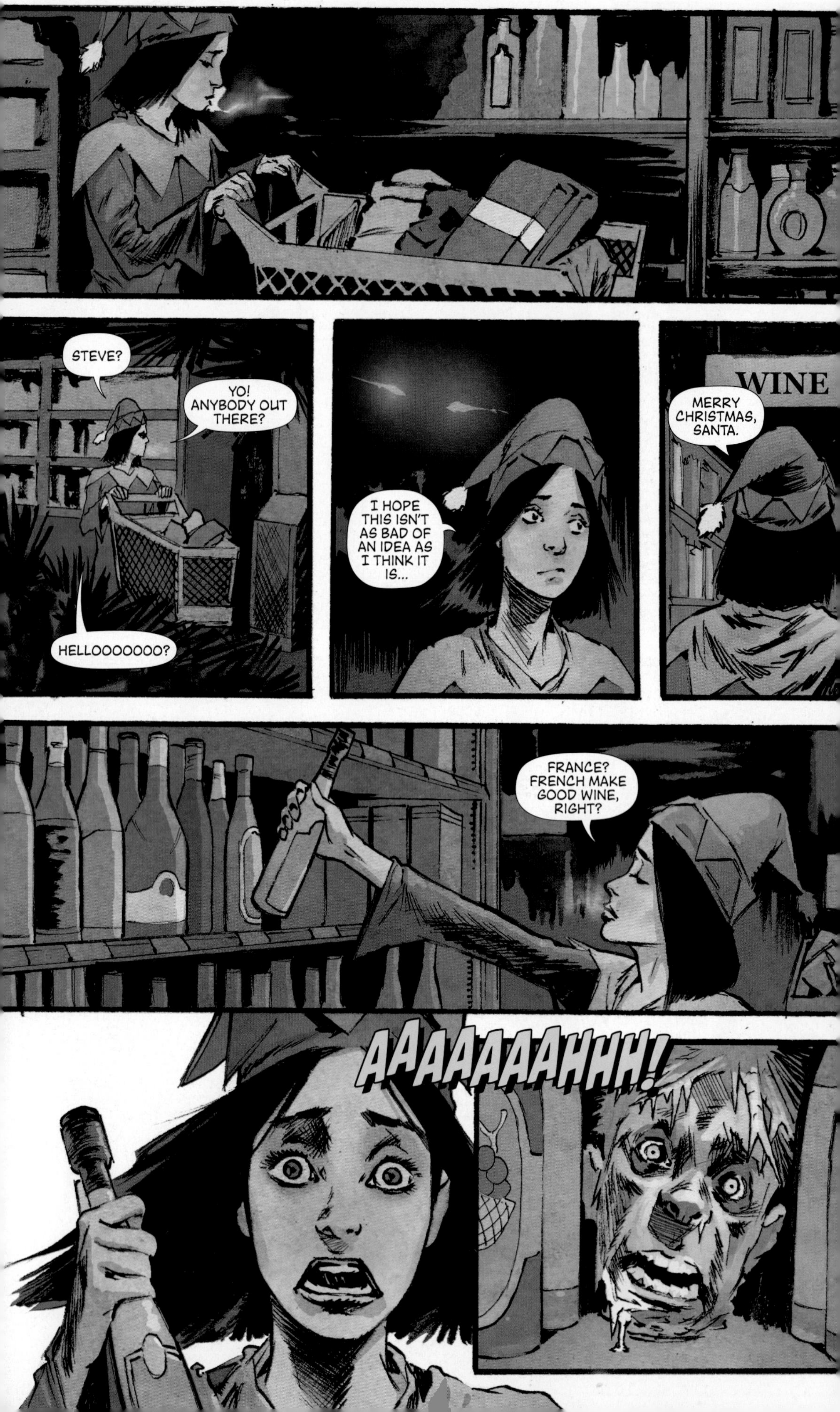
STEVE?
YO! ANYBODY OUT THERE?
HELLOOOOOOO?
I HOPE THIS ISN'T AS BAD OF AN IDEA AS I THINK IT IS...
WINE
MERRY CHRISTMAS, SANTA.
FRANCE? FRENCH MAKE GOOD WINE, RIGHT?
AAAAAAAHHH!

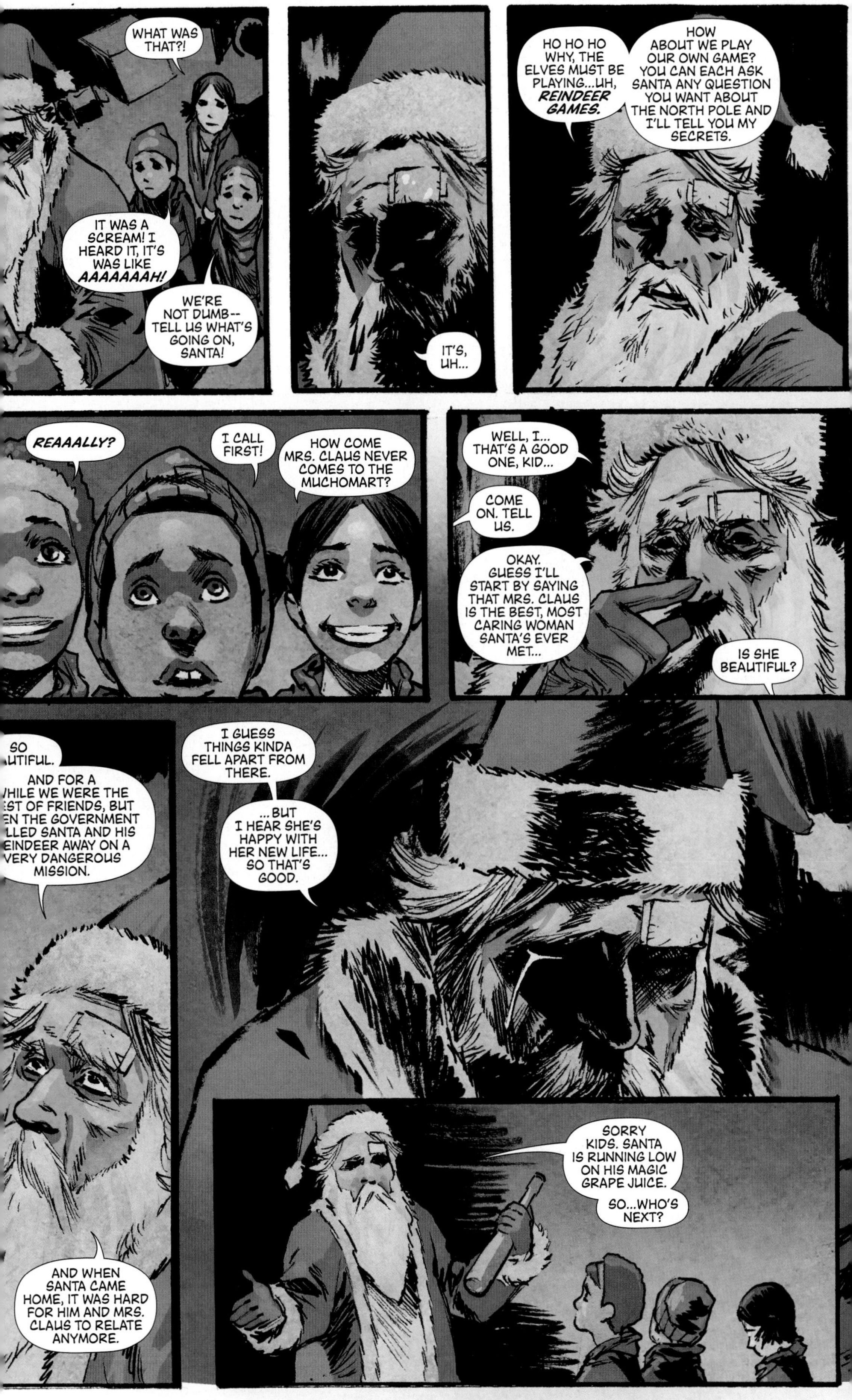
WHAT WAS THAT?!
IT WAS A SCREAM! I HEARD IT, IT'S WAS LIKE *AAAAAAAH!*
WE'RE NOT DUMB-- TELL US WHAT'S GOING ON, SANTA!
IT'S, UH...
HO HO HO WHY, THE ELVES MUST BE PLAYING...UH, ***REINDEER GAMES.***
HOW ABOUT WE PLAY OUR OWN GAME? YOU CAN EACH ASK SANTA ANY QUESTION YOU WANT ABOUT THE NORTH POLE AND I'LL TELL YOU MY SECRETS.
REAAALLY?
I CALL FIRST!
HOW COME MRS. CLAUS NEVER COMES TO THE MUCHOMART?
WELL, I... THAT'S A GOOD ONE, KID...
COME ON. TELL US.
OKAY. GUESS I'LL START BY SAYING THAT MRS. CLAUS IS THE BEST, MOST CARING WOMAN SANTA'S EVER MET...
IS SHE BEAUTIFUL?
SO UTIFUL.
AND FOR A HILE WE WERE THE EST OF FRIENDS, BUT EN THE GOVERNMENT LLED SANTA AND HIS EINDEER AWAY ON A VERY DANGEROUS MISSION.
AND WHEN SANTA CAME HOME, IT WAS HARD FOR HIM AND MRS. CLAUS TO RELATE ANYMORE.
I GUESS THINGS KINDA FELL APART FROM THERE.
...BUT I HEAR SHE'S HAPPY WITH HER NEW LIFE... SO THAT'S GOOD.
SORRY KIDS. SANTA IS RUNNING LOW ON HIS MAGIC GRAPE JUICE.
SO...WHO'S NEXT?

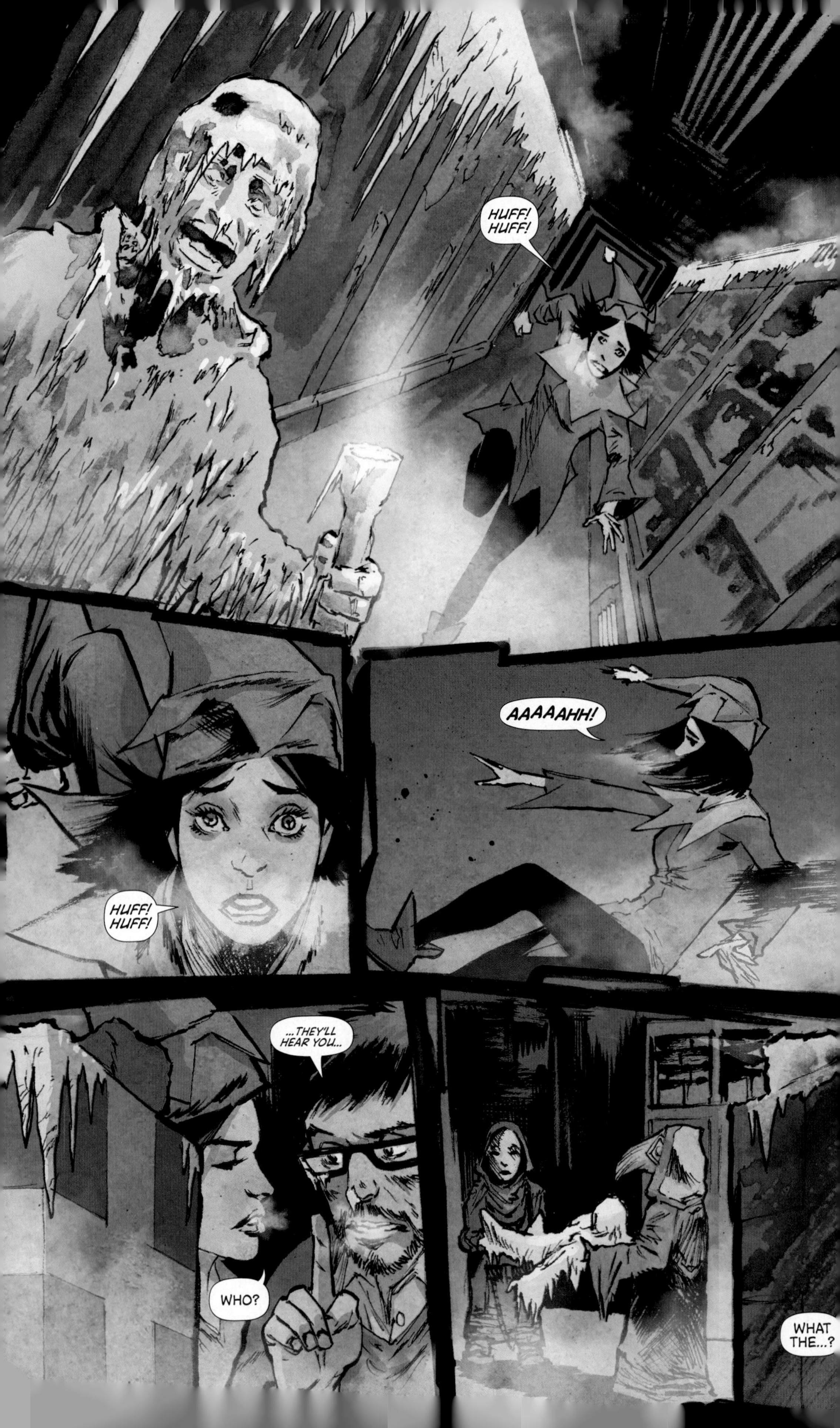
HUFF! HUFF!
HUFF! HUFF!
AAAAAHH!
...THEY'LL HEAR YOU...
WHO?
WHAT THE...?

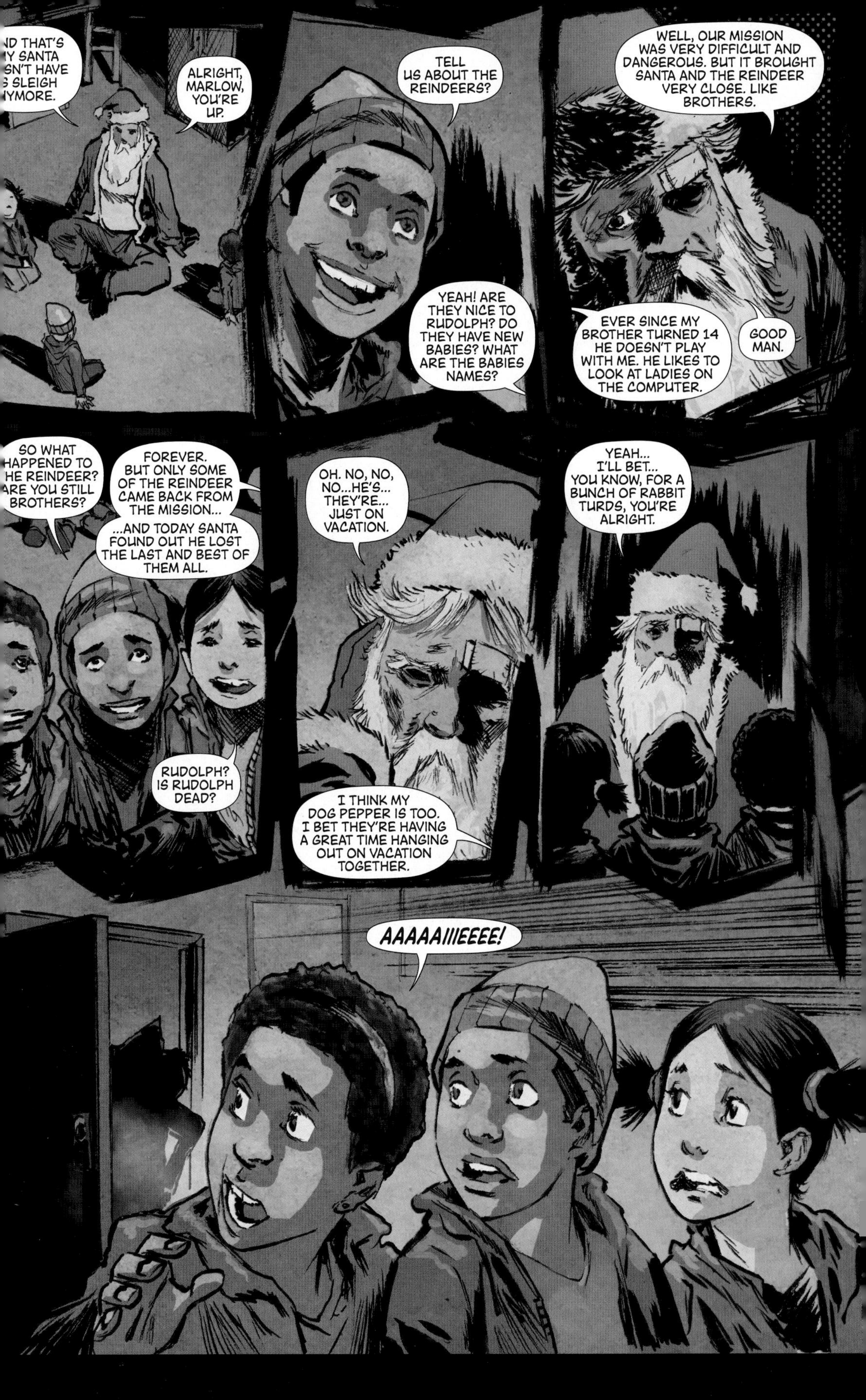

ND THAT'S Y SANTA SN'T HAVE S SLEIGH NYMORE.
ALRIGHT, MARLOW, YOU'RE UP.
TELL US ABOUT THE REINDEERS?
YEAH! ARE THEY NICE TO RUDOLPH? DO THEY HAVE NEW BABIES? WHAT ARE THE BABIES NAMES?
WELL, OUR MISSION WAS VERY DIFFICULT AND DANGEROUS. BUT IT BROUGHT SANTA AND THE REINDEER VERY CLOSE. LIKE BROTHERS.
EVER SINCE MY BROTHER TURNED 14 HE DOESN'T PLAY WITH ME. HE LIKES TO LOOK AT LADIES ON THE COMPUTER.
GOOD MAN.
SO WHAT HAPPENED TO HE REINDEER? ARE YOU STILL BROTHERS?
FOREVER. BUT ONLY SOME OF THE REINDEER CAME BACK FROM THE MISSION...
...AND TODAY SANTA FOUND OUT HE LOST THE LAST AND BEST OF THEM ALL.
RUDOLPH? IS RUDOLPH DEAD?
OH. NO, NO, NO...HE'S... THEY'RE... JUST ON VACATION.
I THINK MY DOG PEPPER IS TOO. I BET THEY'RE HAVING A GREAT TIME HANGING OUT ON VACATION TOGETHER.
YEAH... I'LL BET... YOU KNOW, FOR A BUNCH OF RABBIT TURDS, YOU'RE ALRIGHT.
AAAAAIIIEEEE!

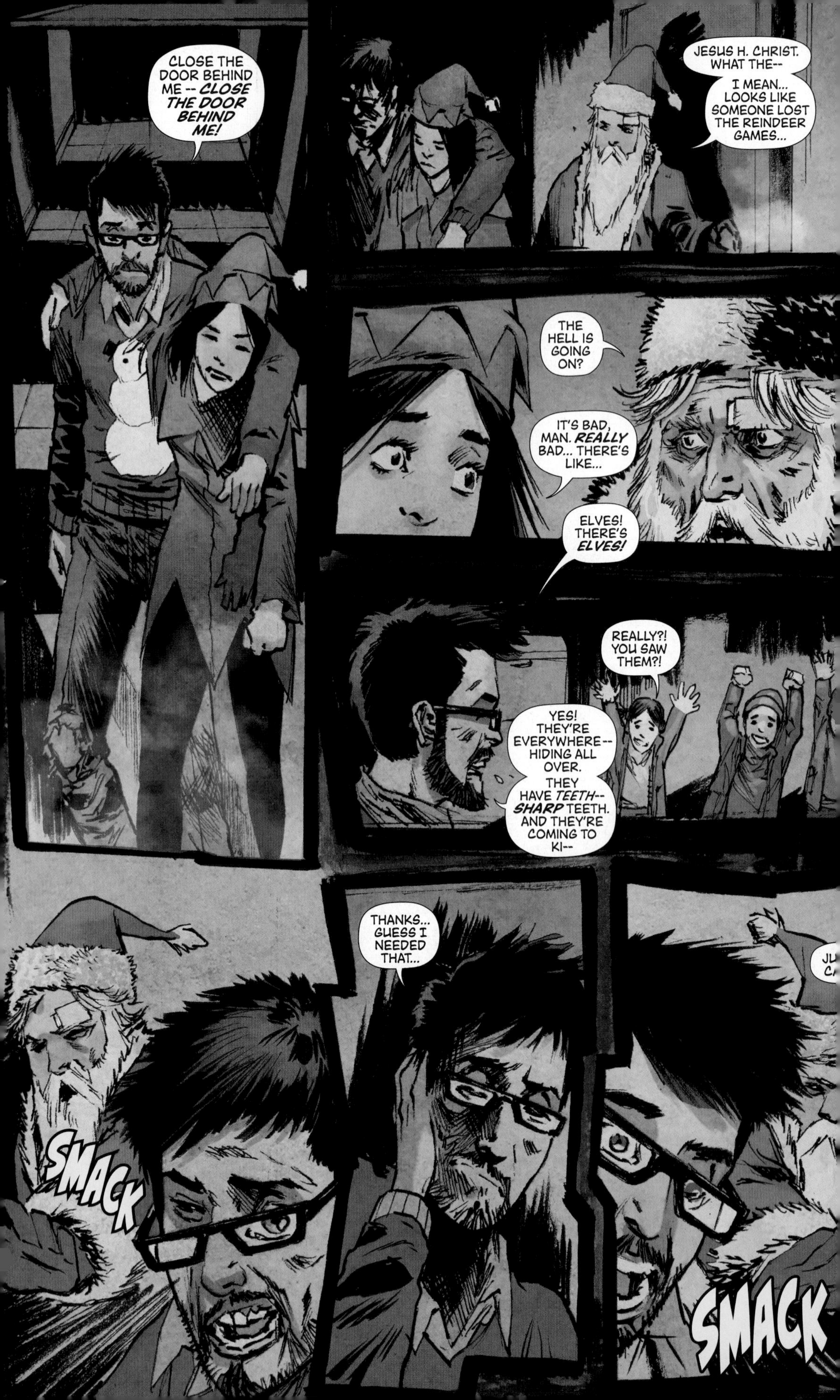
CLOSE THE DOOR BEHIND ME -- CLOSE THE DOOR BEHIND ME!
JESUS H. CHRIST. WHAT THE--
I MEAN... LOOKS LIKE SOMEONE LOST THE REINDEER GAMES...
THE HELL IS GOING ON?
IT'S BAD, MAN. REALLY BAD... THERE'S LIKE...
ELVES! THERE'S ELVES!
REALLY?! YOU SAW THEM?!
YES! THEY'RE EVERYWHERE-- HIDING ALL OVER.
THEY HAVE TEETH-- SHARP TEETH. AND THEY'RE COMING TO KI--
SMACK
THANKS... GUESS I NEEDED THAT...
SMACK

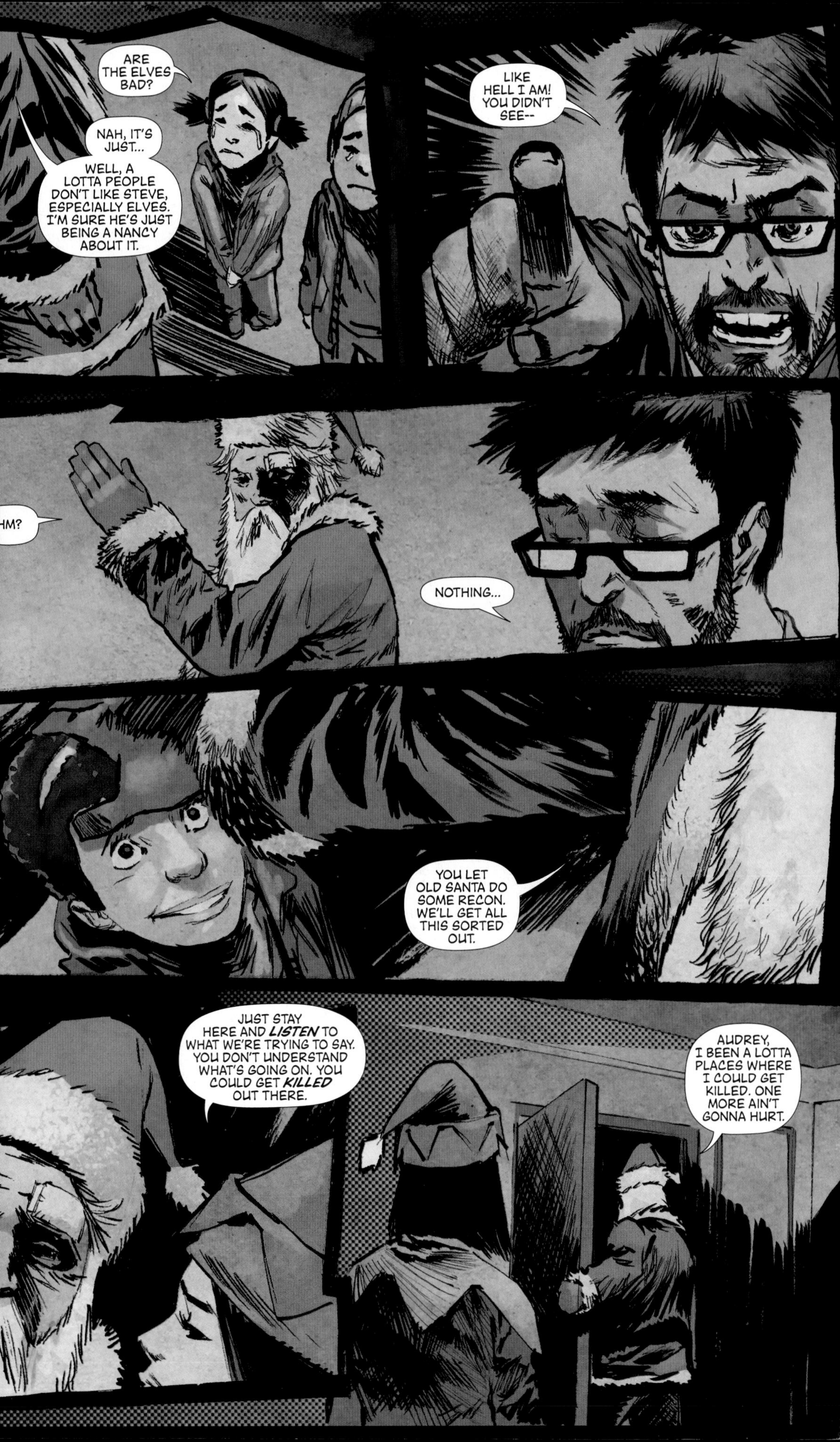
ARE THE ELVES BAD?
NAH, IT'S JUST...
WELL, A LOTTA PEOPLE DON'T LIKE STEVE, ESPECIALLY ELVES. I'M SURE HE'S JUST BEING A NANCY ABOUT IT.
LIKE HELL I AM! YOU DIDN'T SEE--
HM?
NOTHING...
YOU LET OLD SANTA DO SOME RECON. WE'LL GET ALL THIS SORTED OUT.
JUST STAY HERE AND LISTEN TO WHAT WE'RE TRYING TO SAY. YOU DON'T UNDERSTAND WHAT'S GOING ON. YOU COULD GET KILLED OUT THERE.
AUDREY, I BEEN A LOTTA PLACES WHERE I COULD GET KILLED. ONE MORE AIN'T GONNA HURT.

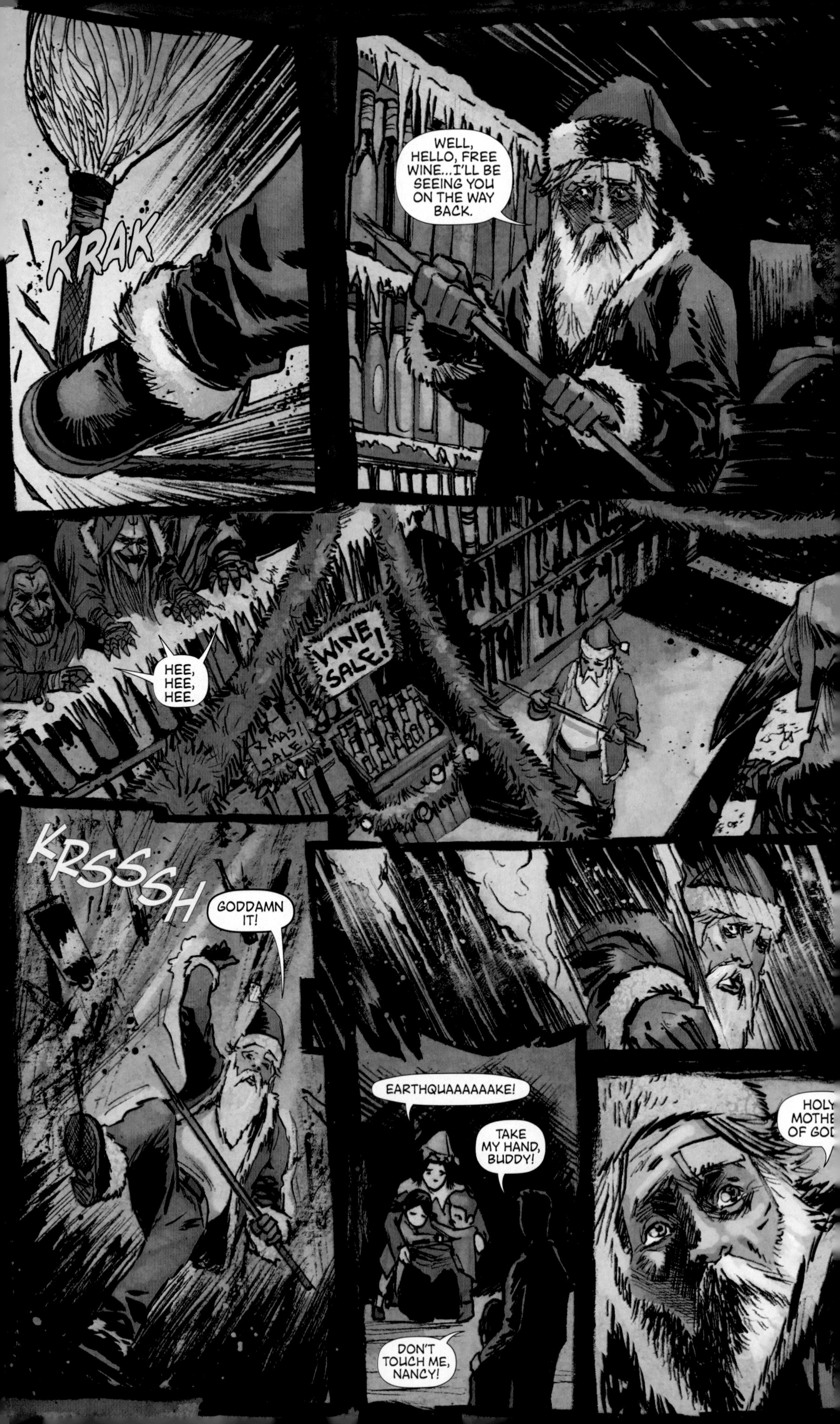
KRAK
WELL, HELLO, FREE WINE...I'LL BE SEEING YOU ON THE WAY BACK.
HEE, HEE, HEE.
WINE SALE!
X-MAS SALE
KRSSSH
GODDAMN IT!
EARTHQUAAAAAAKE!
TAKE MY HAND, BUDDY!
DON'T TOUCH ME, NANCY!
HOLY MOTHER OF GOD

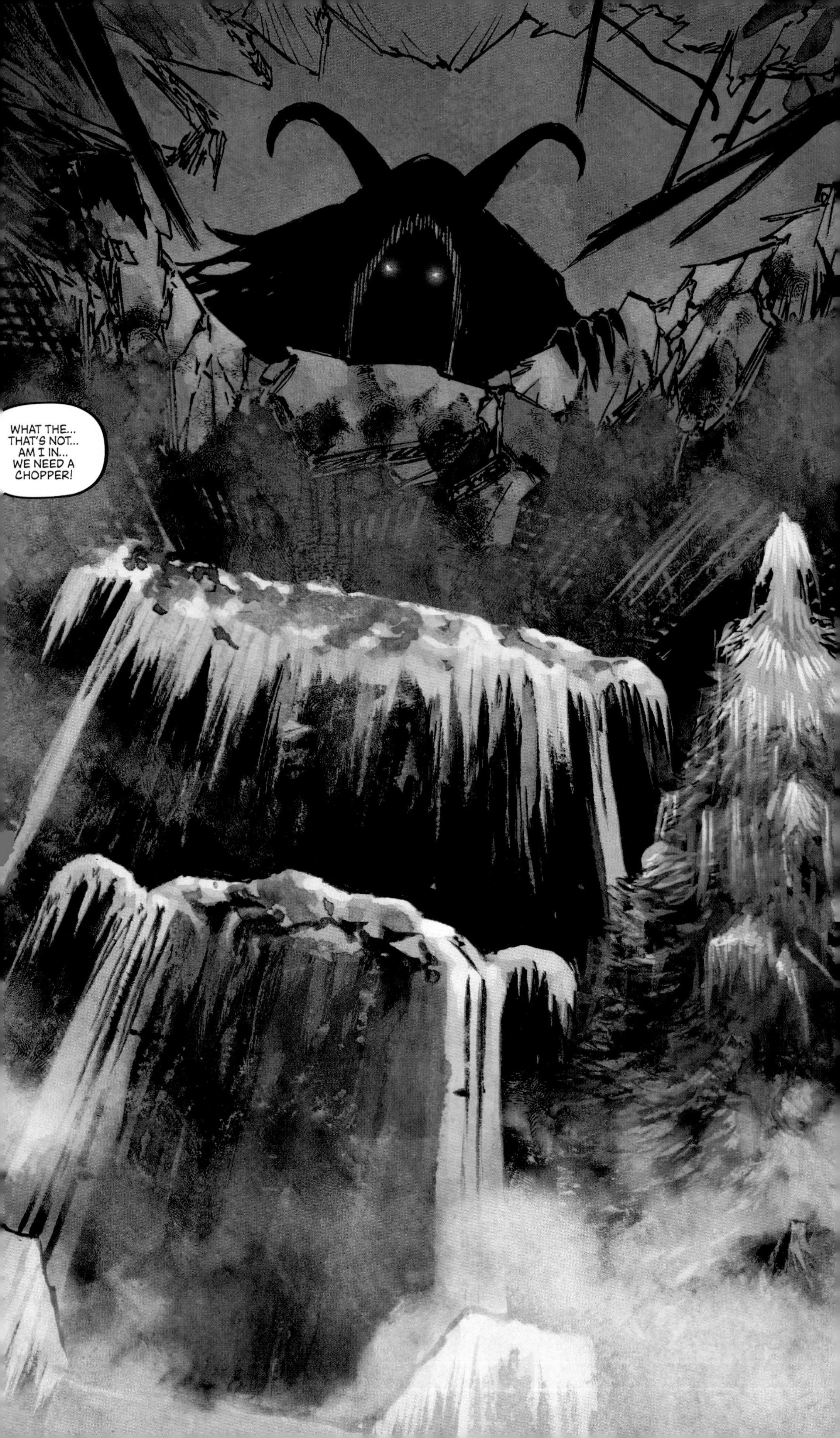
WHAT THE... THAT'S NOT... AM I IN... WE NEED A CHOPPER!

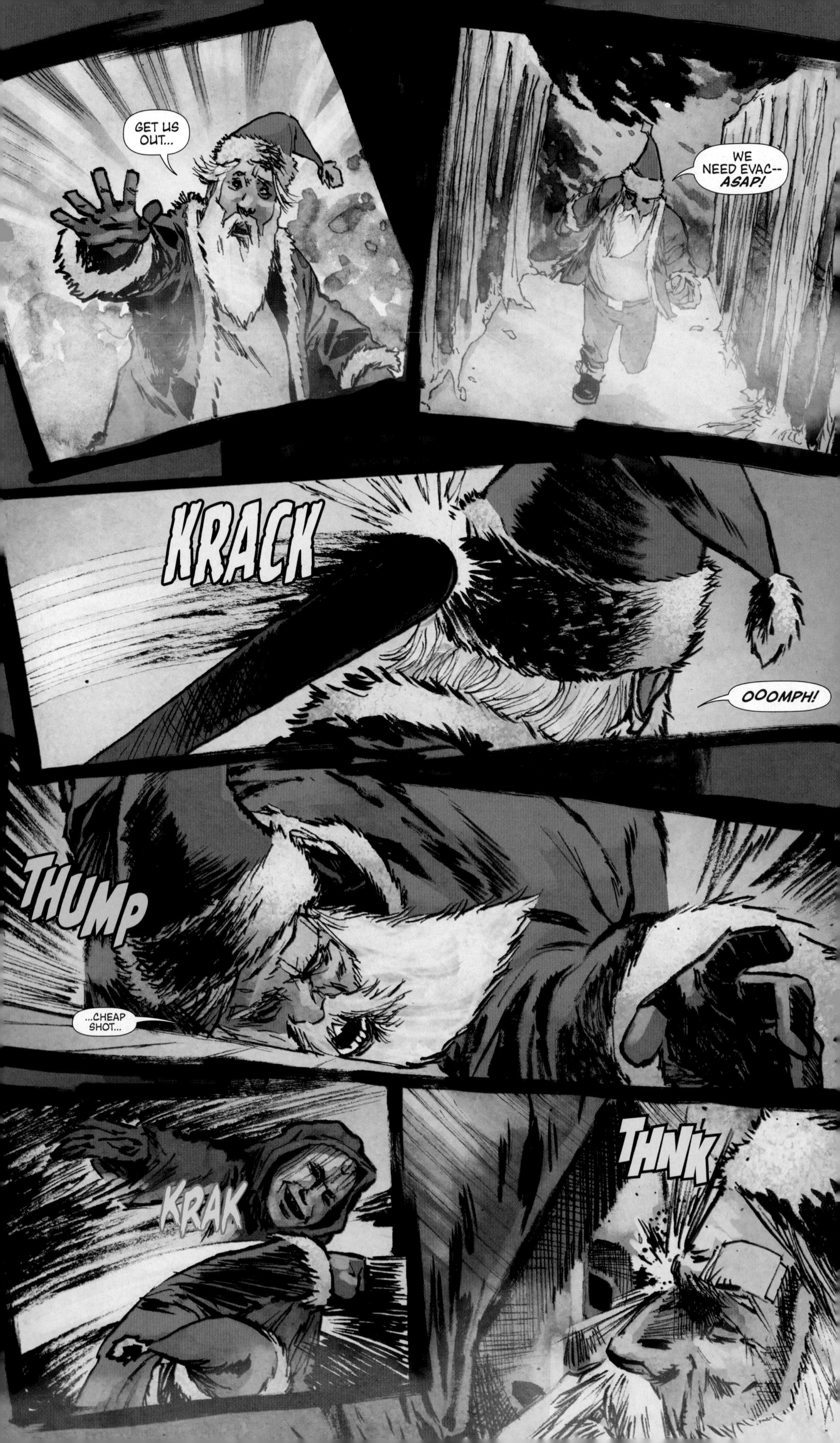
GET US OUT...
WE NEED EVAC-- ASAP!
KRACK
OOOMPH!
THUMP
...CHEAP SHOT...
KRAK
THNK

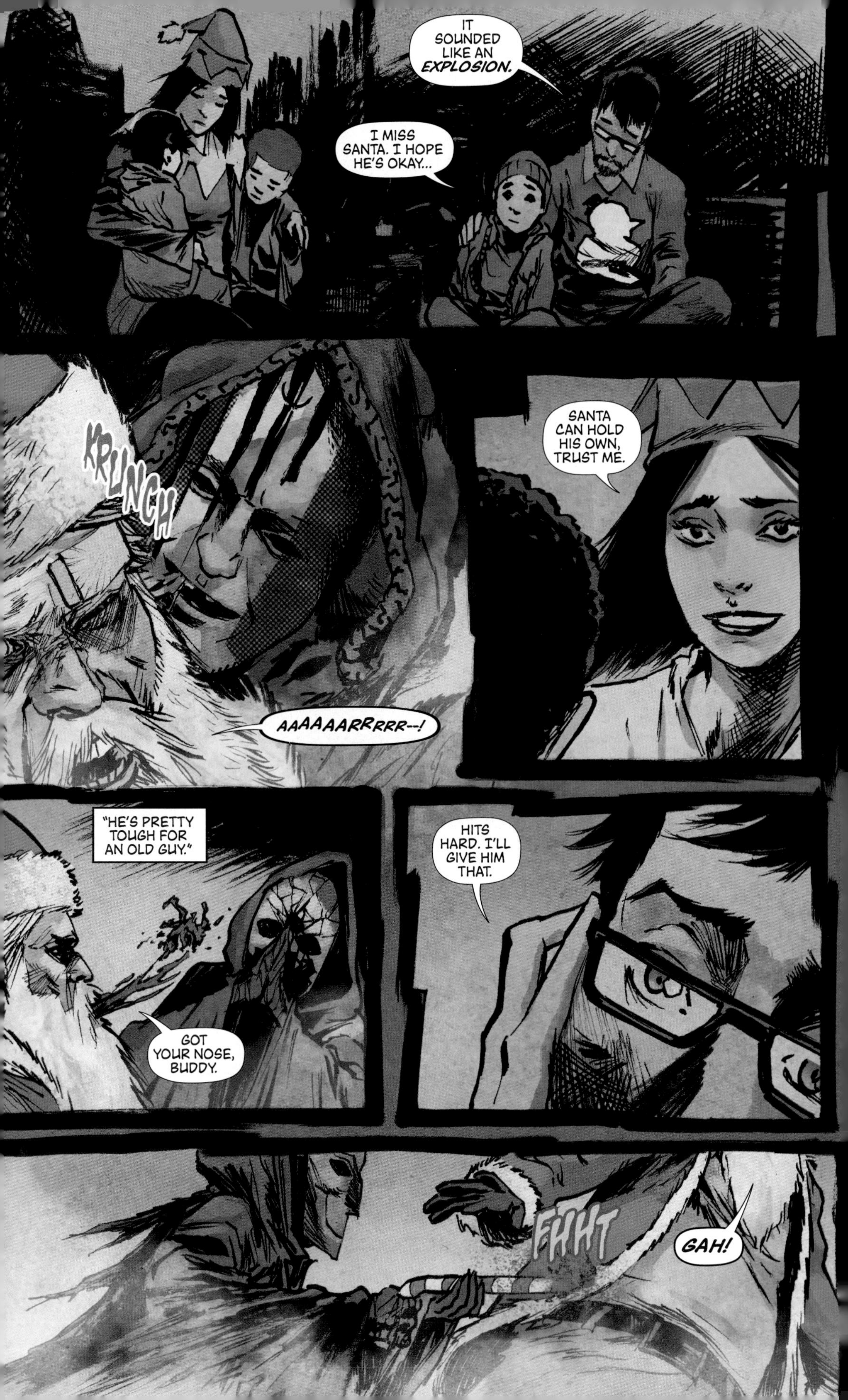
IT SOUNDED LIKE AN EXPLOSION.
I MISS SANTA. I HOPE HE'S OKAY...
KRUNCH
AAAAAARRrrr--!
SANTA CAN HOLD HIS OWN, TRUST ME.
"HE'S PRETTY TOUGH FOR AN OLD GUY."
GOT YOUR NOSE, BUDDY.
HITS HARD. I'LL GIVE HIM THAT.
FHHT
GAH!

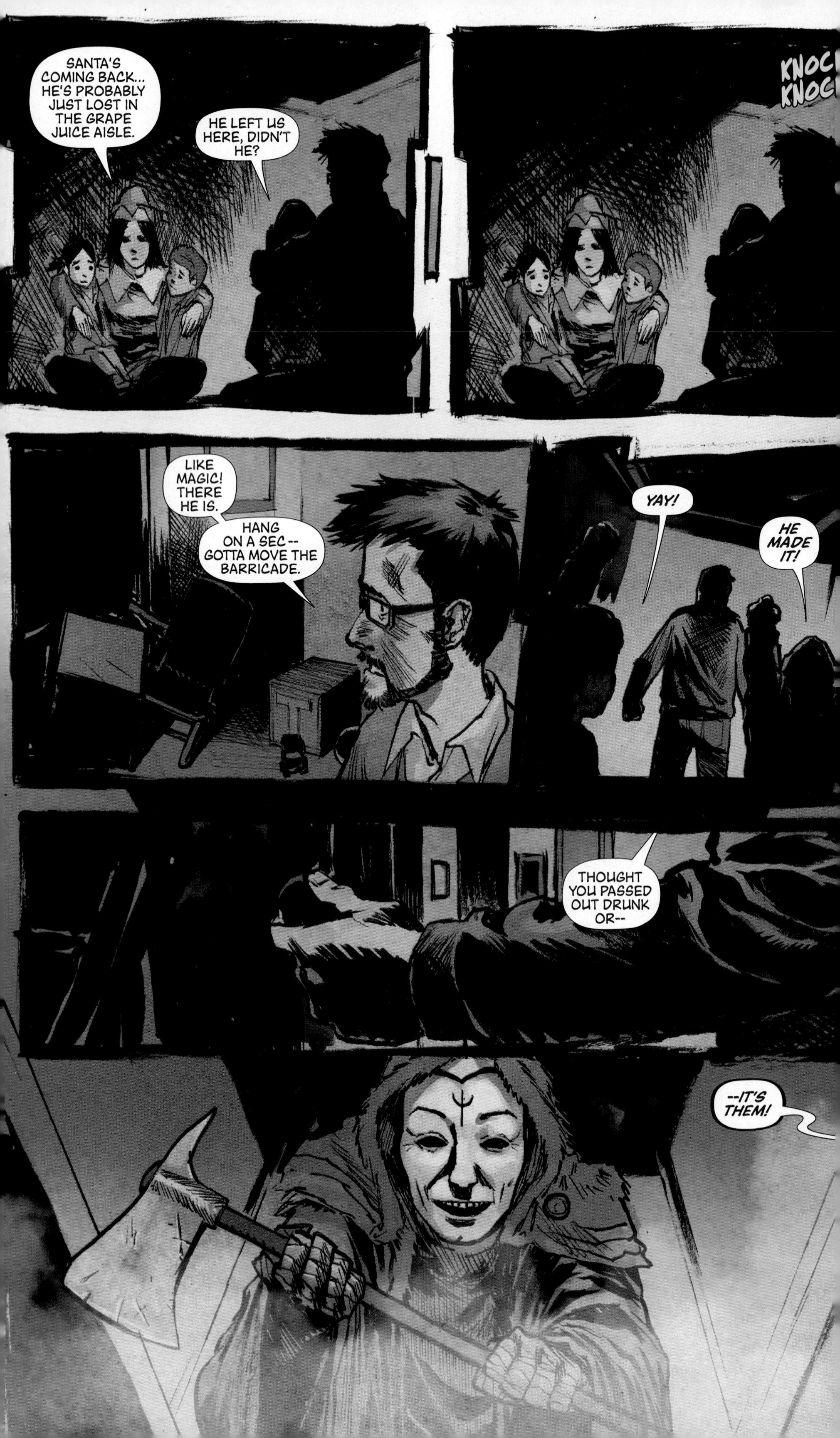
SANTA'S COMING BACK... HE'S PROBABLY JUST LOST IN THE GRAPE JUICE AISLE.
HE LEFT US HERE, DIDN'T HE?
KNOC KNOC
LIKE MAGIC! THERE HE IS.
HANG ON A SEC-- GOTTA MOVE THE BARRICADE.
YAY!
HE MADE IT!
THOUGHT YOU PASSED OUT DRUNK OR--
--IT'S THEM!

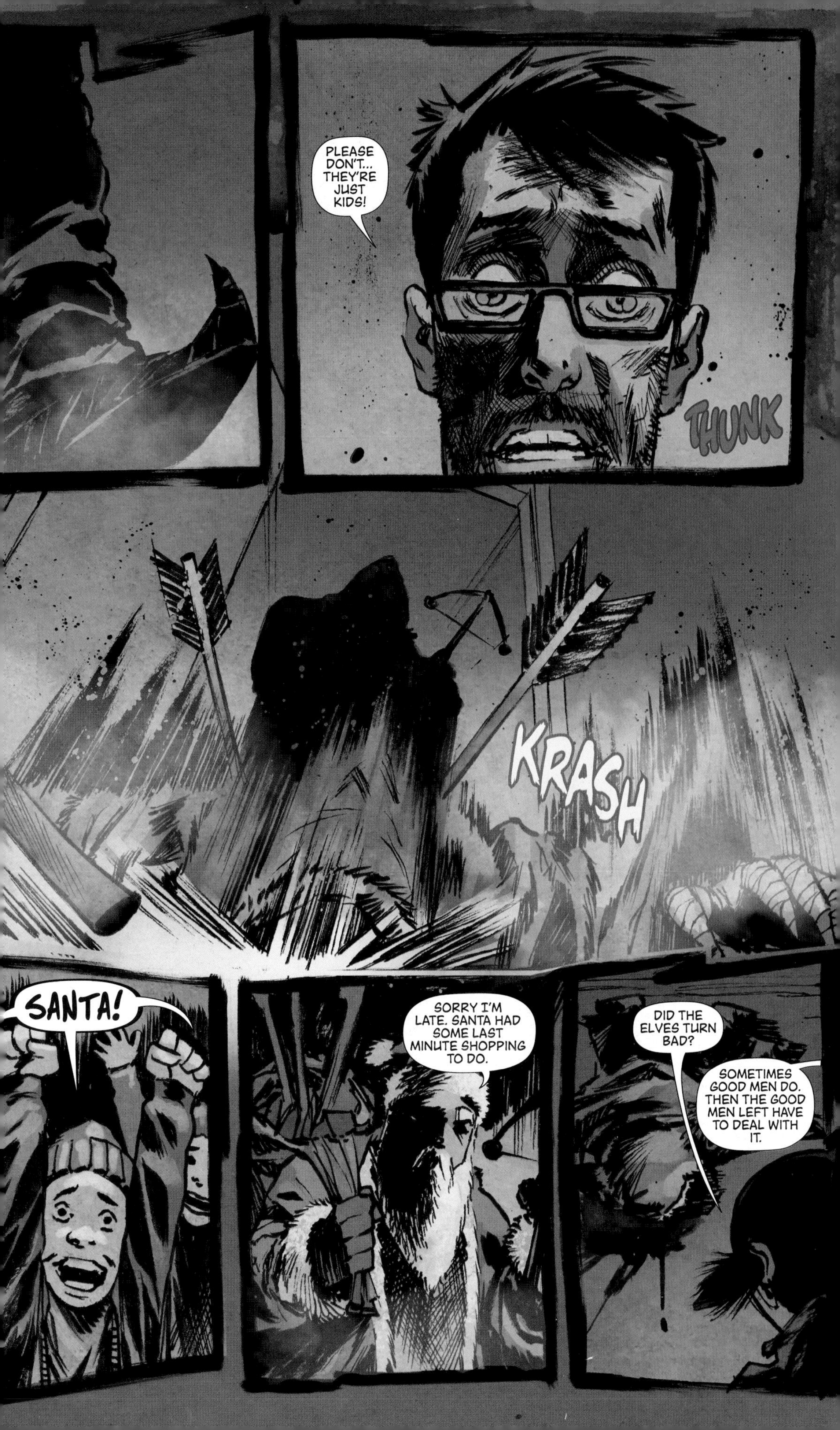
PLEASE DON'T... THEY'RE JUST KIDS!
THUNK
KRASH
SANTA!
SORRY I'M LATE. SANTA HAD SOME LAST MINUTE SHOPPING TO DO.
DID THE ELVES TURN BAD?
SOMETIMES GOOD MEN DO. THEN THE GOOD MEN LEFT HAVE TO DEAL WITH IT.

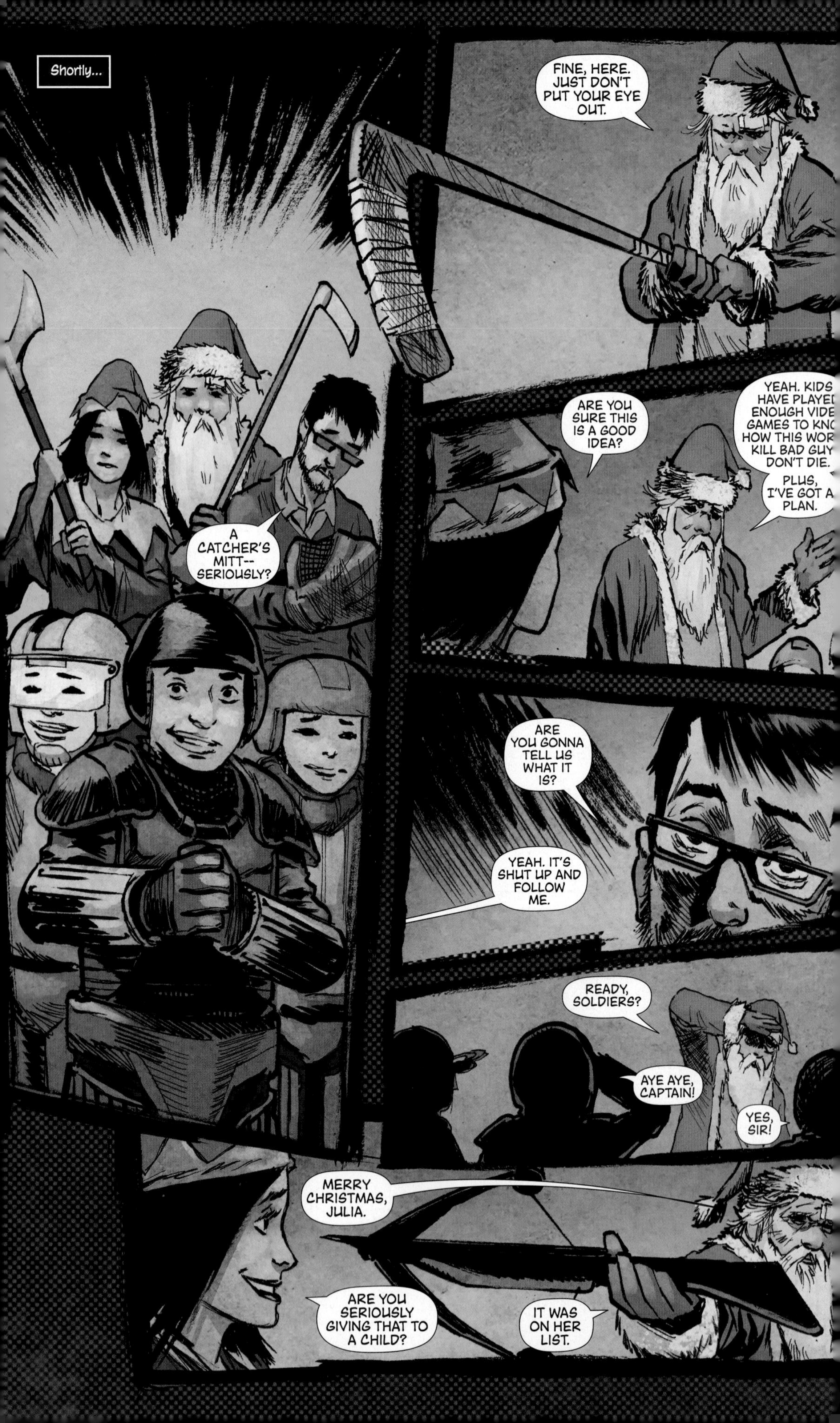
Shortly...
FINE, HERE. JUST DON'T PUT YOUR EYE OUT.
A CATCHER'S MITT-- SERIOUSLY?
ARE YOU SURE THIS IS A GOOD IDEA?
YEAH. KIDS HAVE PLAYED ENOUGH VIDE GAMES TO KNO HOW THIS WOR KILL BAD GUY DON'T DIE.
PLUS, I'VE GOT A PLAN.
ARE YOU GONNA TELL US WHAT IT IS?
YEAH. IT'S SHUT UP AND FOLLOW ME.
READY, SOLDIERS?
AYE AYE, CAPTAIN!
YES, SIR!
MERRY CHRISTMAS, JULIA.
ARE YOU SERIOUSLY GIVING THAT TO A CHILD?
IT WAS ON HER LIST.

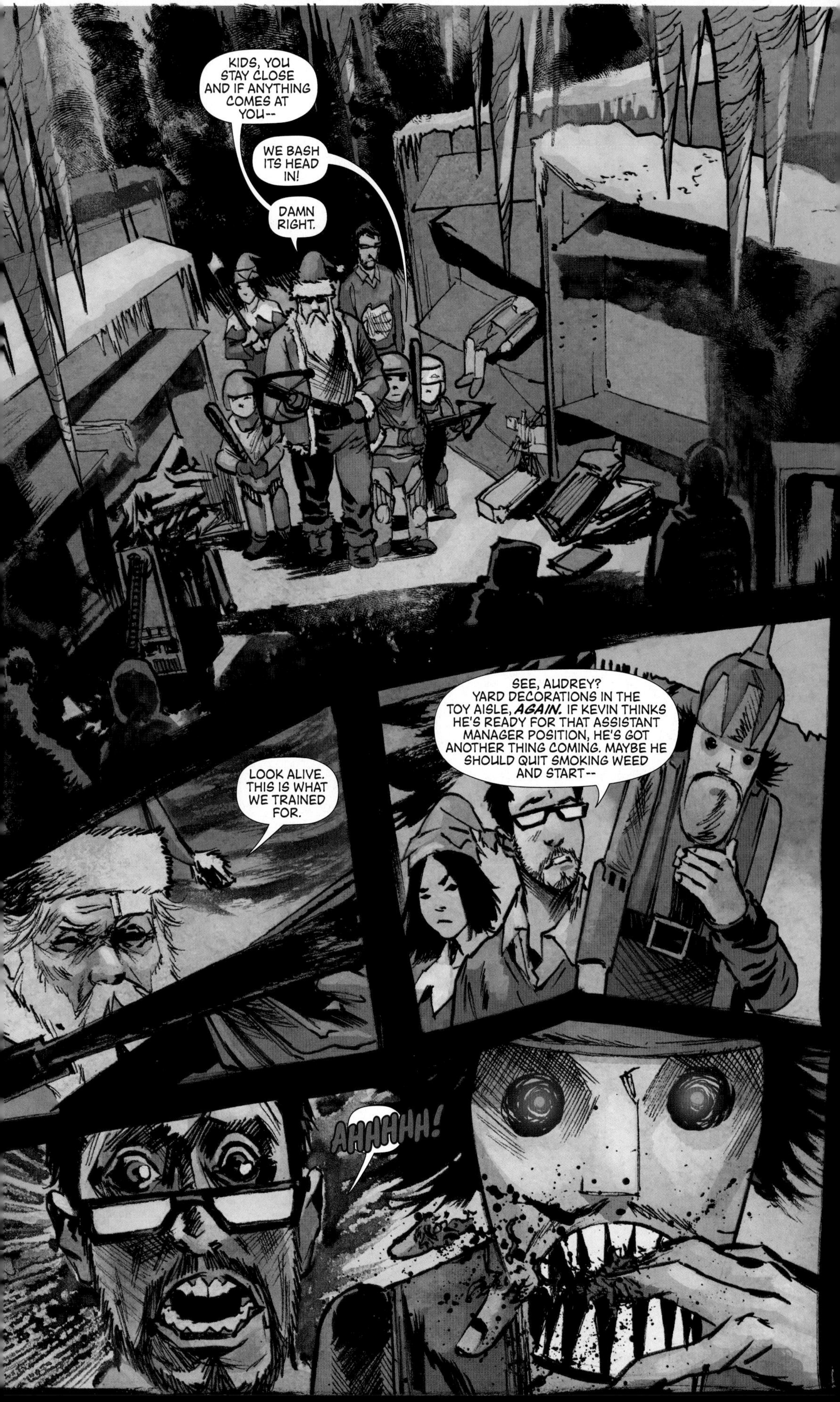
KIDS, YOU STAY CLOSE AND IF ANYTHING COMES AT YOU--
WE BASH ITS HEAD IN!
DAMN RIGHT.
LOOK ALIVE. THIS IS WHAT WE TRAINED FOR.
SEE, AUDREY? YARD DECORATIONS IN THE TOY AISLE, *AGAIN.* IF KEVIN THINKS HE'S READY FOR THAT ASSISTANT MANAGER POSITION, HE'S GOT ANOTHER THING COMING. MAYBE HE SHOULD QUIT SMOKING WEED AND START--
AHHHHH!

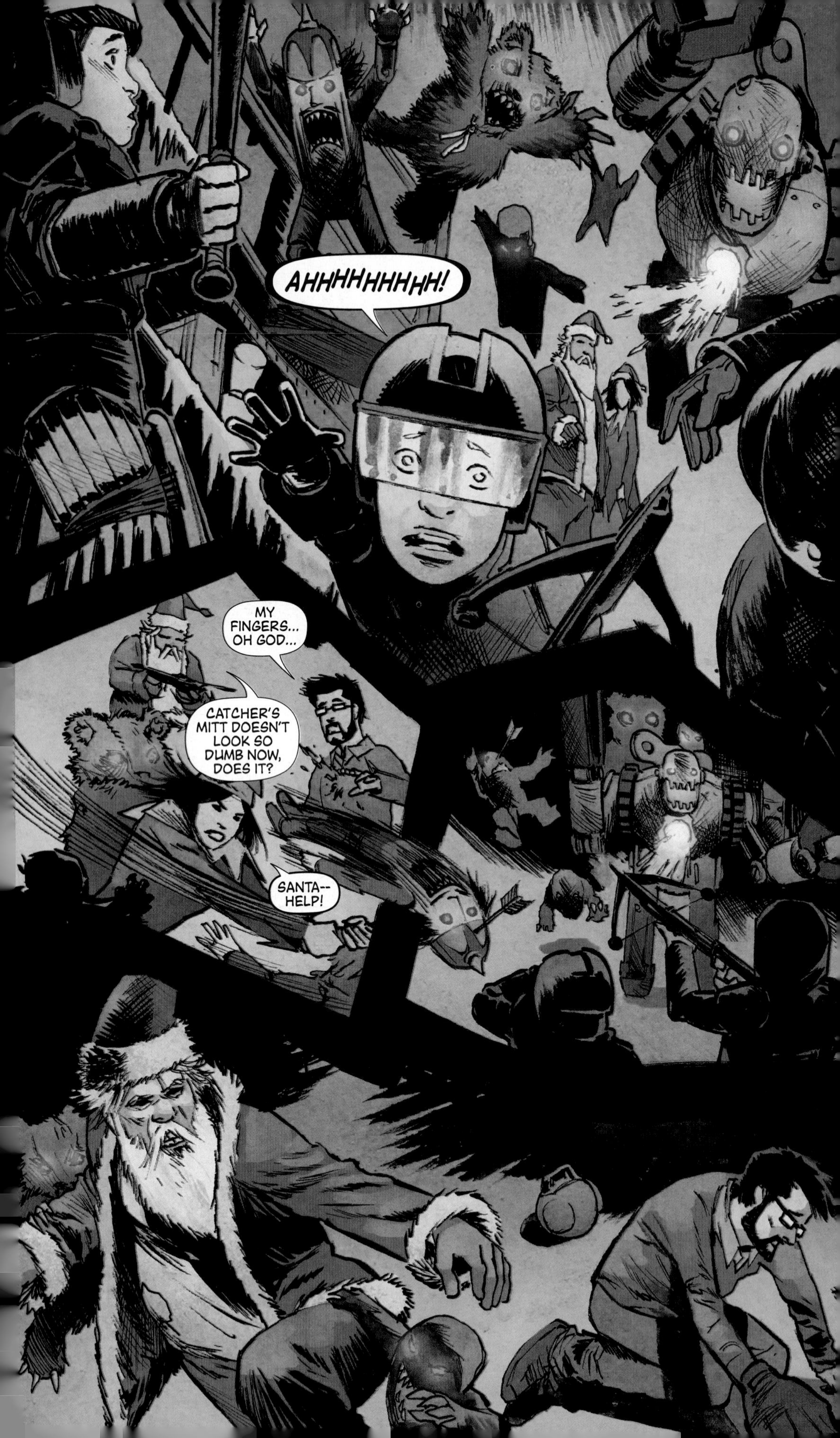
AHHHHHHHHH!
MY FINGERS... OH GOD...
CATCHER'S MITT DOESN'T LOOK SO DUMB NOW, DOES IT?
SANTA-- HELP!

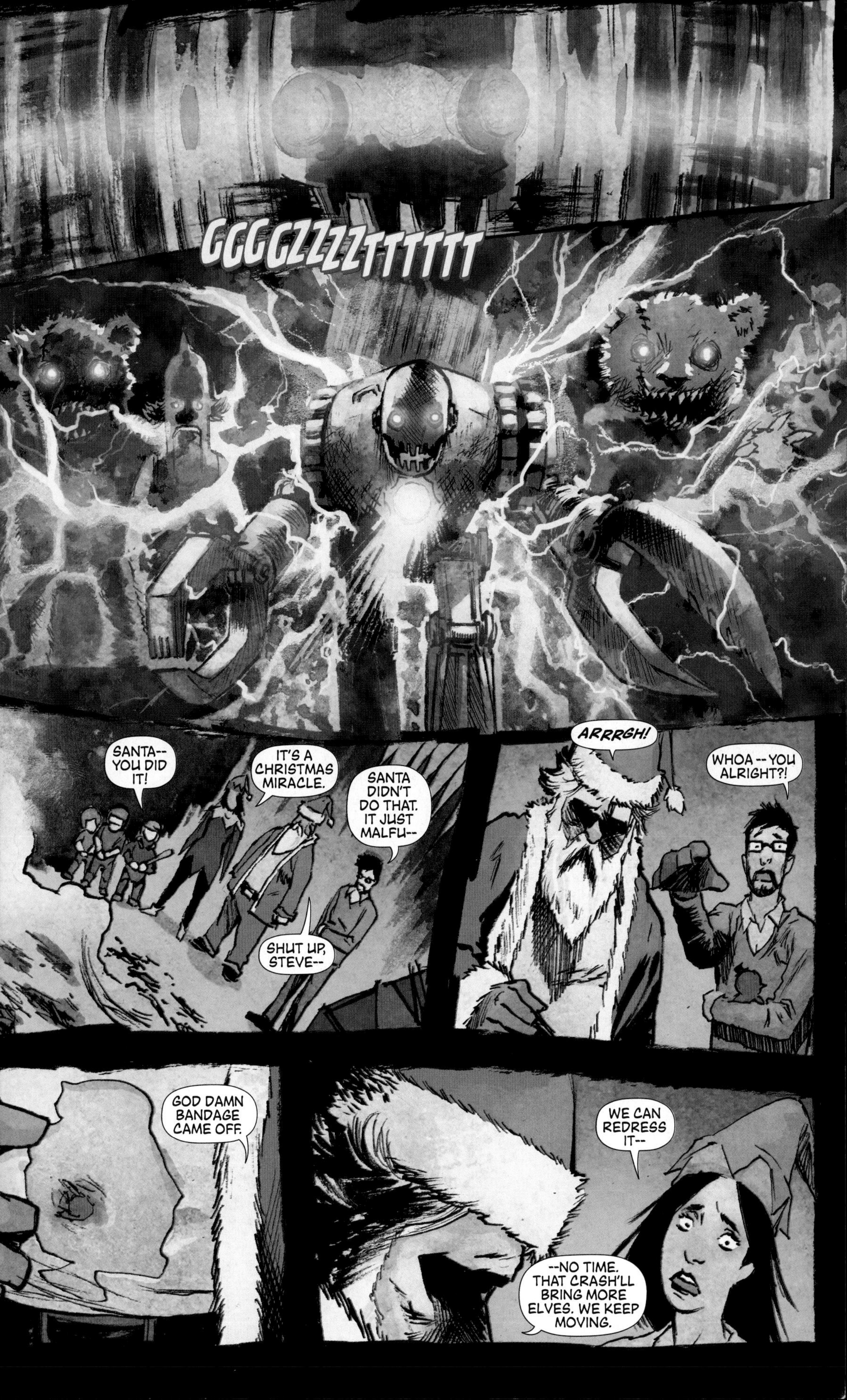
GGGGZZZZTTTTTT
SANTA-- YOU DID IT!
IT'S A CHRISTMAS MIRACLE.
SANTA DIDN'T DO THAT. IT JUST MALFU--
SHUT UP, STEVE--
ARRRGH!
WHOA -- YOU ALRIGHT?!
GOD DAMN BANDAGE CAME OFF.
WE CAN REDRESS IT--
--NO TIME. THAT CRASH'LL BRING MORE ELVES. WE KEEP MOVING.

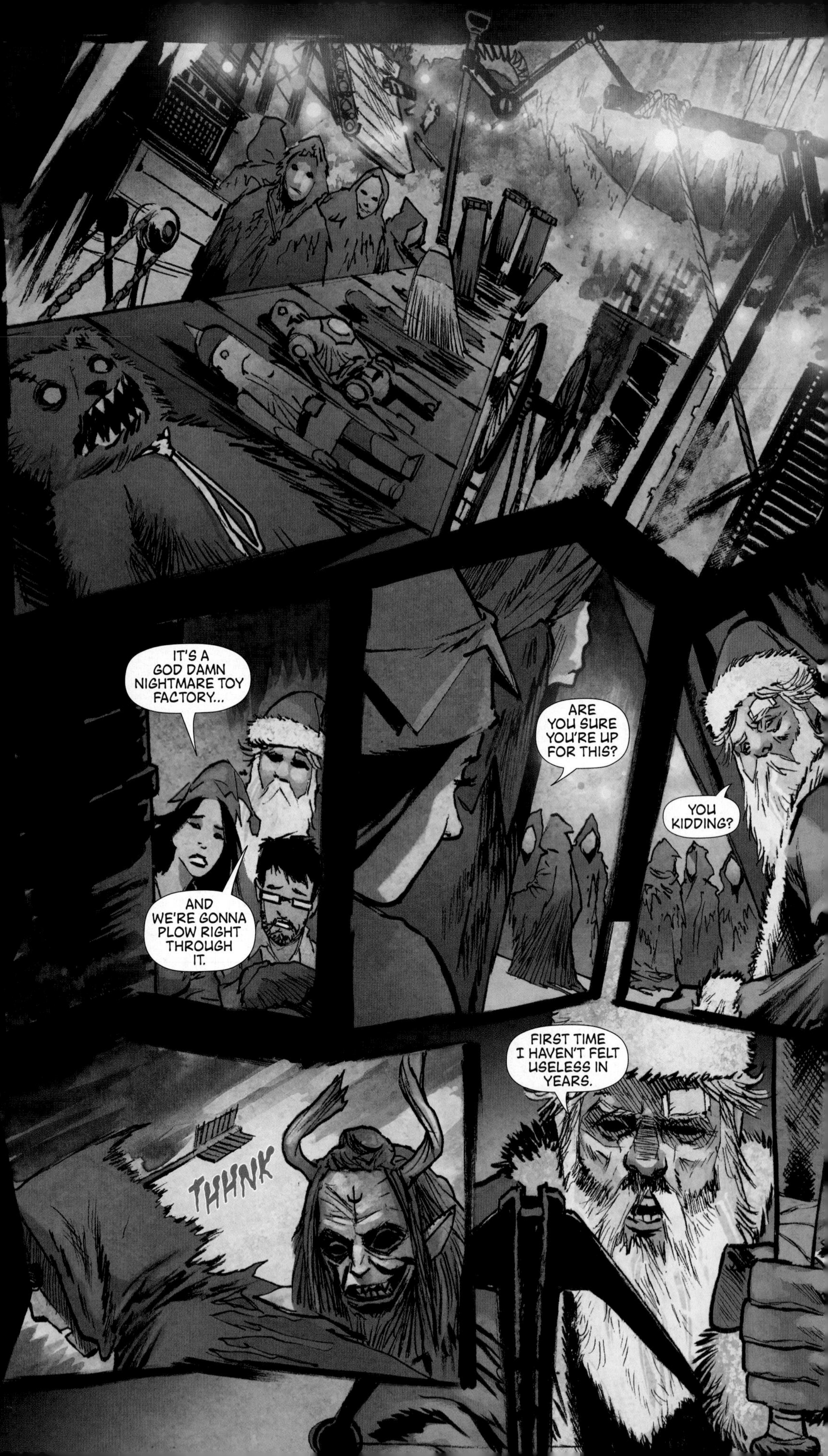
IT'S A GOD DAMN NIGHTMARE TOY FACTORY...
AND WE'RE GONNA PLOW RIGHT THROUGH IT.
ARE YOU SURE YOU'RE UP FOR THIS?
YOU KIDDING?
THHNK
FIRST TIME I HAVEN'T FELT USELESS IN YEARS.

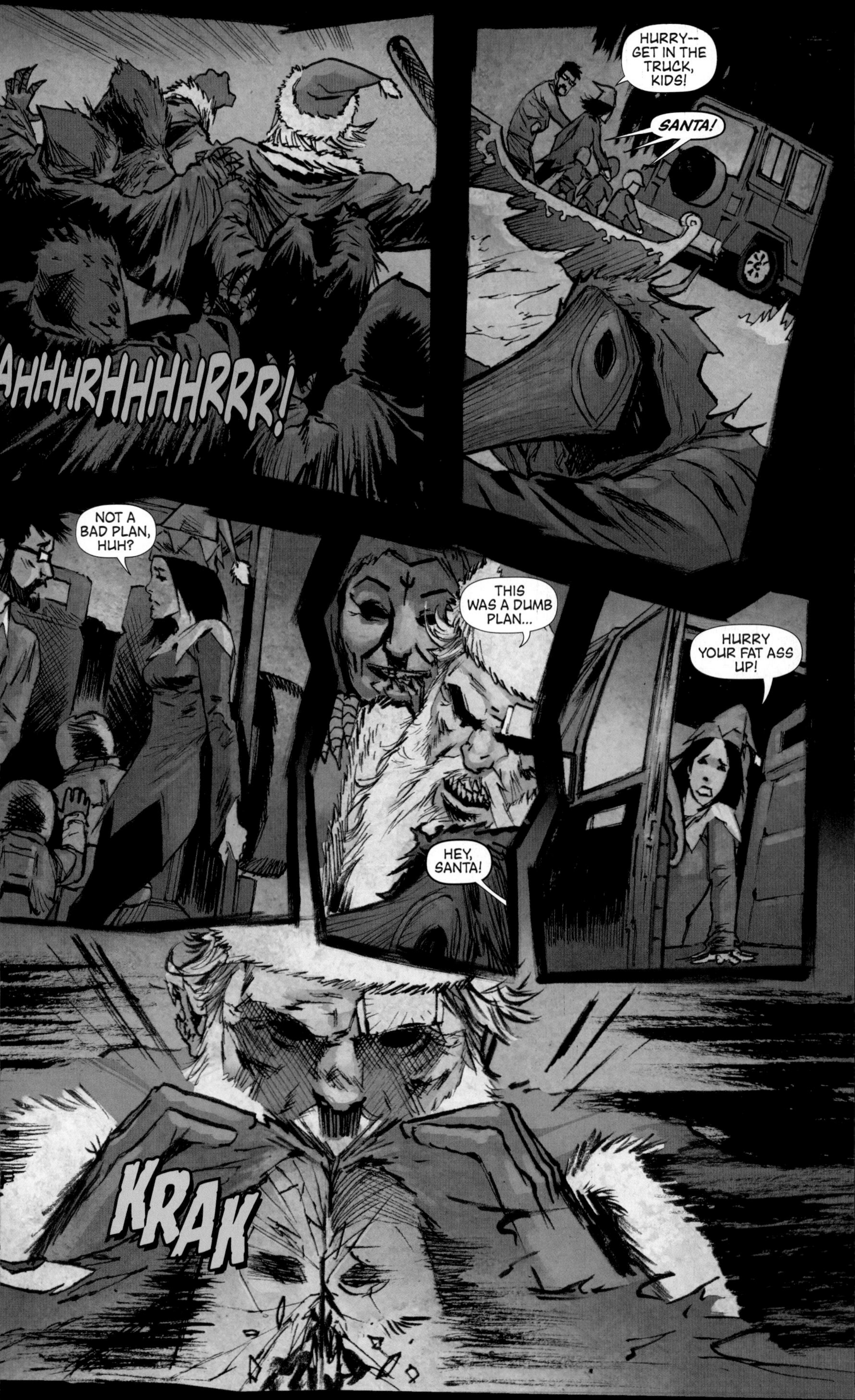

AHHHRHHHHRRR!
HURRY-- GET IN THE TRUCK, KIDS!
SANTA!
NOT A BAD PLAN, HUH?
THIS WAS A DUMB PLAN...
HEY, SANTA!
HURRY YOUR FAT ASS UP!
KRAK

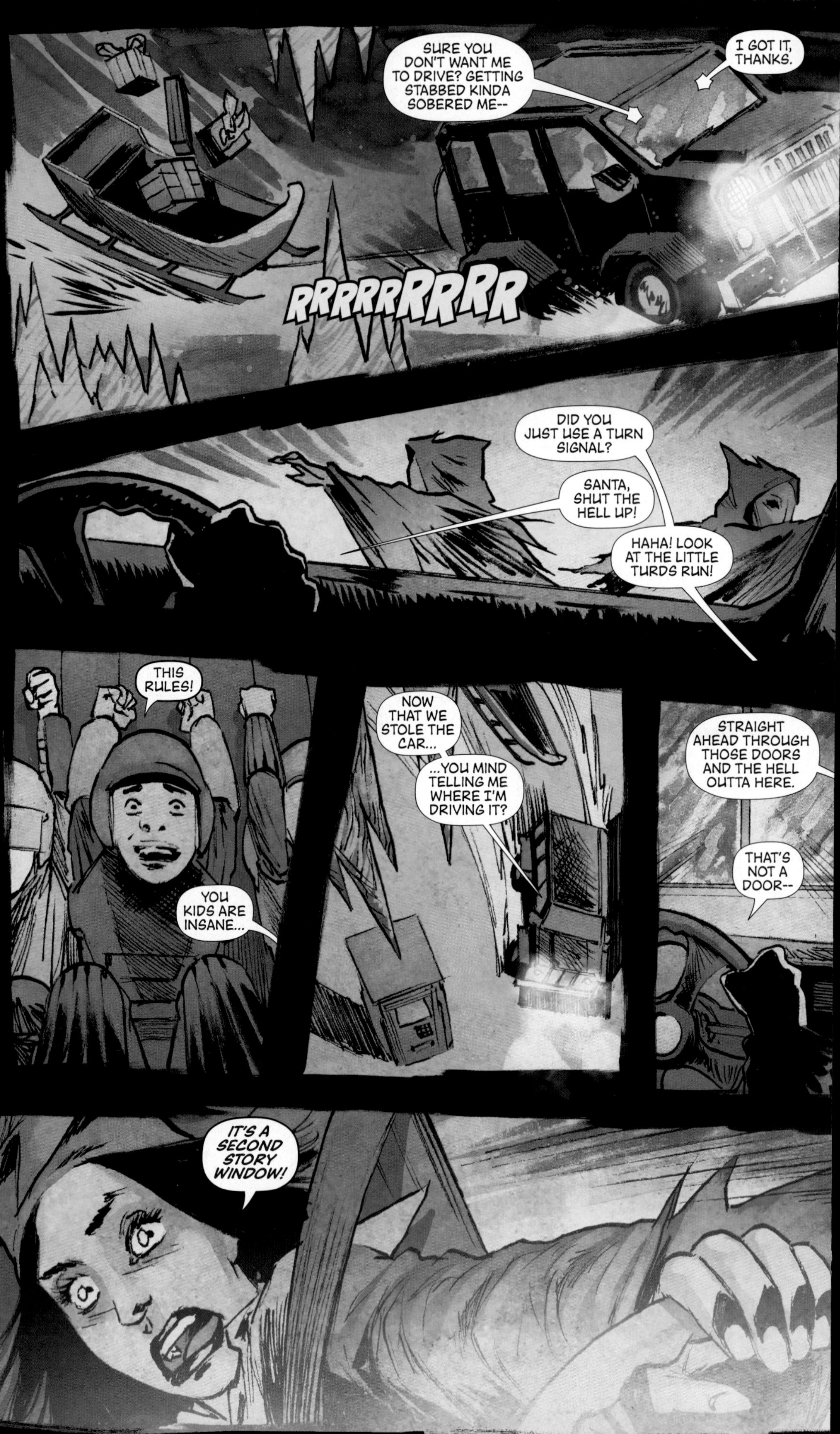
SURE YOU DON'T WANT ME TO DRIVE? GETTING STABBED KINDA SOBERED ME--
I GOT IT, THANKS.
RRRRRRRRR
DID YOU JUST USE A TURN SIGNAL?
SANTA, SHUT THE HELL UP!
HAHA! LOOK AT THE LITTLE TURDS RUN!
THIS RULES!
YOU KIDS ARE INSANE...
NOW THAT WE STOLE THE CAR...
...YOU MIND TELLING ME WHERE I'M DRIVING IT?
STRAIGHT AHEAD THROUGH THOSE DOORS AND THE HELL OUTTA HERE.
THAT'S NOT A DOOR--
IT'S A SECOND STORY WINDOW!

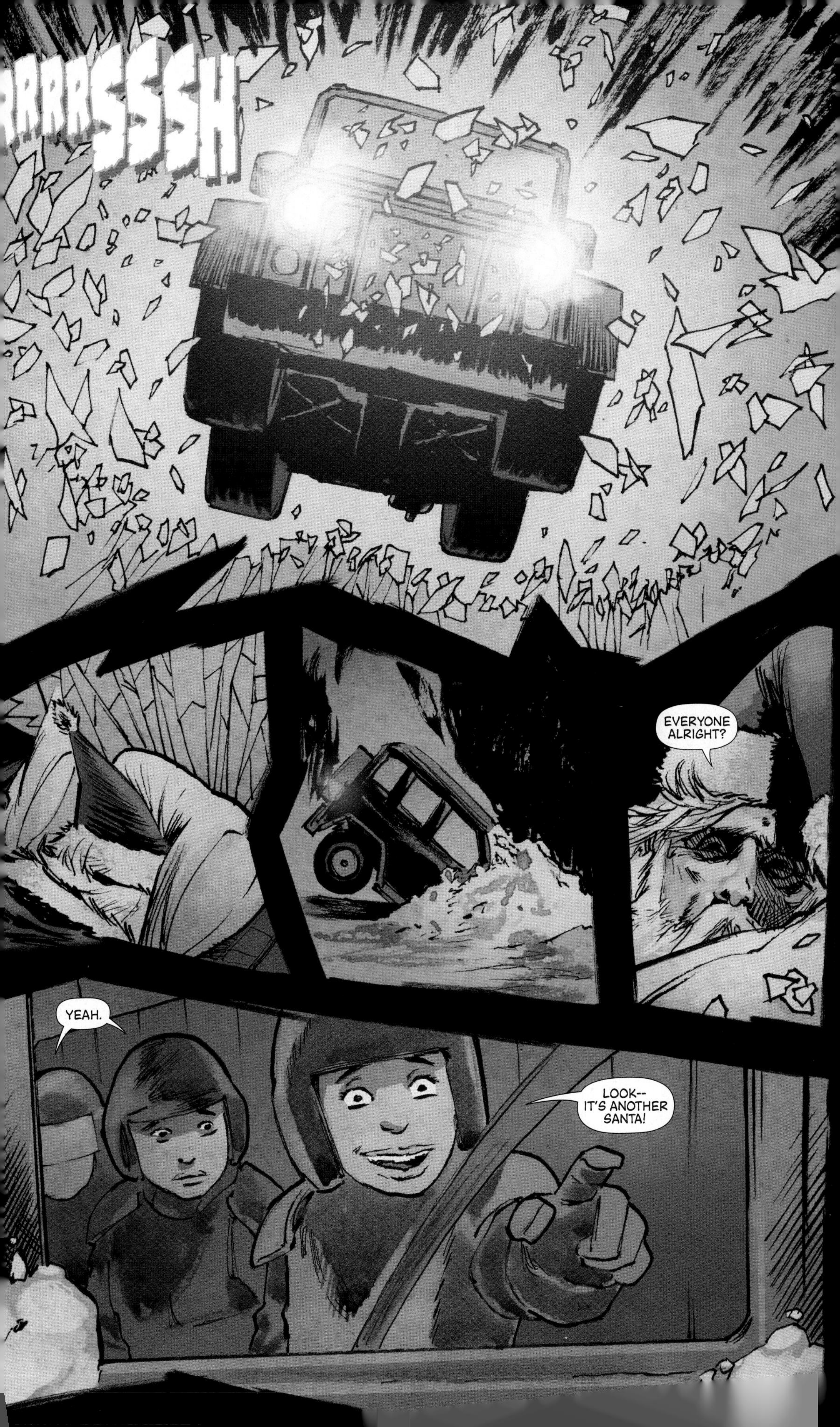
RRRRSSSH
EVERYONE ALRIGHT?
YEAH.
LOOK-- IT'S ANOTHER SANTA!

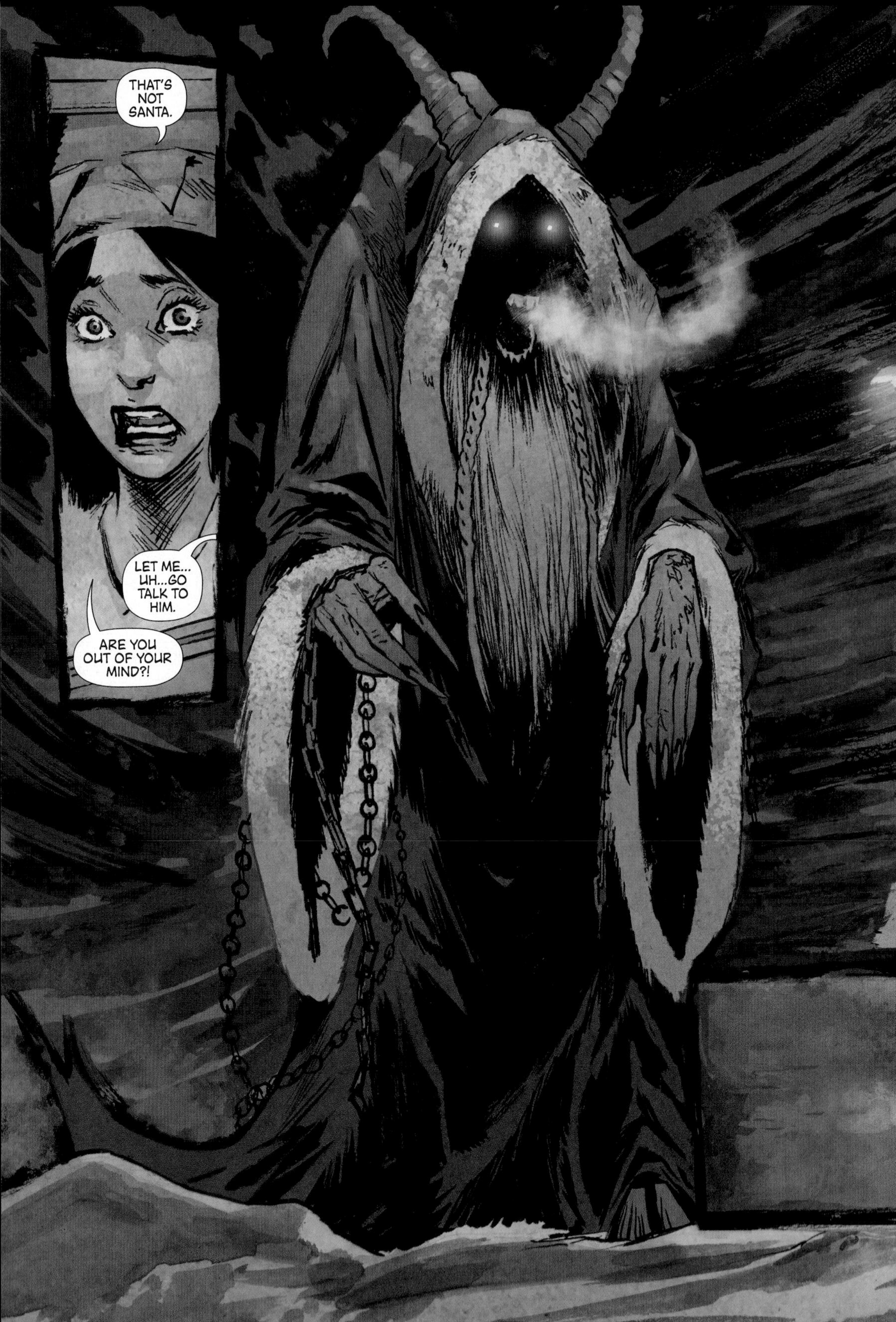
THAT'S NOT SANTA.
LET ME... UH...GO TALK TO HIM.
ARE YOU OUT OF YOUR MIND?!

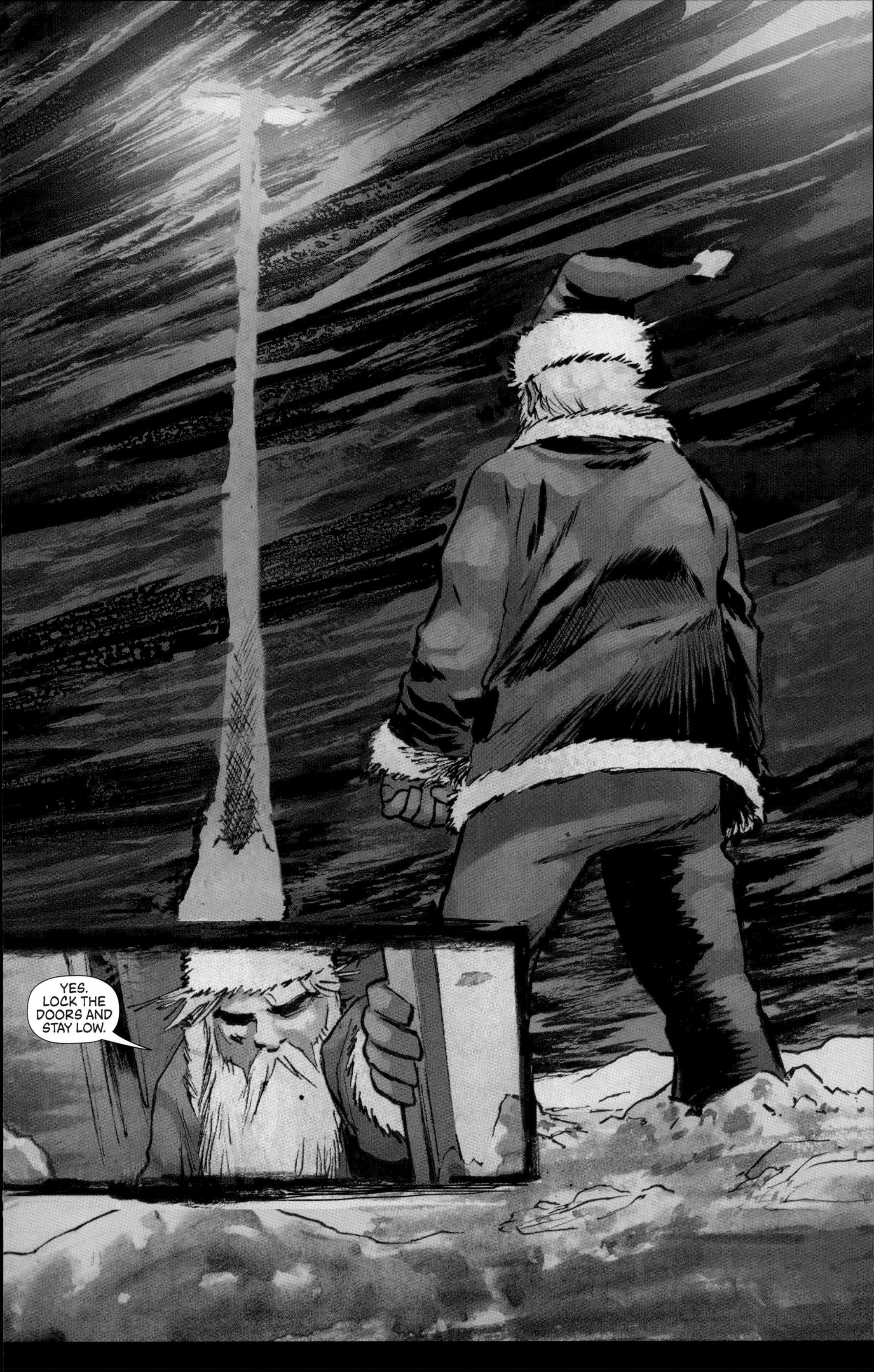
YES. LOCK THE DOORS AND STAY LOW.

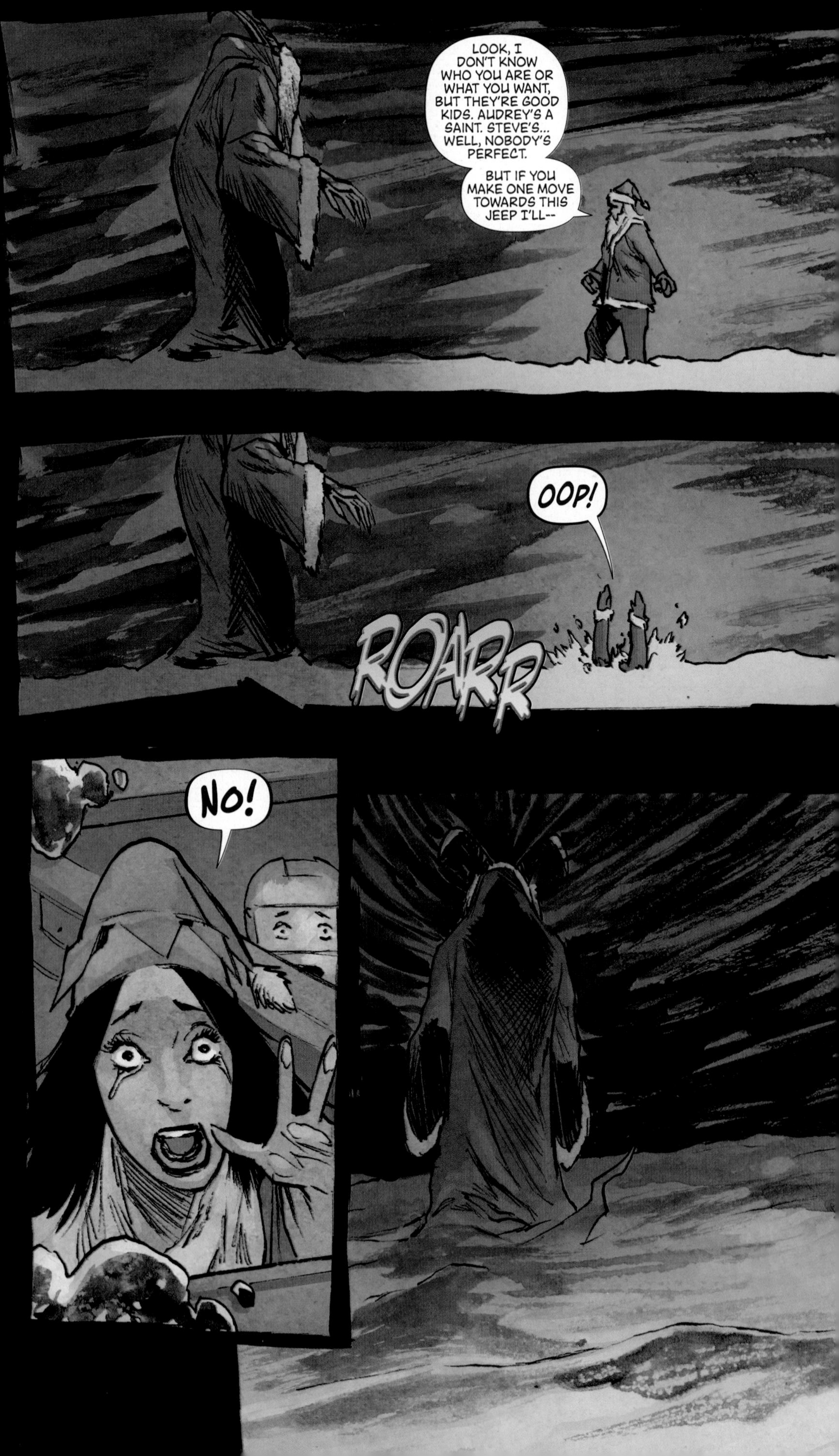
LOOK, I DON'T KNOW WHO YOU ARE OR WHAT YOU WANT, BUT THEY'RE GOOD KIDS. AUDREY'S A SAINT. STEVE'S... WELL, NOBODY'S PERFECT.
BUT IF YOU MAKE ONE MOVE TOWARDS THIS JEEP I'LL--
OOP!
ROARR
NO!

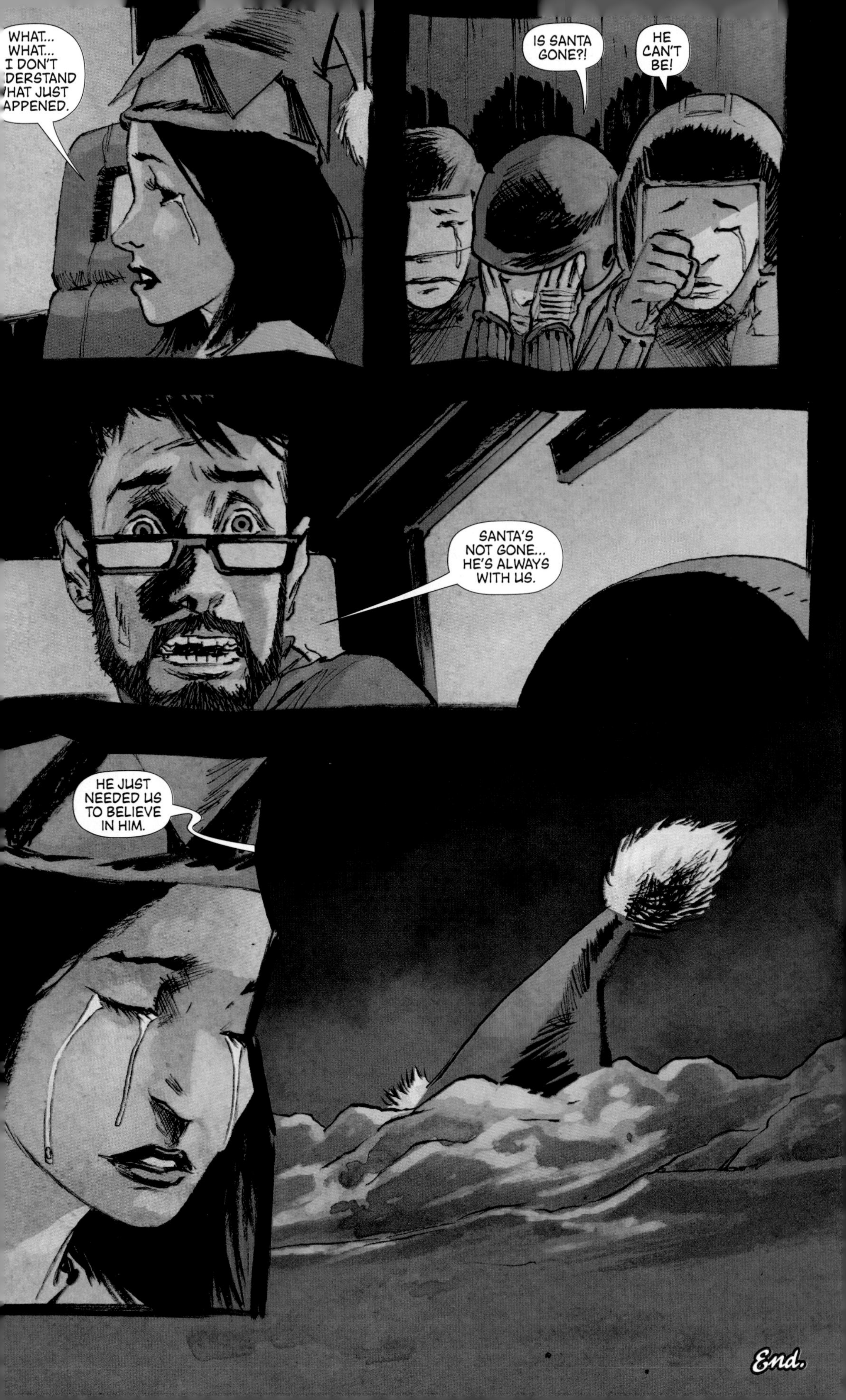
WHAT... WHAT... I DON'T DERSTAND HAT JUST APPENED.
IS SANTA GONE?!
HE CAN'T BE!
SANTA'S NOT GONE... HE'S ALWAYS WITH US.
HE JUST NEEDED US TO BELIEVE IN HIM.
End.

II

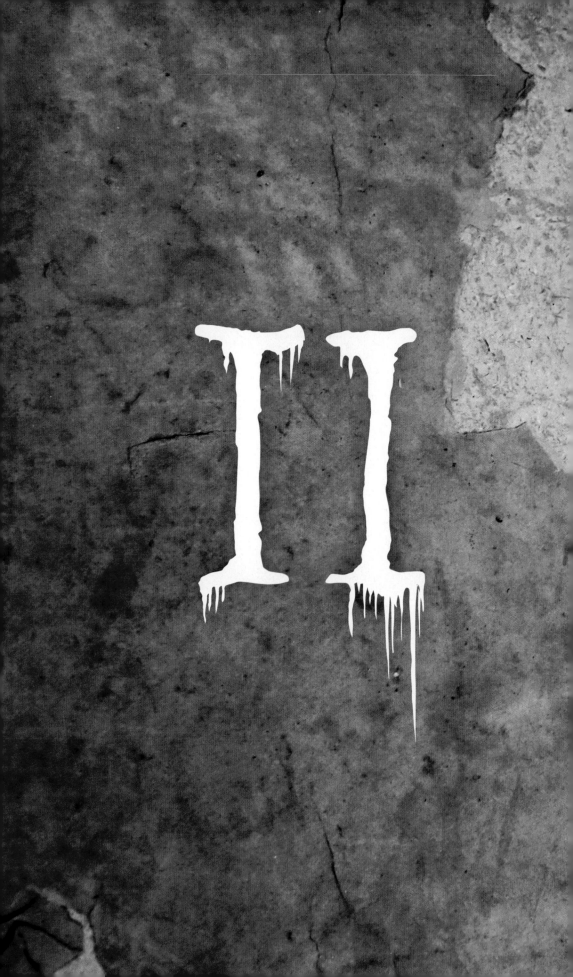

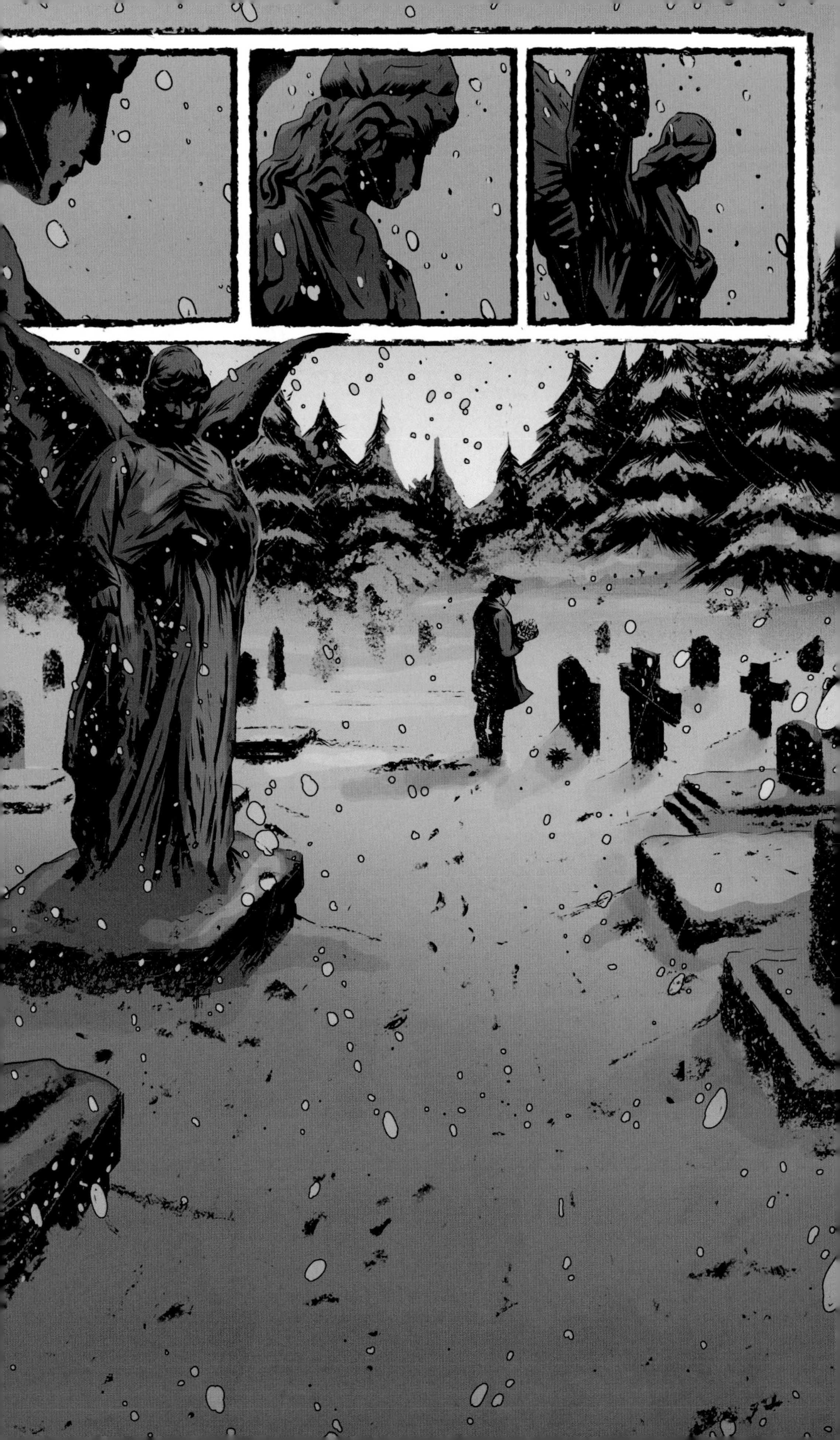

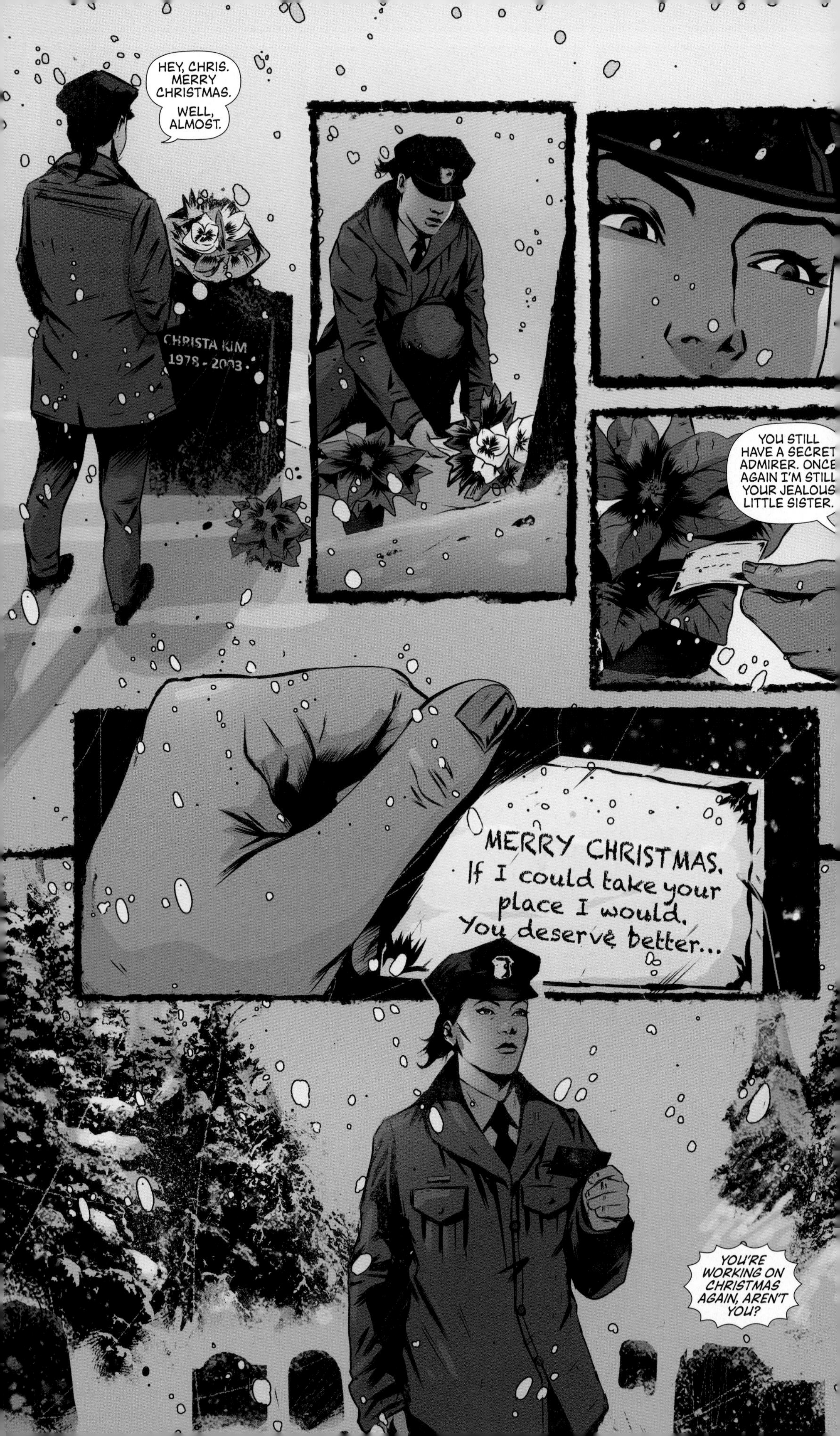
HEY, CHRIS. MERRY CHRISTMAS.
WELL, ALMOST.
CHRISTA KIM 1978 - 2003
YOU STILL HAVE A SECRET ADMIRER. ONCE AGAIN I'M STILL YOUR JEALOUS LITTLE SISTER.
MERRY CHRISTMAS. If I could take your place I would. You deserve better...
YOU'RE WORKING ON CHRISTMAS AGAIN, AREN'T YOU?

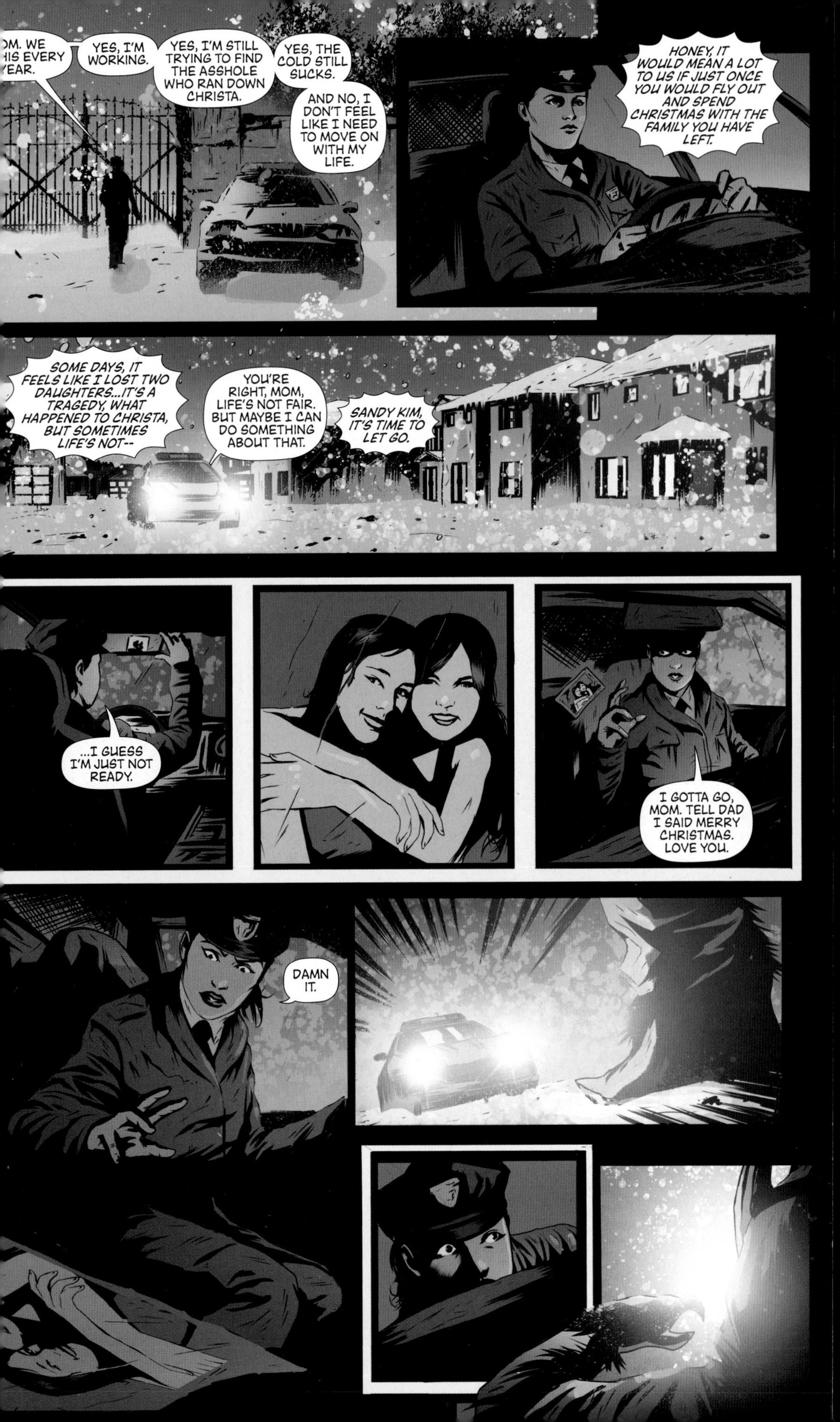

...OM. WE ...HIS EVERY YEAR.
YES, I'M WORKING.
YES, I'M STILL TRYING TO FIND THE ASSHOLE WHO RAN DOWN CHRISTA.
YES, THE COLD STILL SUCKS.
AND NO, I DON'T FEEL LIKE I NEED TO MOVE ON WITH MY LIFE.
HONEY, IT WOULD MEAN A LOT TO US IF JUST ONCE YOU WOULD FLY OUT AND SPEND CHRISTMAS WITH THE FAMILY YOU HAVE LEFT.
SOME DAYS, IT FEELS LIKE I LOST TWO DAUGHTERS...IT'S A TRAGEDY, WHAT HAPPENED TO CHRISTA, BUT SOMETIMES LIFE'S NOT--
YOU'RE RIGHT, MOM, LIFE'S NOT FAIR. BUT MAYBE I CAN DO SOMETHING ABOUT THAT.
SANDY KIM, IT'S TIME TO LET GO.
...I GUESS I'M JUST NOT READY.
I GOTTA GO, MOM. TELL DAD I SAID MERRY CHRISTMAS. LOVE YOU.
DAMN IT.

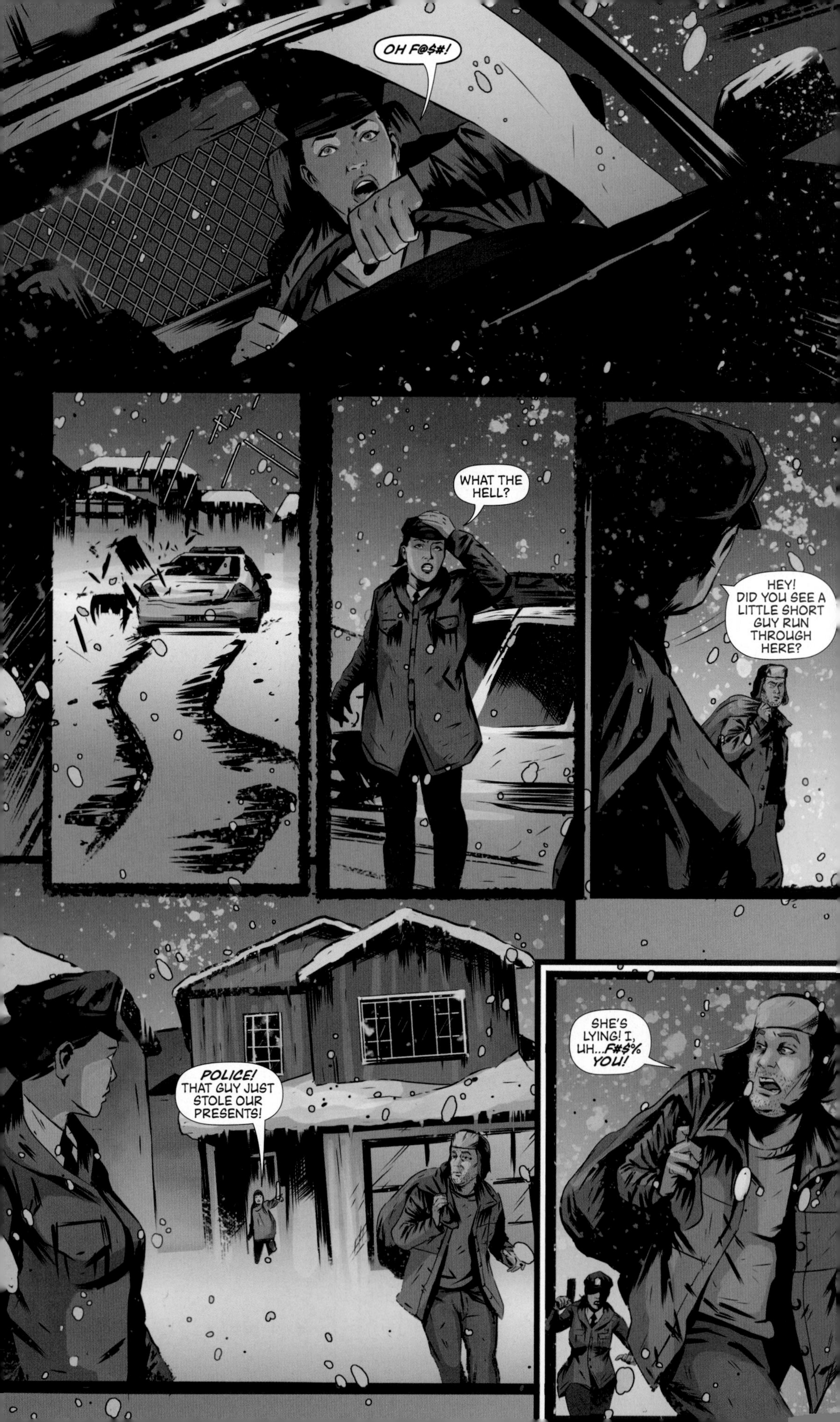
OH F@$#!
WHAT THE HELL?
HEY! DID YOU SEE A LITTLE SHORT GUY RUN THROUGH HERE?
POLICE! THAT GUY JUST STOLE OUR PRESENTS!
SHE'S LYING! I, UH...F#$% YOU!

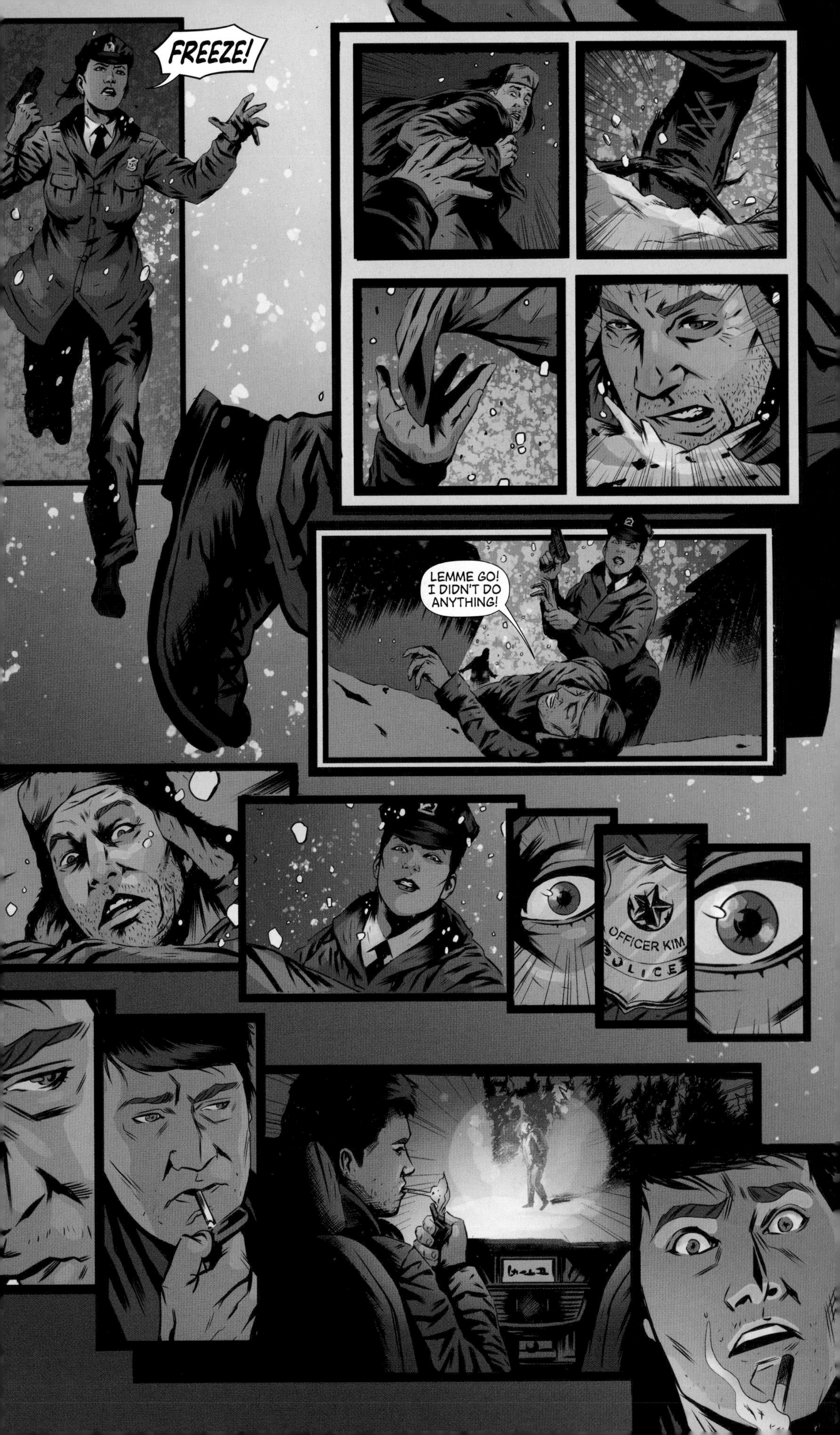
FREEZE!
LEMME GO! I DIDN'T DO ANYTHING!
OFFICER KIM
POLICE

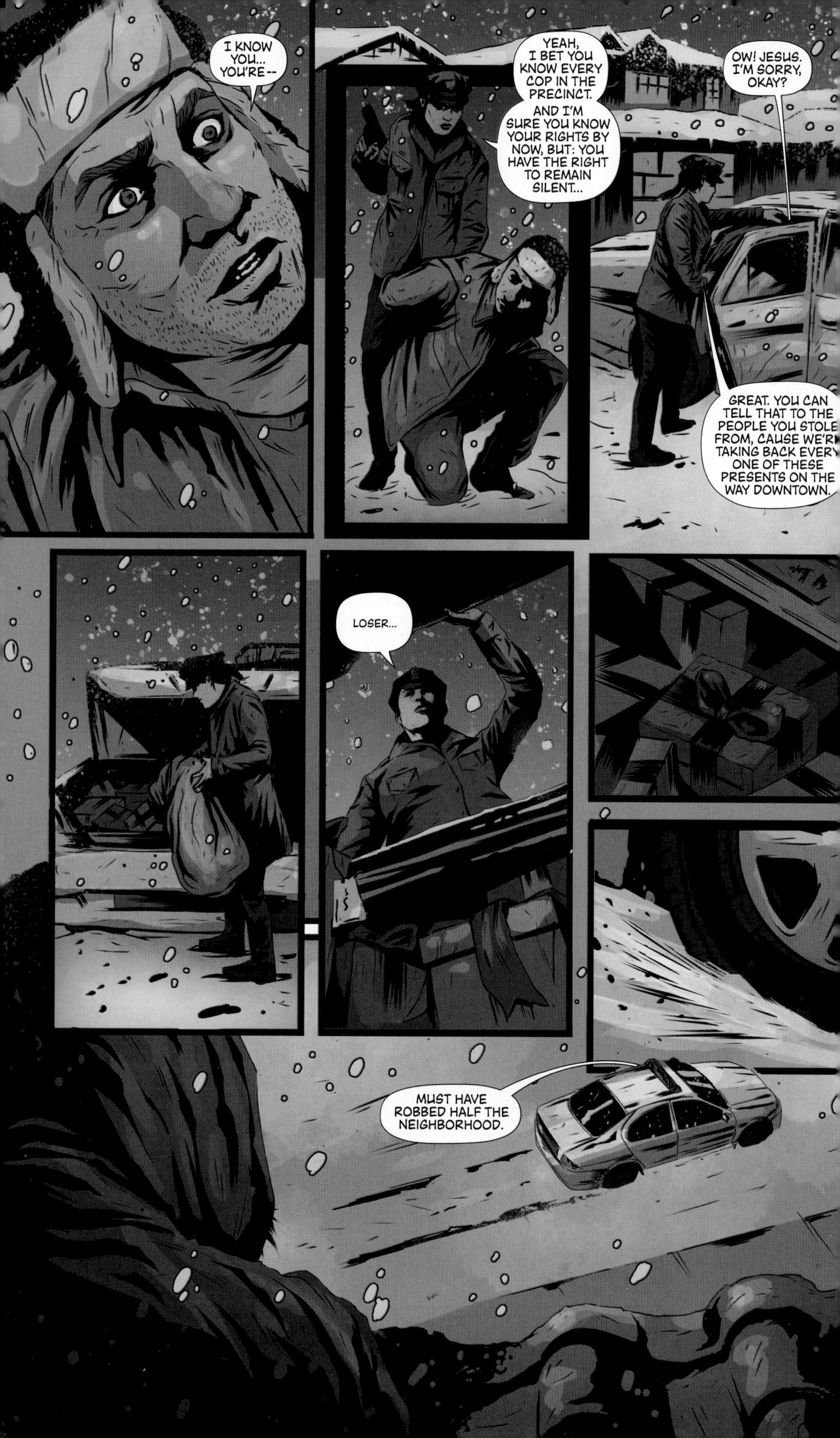
I KNOW YOU... YOU'RE--
YEAH, I BET YOU KNOW EVERY COP IN THE PRECINCT.
AND I'M SURE YOU KNOW YOUR RIGHTS BY NOW, BUT: YOU HAVE THE RIGHT TO REMAIN SILENT...
OW! JESUS. I'M SORRY, OKAY?
GREAT. YOU CAN TELL THAT TO THE PEOPLE YOU STOLE FROM, CAUSE WE'RE TAKING BACK EVERY ONE OF THESE PRESENTS ON THE WAY DOWNTOWN.
LOSER...
MUST HAVE ROBBED HALF THE NEIGHBORHOOD.

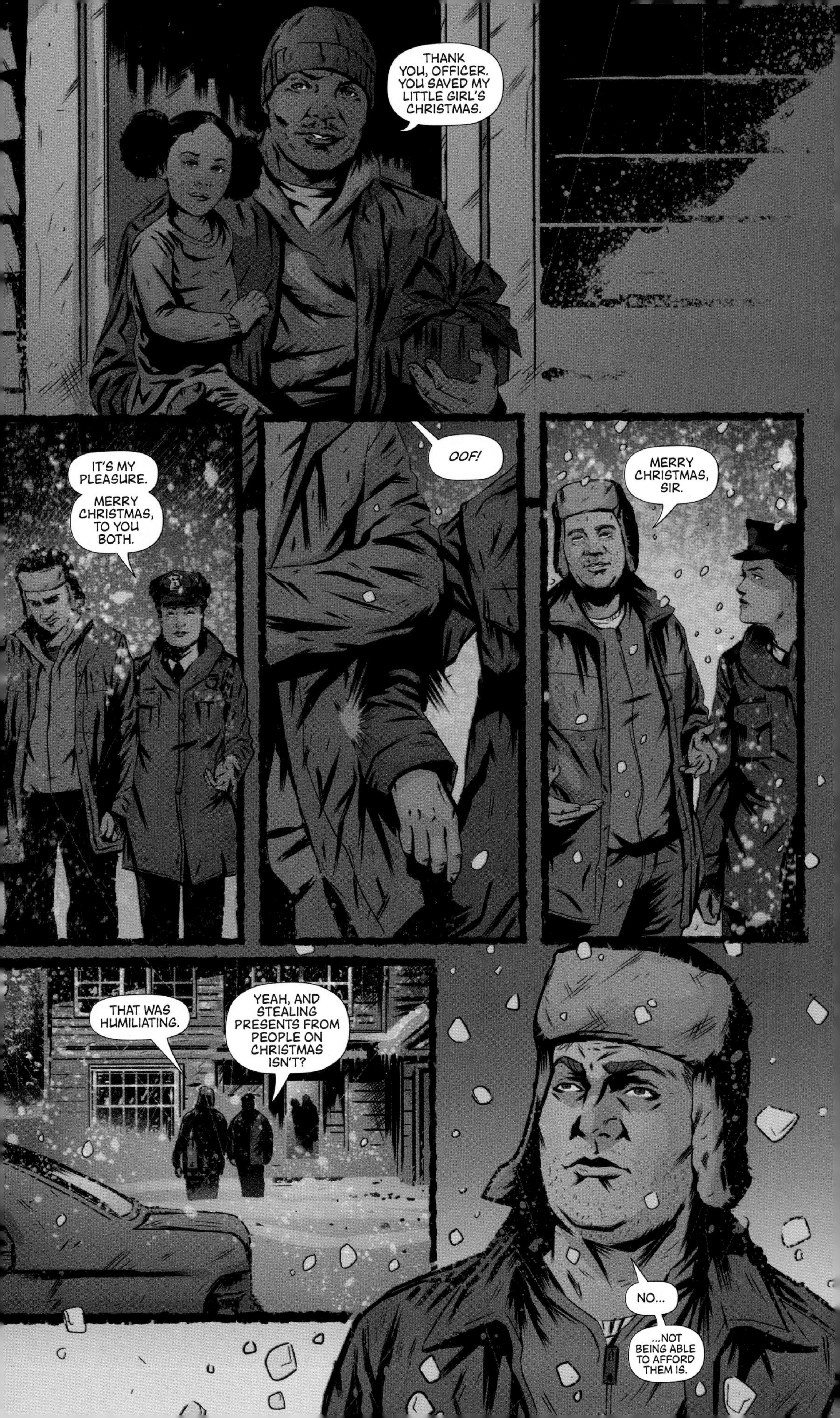
THANK YOU, OFFICER. YOU SAVED MY LITTLE GIRL'S CHRISTMAS.
IT'S MY PLEASURE.
MERRY CHRISTMAS, TO YOU BOTH.
OOF!
MERRY CHRISTMAS, SIR.
THAT WAS HUMILIATING.
YEAH, AND STEALING PRESENTS FROM PEOPLE ON CHRISTMAS ISN'T?
NO...
...NOT BEING ABLE TO AFFORD THEM IS.

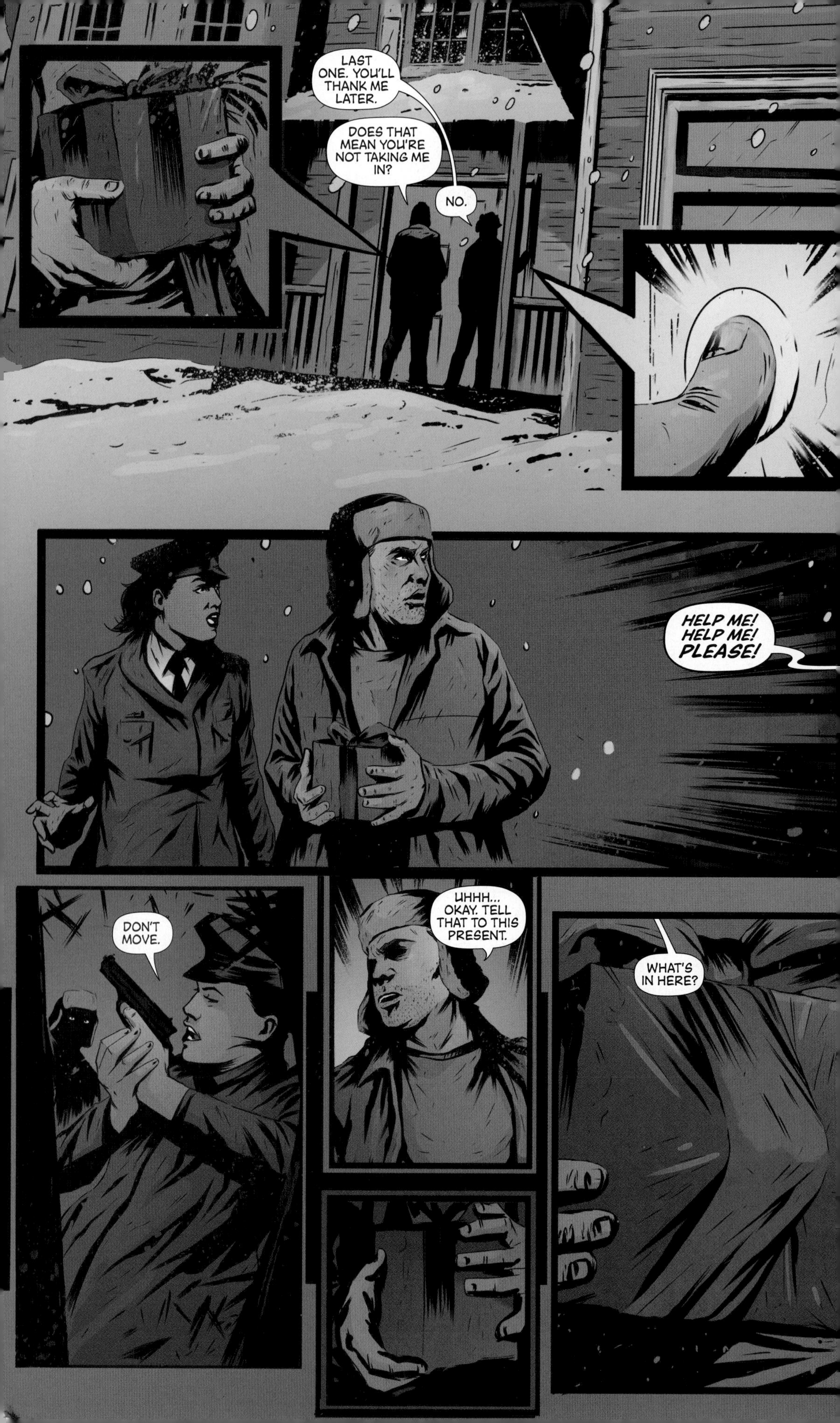
LAST ONE. YOU'LL THANK ME LATER.
DOES THAT MEAN YOU'RE NOT TAKING ME IN?
NO.
HELP ME! HELP ME! PLEASE!
DON'T MOVE.
UHHH... OKAY. TELL THAT TO THIS PRESENT.
WHAT'S IN HERE?

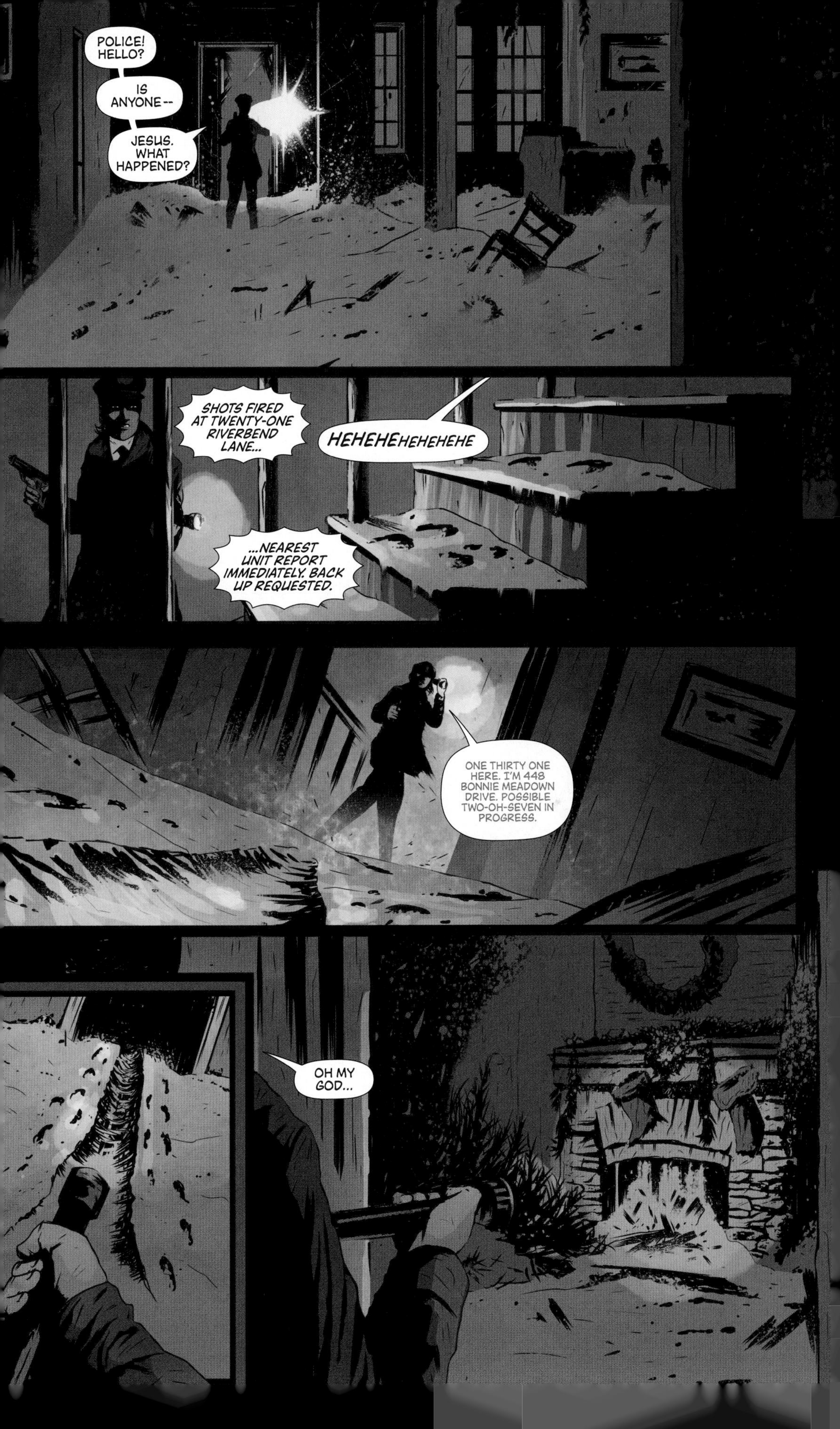
POLICE! HELLO?
IS ANYONE --
JESUS. WHAT HAPPENED?
SHOTS FIRED AT TWENTY-ONE RIVERBEND LANE...
HEHEHEHEHEHEHE
...NEAREST UNIT REPORT IMMEDIATELY. BACK UP REQUESTED.
ONE THIRTY ONE HERE. I'M 448 BONNIE MEADOWN DRIVE. POSSIBLE TWO-OH-SEVEN IN PROGRESS.
OH MY GOD...

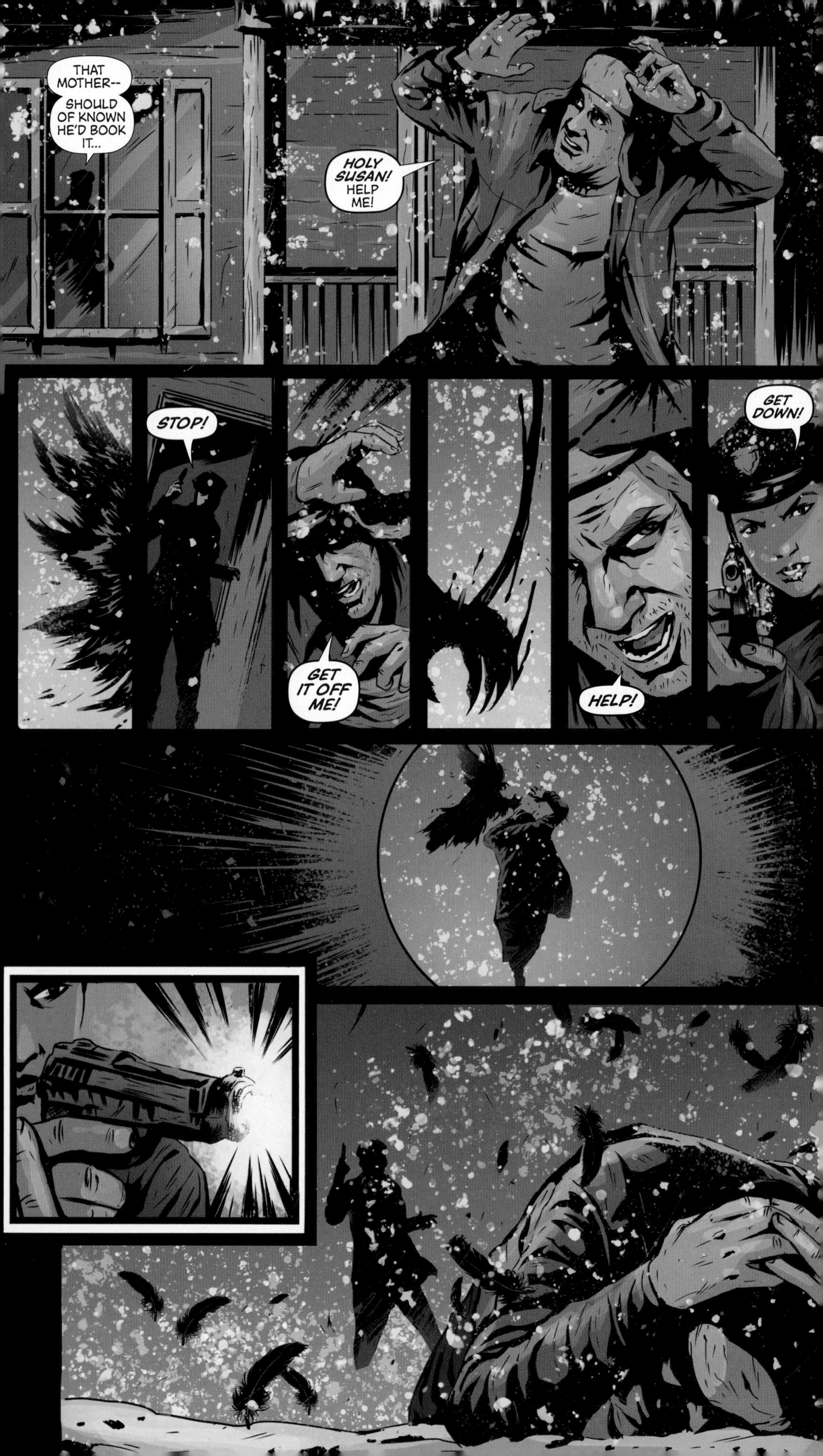
THAT MOTHER-- SHOULD OF KNOWN HE'D BOOK IT...
HOLY SUSAN! HELP ME!
STOP!
GET IT OFF ME!
HELP!
GET DOWN!

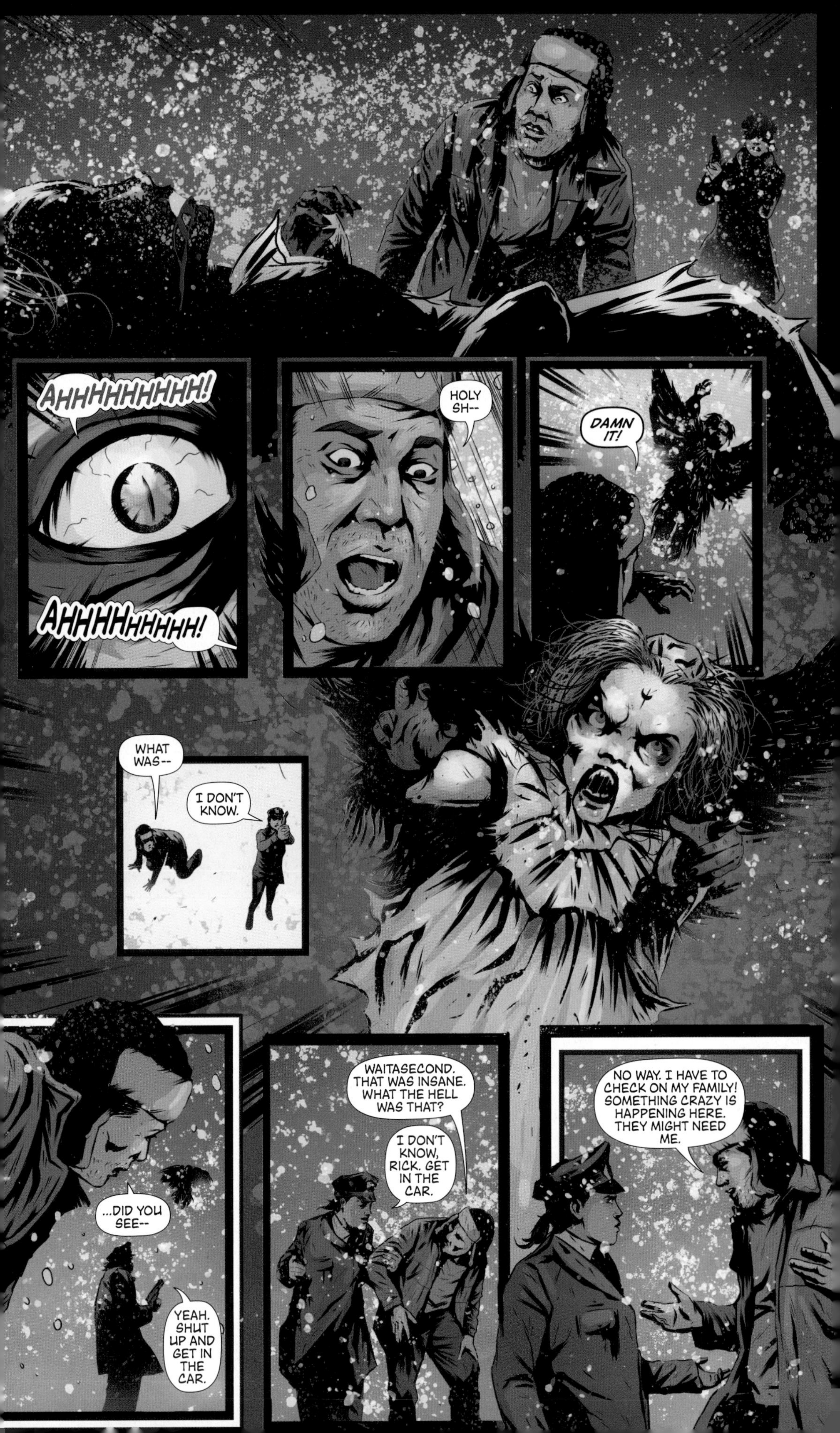
AHHHHHHHHH!
AHHHHHHHHH!
HOLY SH--
DAMN IT!
WHAT WAS--
I DON'T KNOW.
...DID YOU SEE--
YEAH. SHUT UP AND GET IN THE CAR.
WAITASECOND. THAT WAS INSANE. WHAT THE HELL WAS THAT?
I DON'T KNOW, RICK. GET IN THE CAR.
NO WAY. I HAVE TO CHECK ON MY FAMILY! SOMETHING CRAZY IS HAPPENING HERE. THEY MIGHT NEED ME.

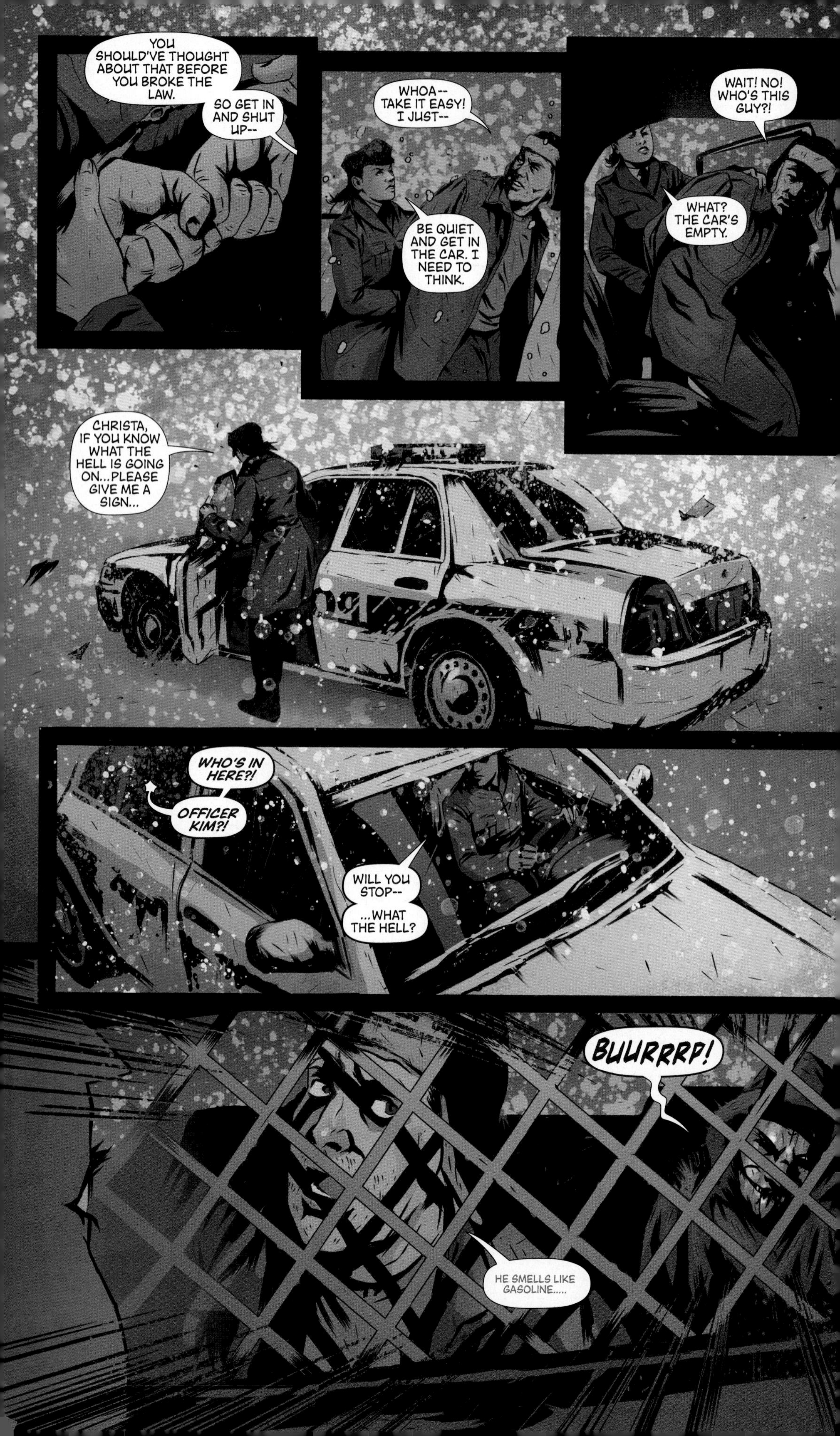

YOU SHOULD'VE THOUGHT ABOUT THAT BEFORE YOU BROKE THE LAW.
SO GET IN AND SHUT UP--
WHOA-- TAKE IT EASY! I JUST--
BE QUIET AND GET IN THE CAR. I NEED TO THINK.
WAIT! NO! WHO'S THIS GUY?!
WHAT? THE CAR'S EMPTY.
CHRISTA, IF YOU KNOW WHAT THE HELL IS GOING ON...PLEASE GIVE ME A SIGN...
WHO'S IN HERE?!
OFFICER KIM?!
WILL YOU STOP--
...WHAT THE HELL?
BUURRRP!
HE SMELLS LIKE GASOLINE.....

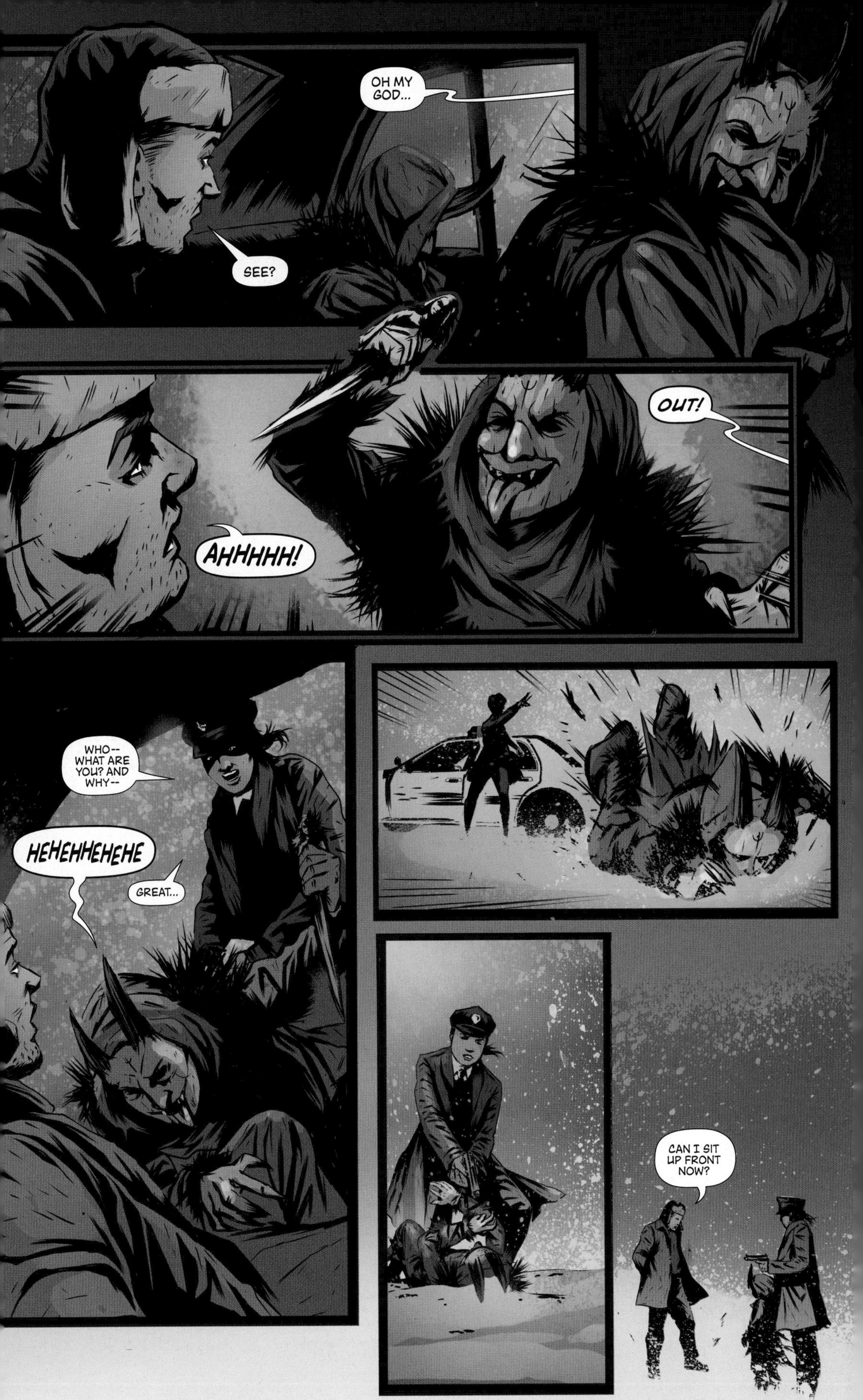
OH MY GOD...
SEE?
OUT!
AHHHHH!
WHO-- WHAT ARE YOU? AND WHY--
HEHEHHEHEHE
GREAT...
CAN I SIT UP FRONT NOW?

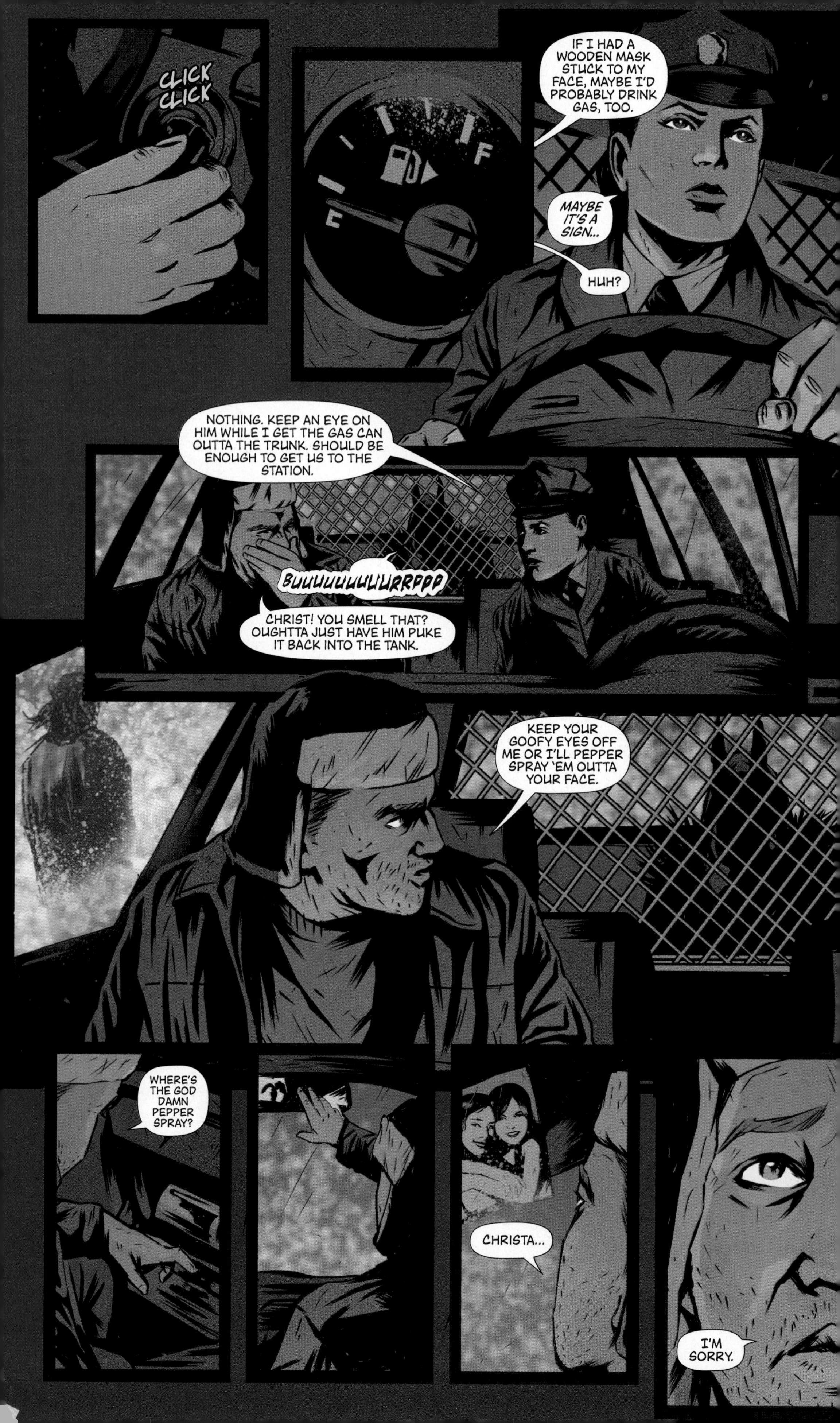
CLICK CLICK
IF I HAD A WOODEN MASK STUCK TO MY FACE, MAYBE I'D PROBABLY DRINK GAS, TOO.
MAYBE IT'S A SIGN...
HUH?
NOTHING. KEEP AN EYE ON HIM WHILE I GET THE GAS CAN OUTTA THE TRUNK. SHOULD BE ENOUGH TO GET US TO THE STATION.
BUUUUUUUUURRPPP
CHRIST! YOU SMELL THAT? OUGHTTA JUST HAVE HIM PUKE IT BACK INTO THE TANK.
KEEP YOUR GOOFY EYES OFF ME OR I'LL PEPPER SPRAY 'EM OUTTA YOUR FACE.
WHERE'S THE GOD DAMN PEPPER SPRAY?
CHRISTA...
I'M SORRY.

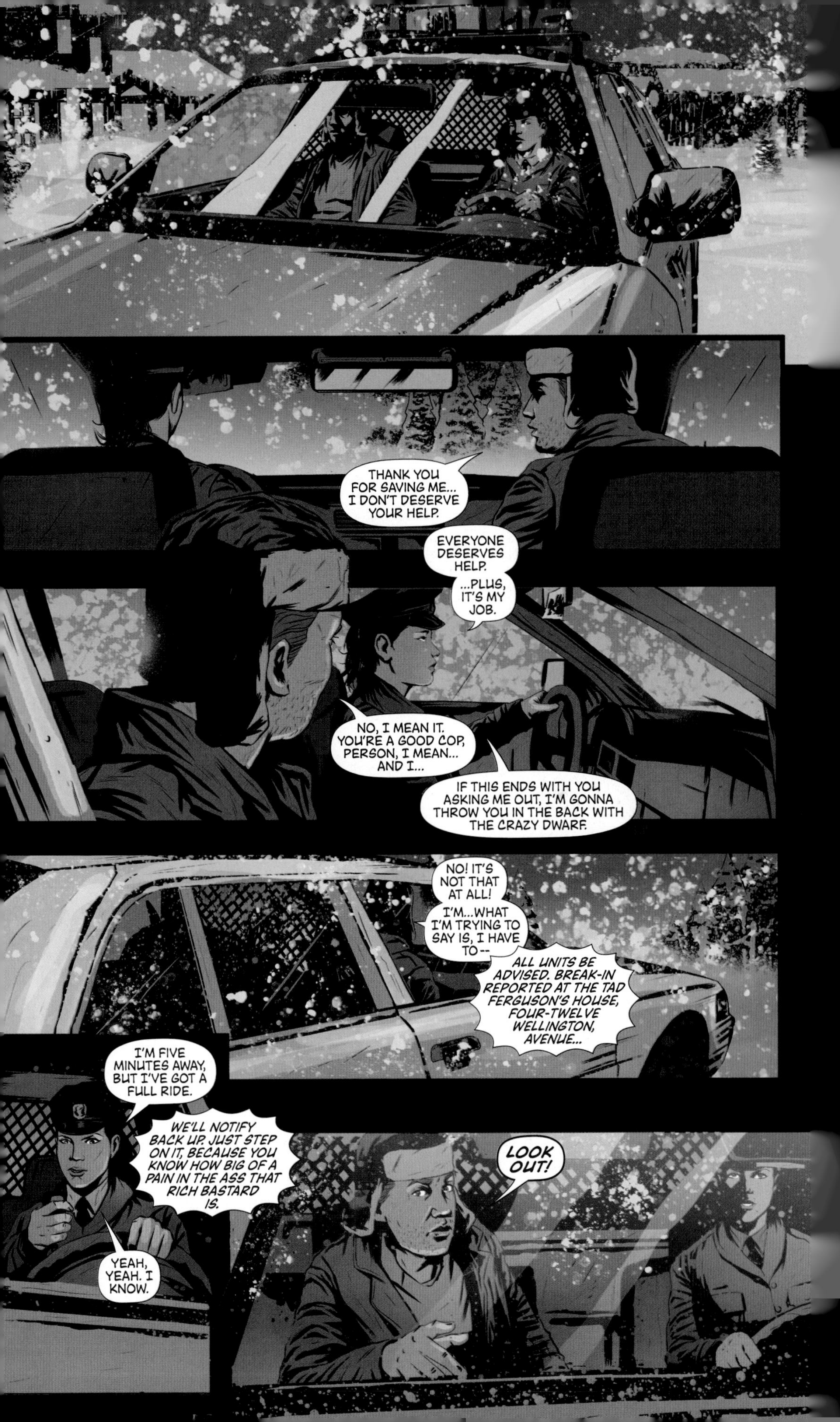
THANK YOU FOR SAVING ME... I DON'T DESERVE YOUR HELP.
EVERYONE DESERVES HELP.
...PLUS, IT'S MY JOB.
NO, I MEAN IT. YOU'RE A GOOD COP, PERSON, I MEAN... AND I...
IF THIS ENDS WITH YOU ASKING ME OUT, I'M GONNA THROW YOU IN THE BACK WITH THE CRAZY DWARF.
NO! IT'S NOT THAT AT ALL!
I'M...WHAT I'M TRYING TO SAY IS, I HAVE TO --
ALL UNITS BE ADVISED. BREAK-IN REPORTED AT THE TAD FERGUSON'S HOUSE, FOUR-TWELVE WELLINGTON, AVENUE...
I'M FIVE MINUTES AWAY, BUT I'VE GOT A FULL RIDE.
WE'LL NOTIFY BACK UP. JUST STEP ON IT, BECAUSE YOU KNOW HOW BIG OF A PAIN IN THE ASS THAT RICH BASTARD IS.
YEAH, YEAH. I KNOW.
LOOK OUT!

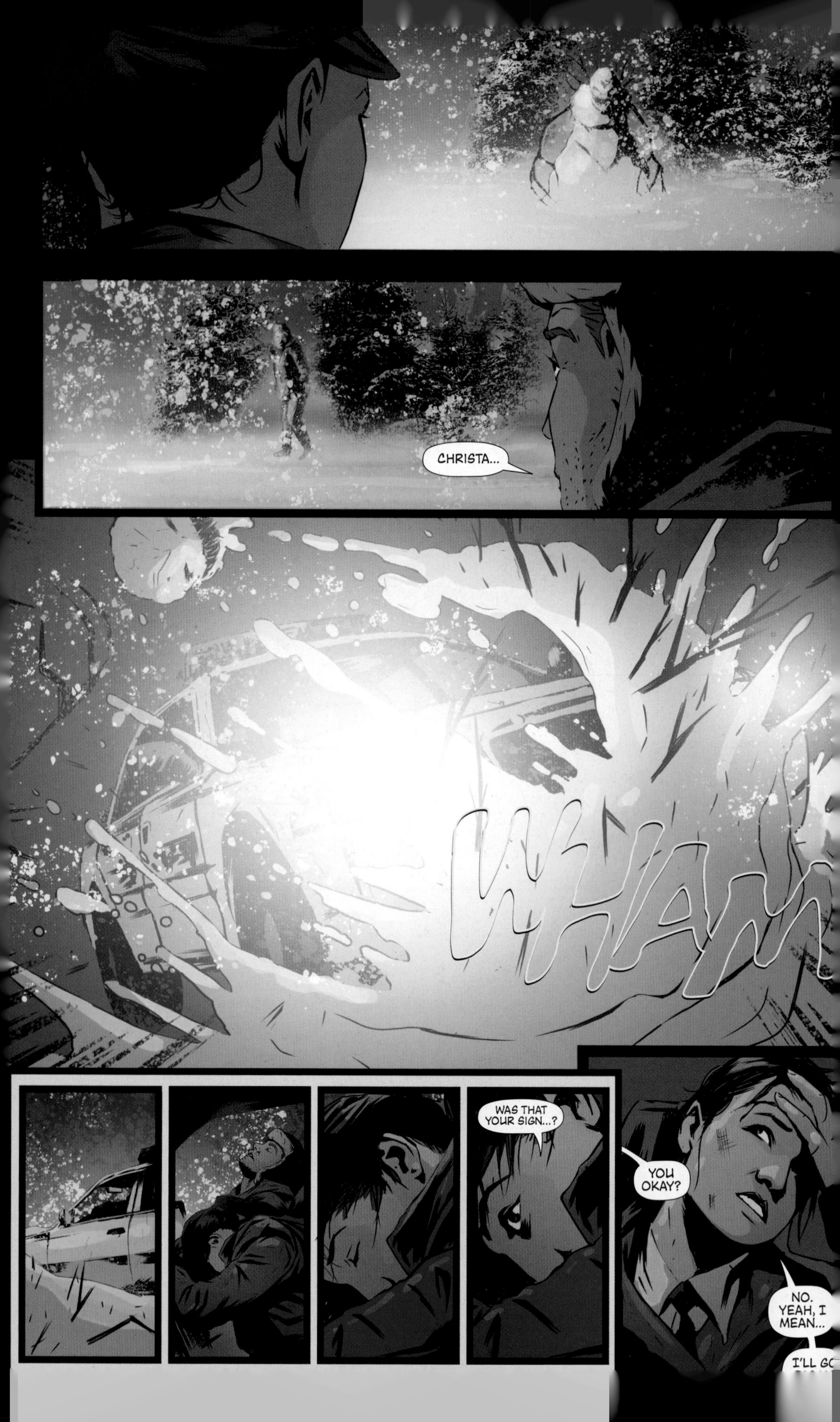

CHRISTA...
WHAM
WAS THAT YOUR SIGN...?
YOU OKAY?
NO. YEAH, I MEAN...
I'LL GO

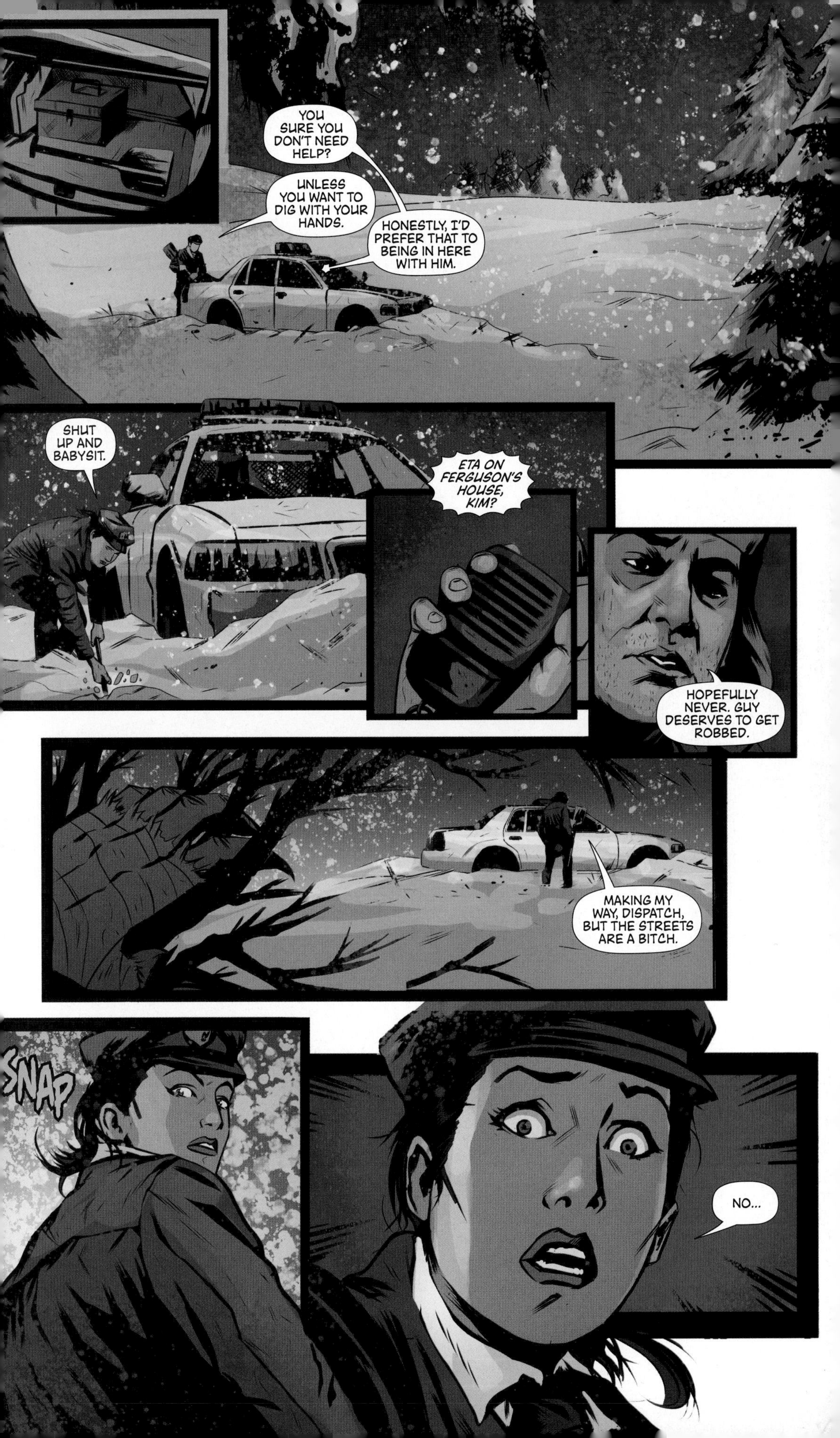
YOU SURE YOU DON'T NEED HELP?
UNLESS YOU WANT TO DIG WITH YOUR HANDS.
HONESTLY, I'D PREFER THAT TO BEING IN HERE WITH HIM.
SHUT UP AND BABYSIT.
ETA ON FERGUSON'S HOUSE, KIM?
HOPEFULLY NEVER. GUY DESERVES TO GET ROBBED.
MAKING MY WAY, DISPATCH, BUT THE STREETS ARE A BITCH.
SNAP
NO...

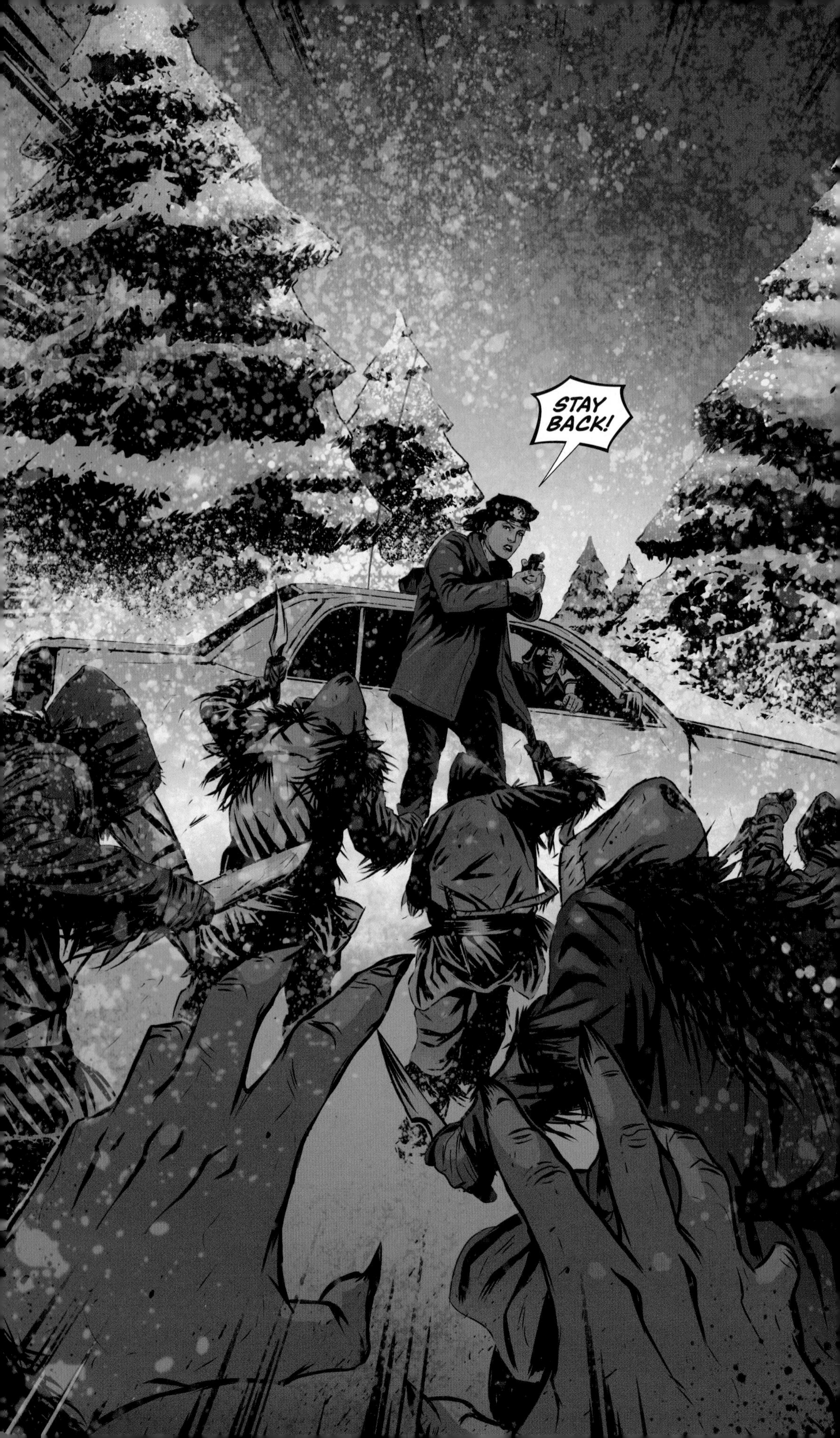
STAY BACK!

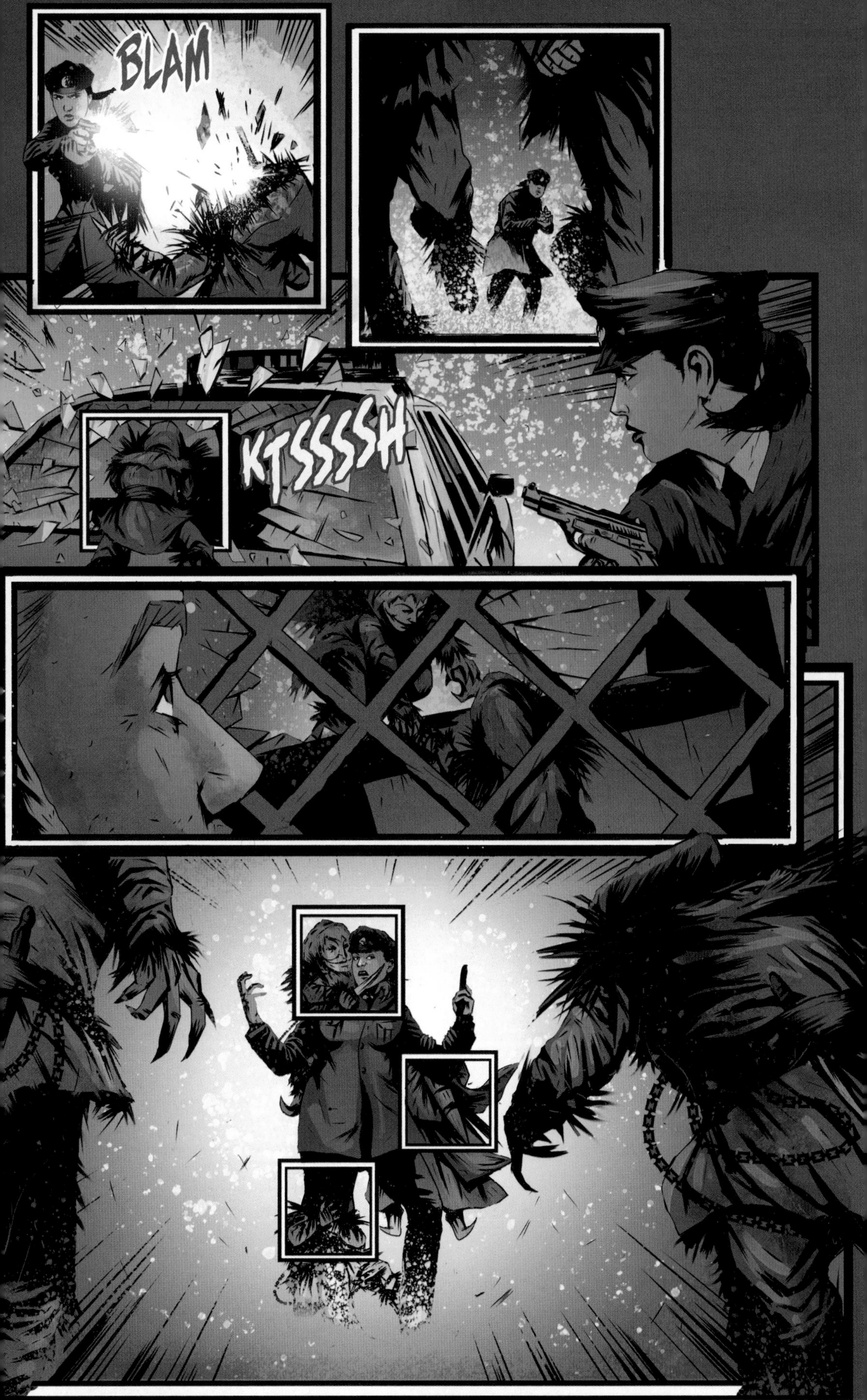
BLAM
KTSSSSSH

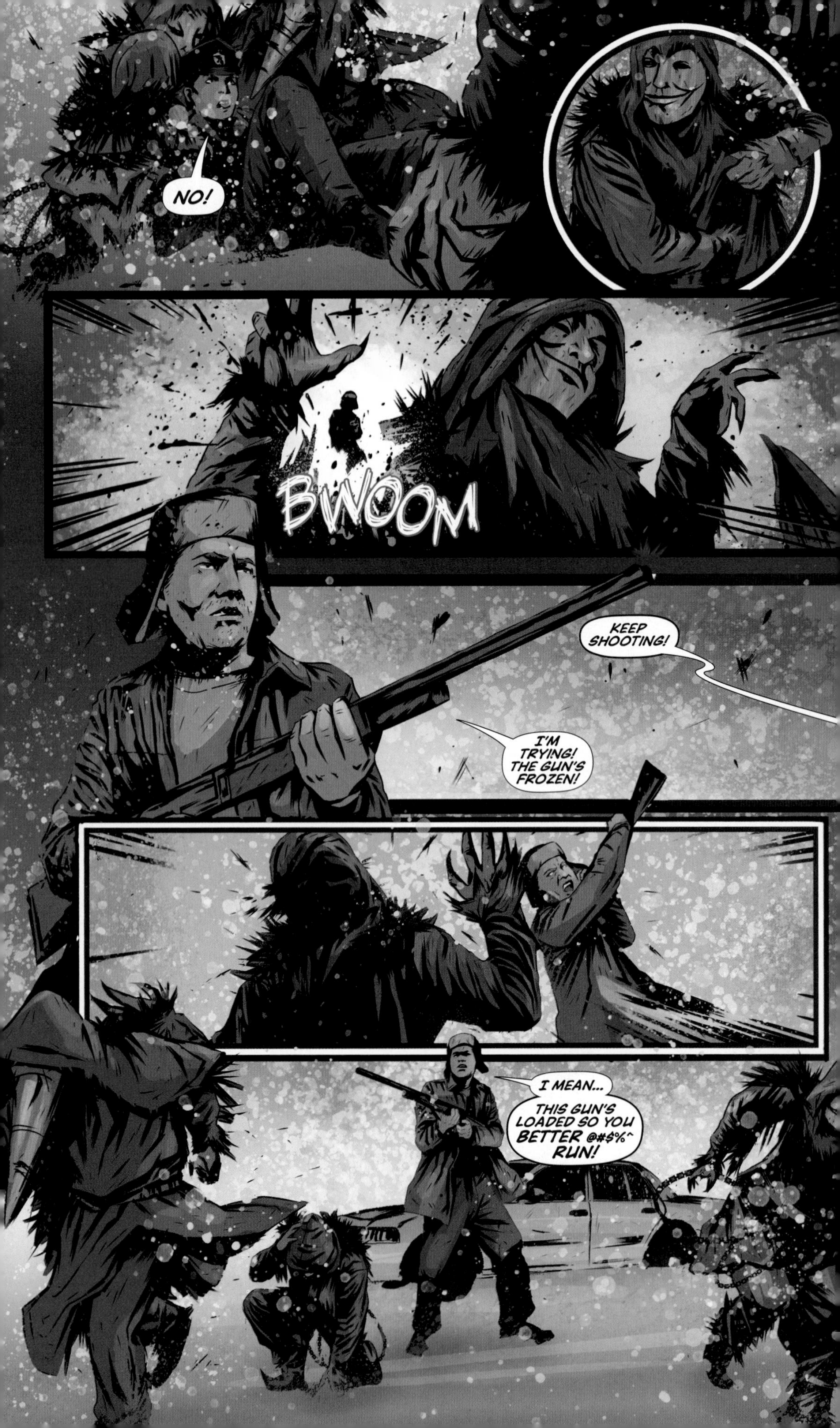
NO!
BWOOM
KEEP SHOOTING!
I'M TRYING! THE GUN'S FROZEN!
I MEAN...
THIS GUN'S LOADED SO YOU BETTER @#$%^ RUN!

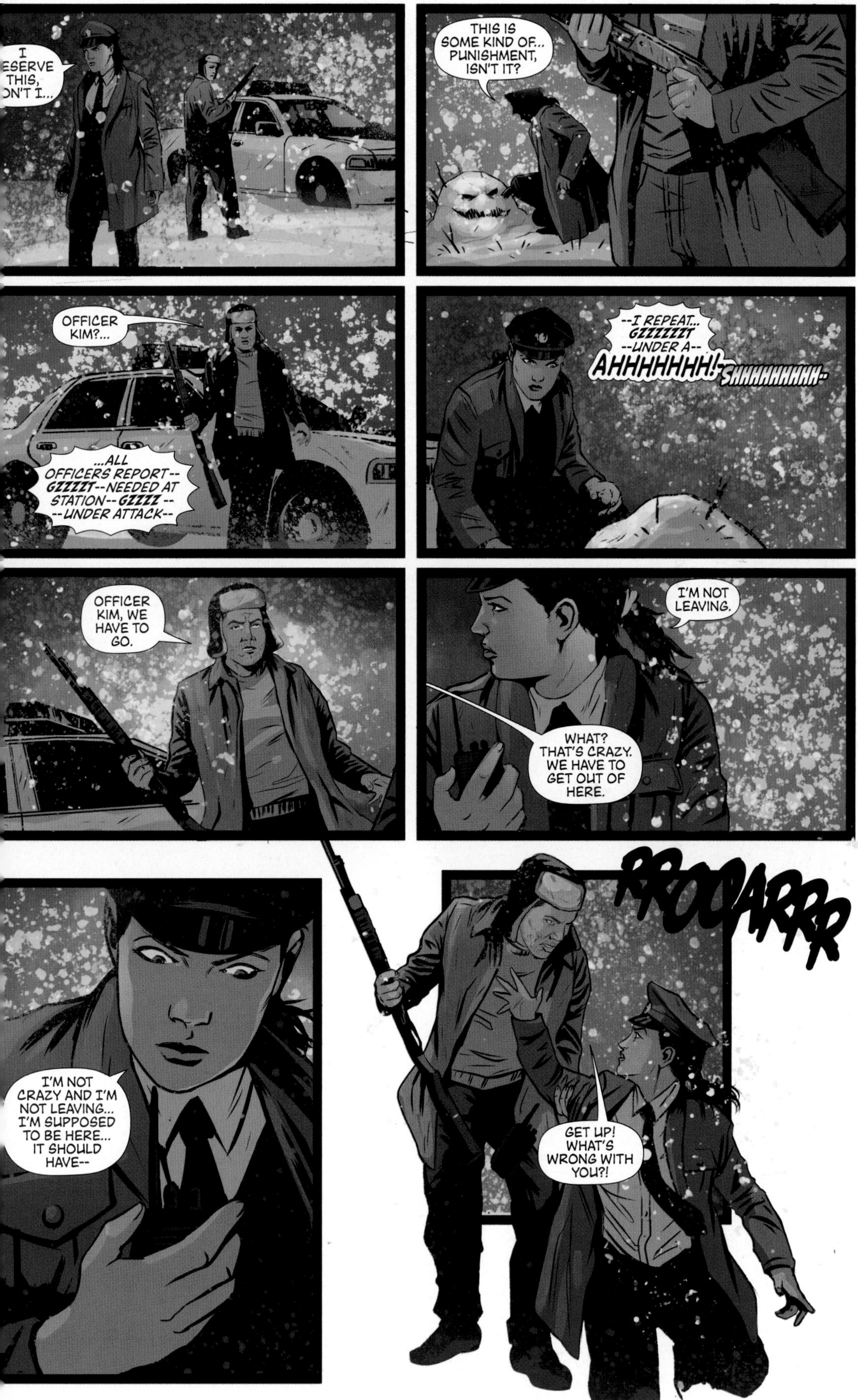
I ESERVE THIS, ON'T I...
THIS IS SOME KIND OF... PUNISHMENT, ISN'T IT?
OFFICER KIM?...
...ALL OFFICERS REPORT-- GZZZZT--NEEDED AT STATION--GZZZZ-- --UNDER ATTACK--
--I REPEAT... GZZZZZZT --UNDER A--
AHHHHHHH!-SHHHHHHHHH-
OFFICER KIM, WE HAVE TO GO.
I'M NOT LEAVING.
WHAT? THAT'S CRAZY. WE HAVE TO GET OUT OF HERE.
I'M NOT CRAZY AND I'M NOT LEAVING... I'M SUPPOSED TO BE HERE... IT SHOULD HAVE--
RROOARRR
GET UP! WHAT'S WRONG WITH YOU?!

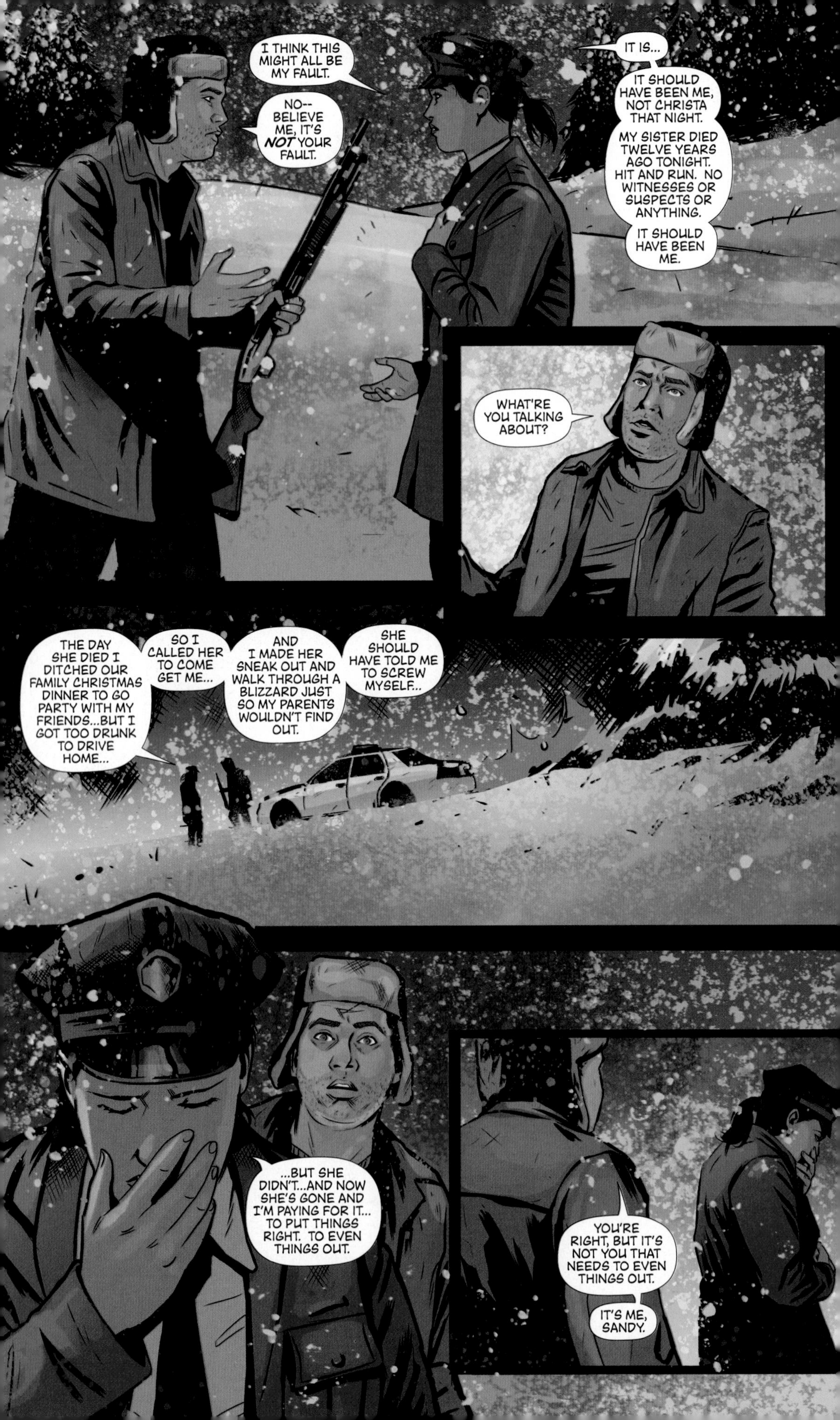
I THINK THIS MIGHT ALL BE MY FAULT.
NO-- BELIEVE ME, IT'S NOT YOUR FAULT.
IT IS...
IT SHOULD HAVE BEEN ME, NOT CHRISTA THAT NIGHT.
MY SISTER DIED TWELVE YEARS AGO TONIGHT. HIT AND RUN. NO WITNESSES OR SUSPECTS OR ANYTHING.
IT SHOULD HAVE BEEN ME.
WHAT'RE YOU TALKING ABOUT?
THE DAY SHE DIED I DITCHED OUR FAMILY CHRISTMAS DINNER TO GO PARTY WITH MY FRIENDS...BUT I GOT TOO DRUNK TO DRIVE HOME...
SO I CALLED HER TO COME GET ME...
AND I MADE HER SNEAK OUT AND WALK THROUGH A BLIZZARD JUST SO MY PARENTS WOULDN'T FIND OUT.
SHE SHOULD HAVE TOLD ME TO SCREW MYSELF...
...BUT SHE DIDN'T...AND NOW SHE'S GONE AND I'M PAYING FOR IT... TO PUT THINGS RIGHT. TO EVEN THINGS OUT.
YOU'RE RIGHT, BUT IT'S NOT YOU THAT NEEDS TO EVEN THINGS OUT.
IT'S ME, SANDY.

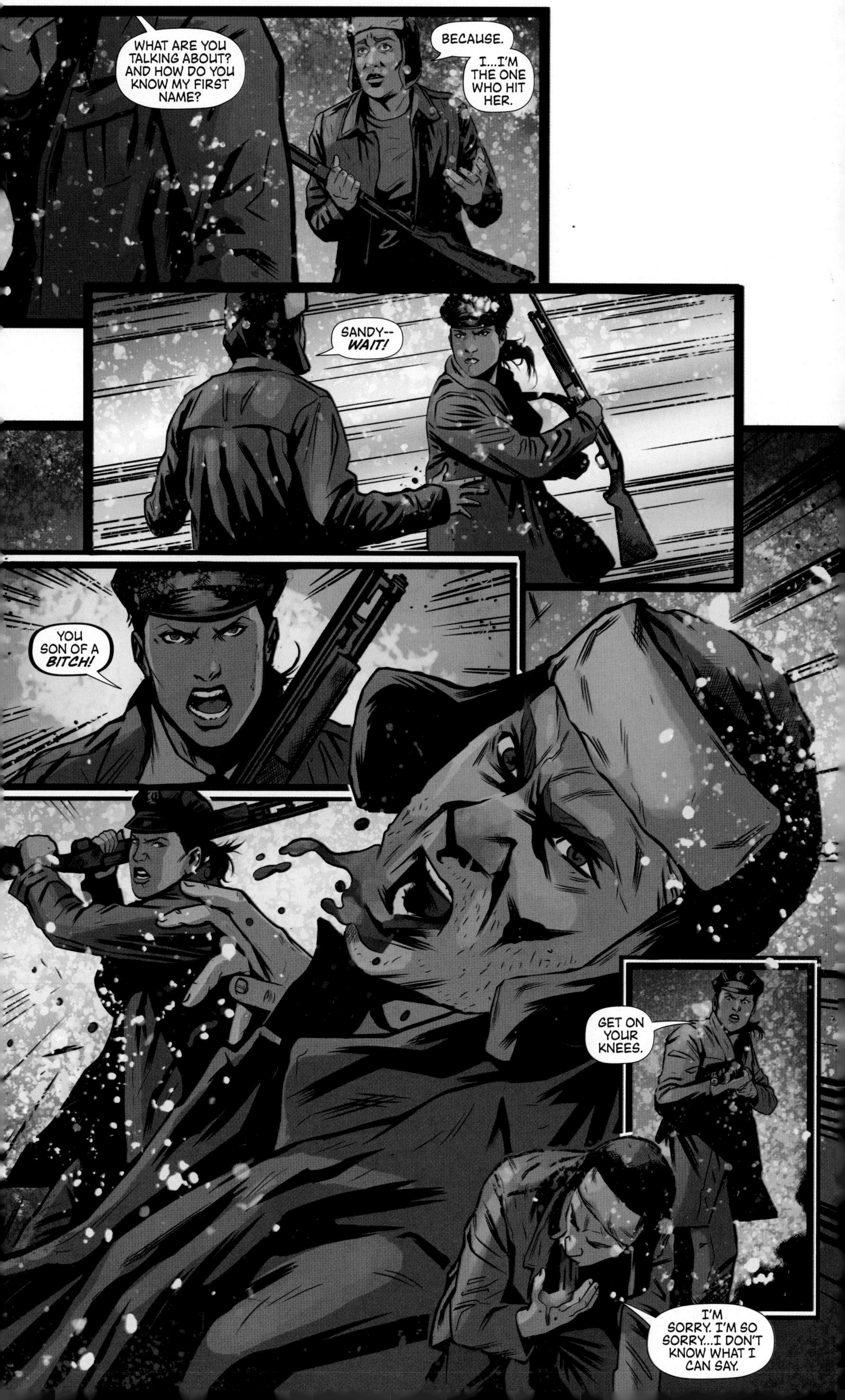
WHAT ARE YOU TALKING ABOUT? AND HOW DO YOU KNOW MY FIRST NAME?
BECAUSE.
I...I'M THE ONE WHO HIT HER.
SANDY-- WAIT!
YOU SON OF A BITCH!
GET ON YOUR KNEES.
I'M SORRY. I'M SO SORRY...I DON'T KNOW WHAT I CAN SAY.

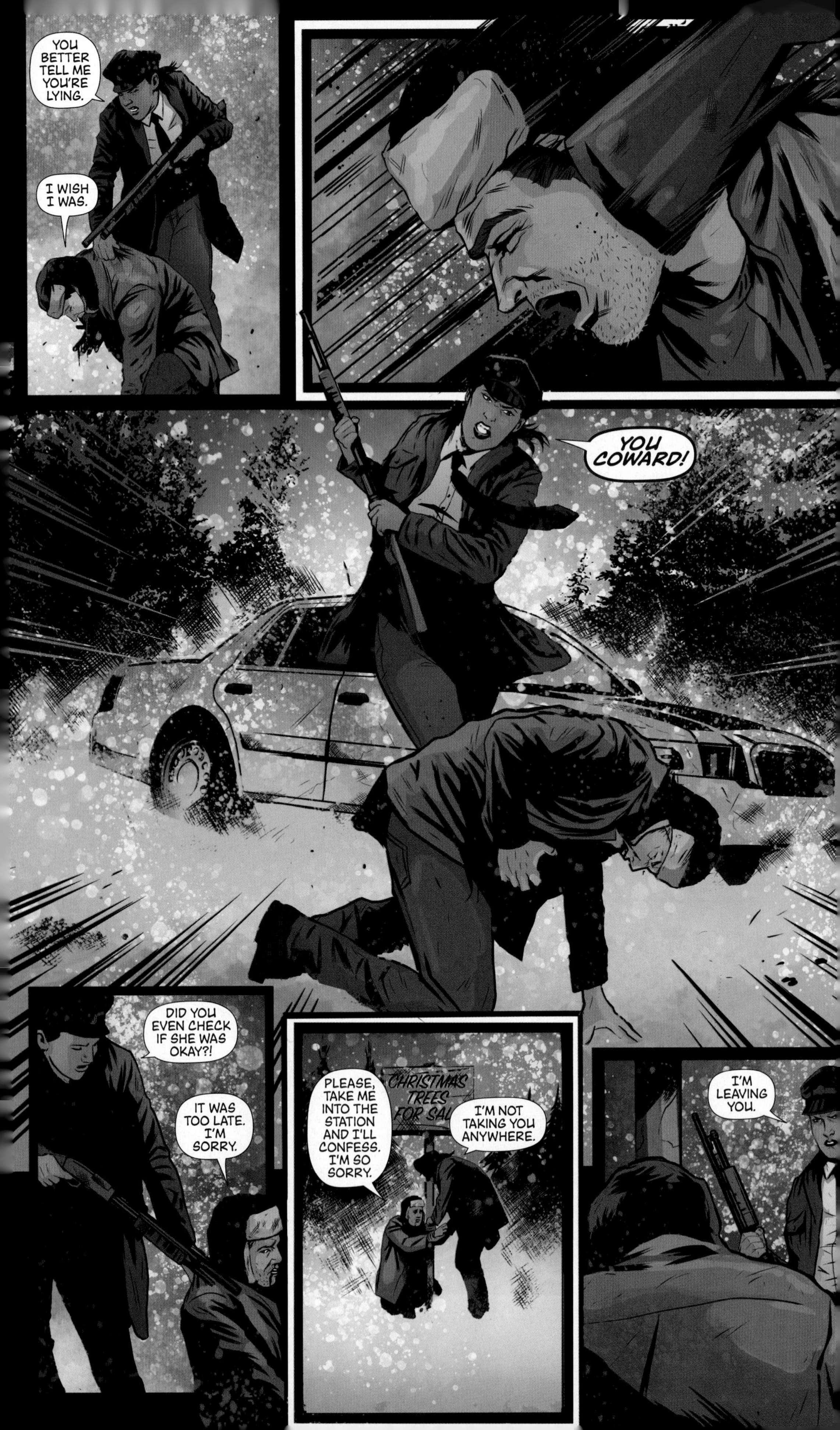
YOU BETTER TELL ME YOU'RE LYING.
I WISH I WAS.
YOU COWARD!
DID YOU EVEN CHECK IF SHE WAS OKAY?!
IT WAS TOO LATE. I'M SORRY.
CHRISTMAS TREES FOR SAL
PLEASE, TAKE ME INTO THE STATION AND I'LL CONFESS. I'M SO SORRY.
I'M NOT TAKING YOU ANYWHERE.
I'M LEAVING YOU.

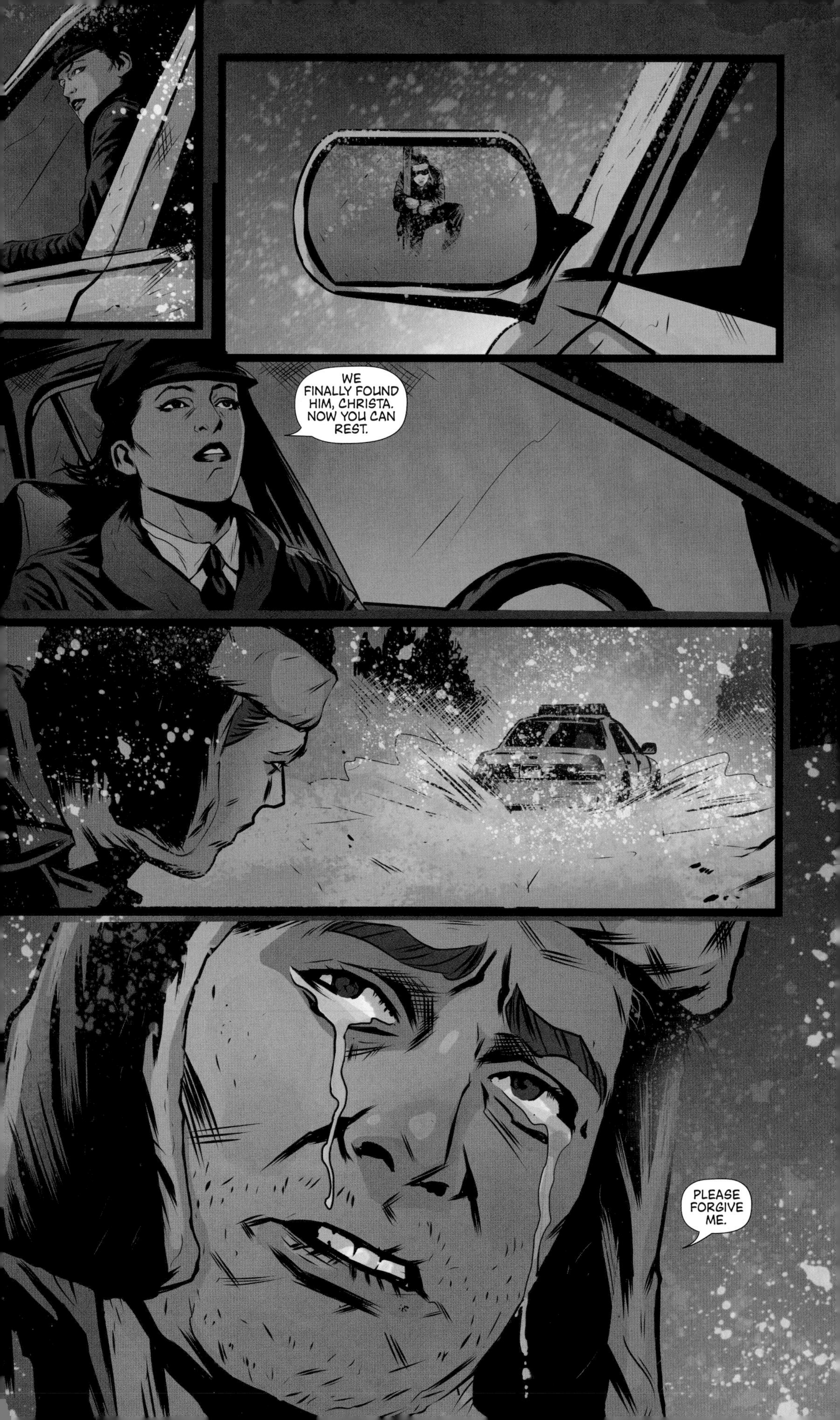
WE FINALLY FOUND HIM, CHRISTA. NOW YOU CAN REST.
PLEASE FORGIVE ME.

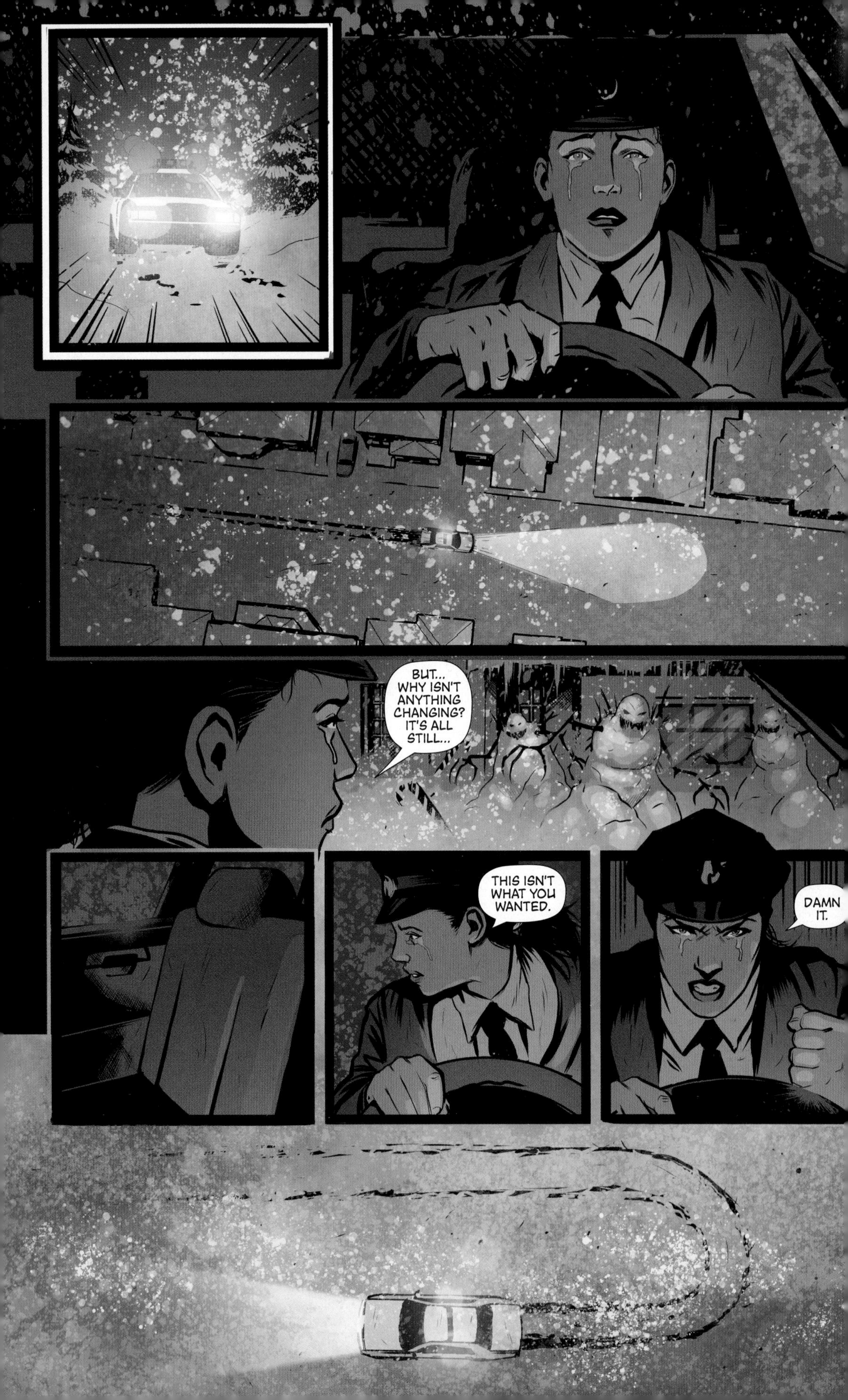
BUT... WHY ISN'T ANYTHING CHANGING? IT'S ALL STILL...
THIS ISN'T WHAT YOU WANTED.
DAMN IT.

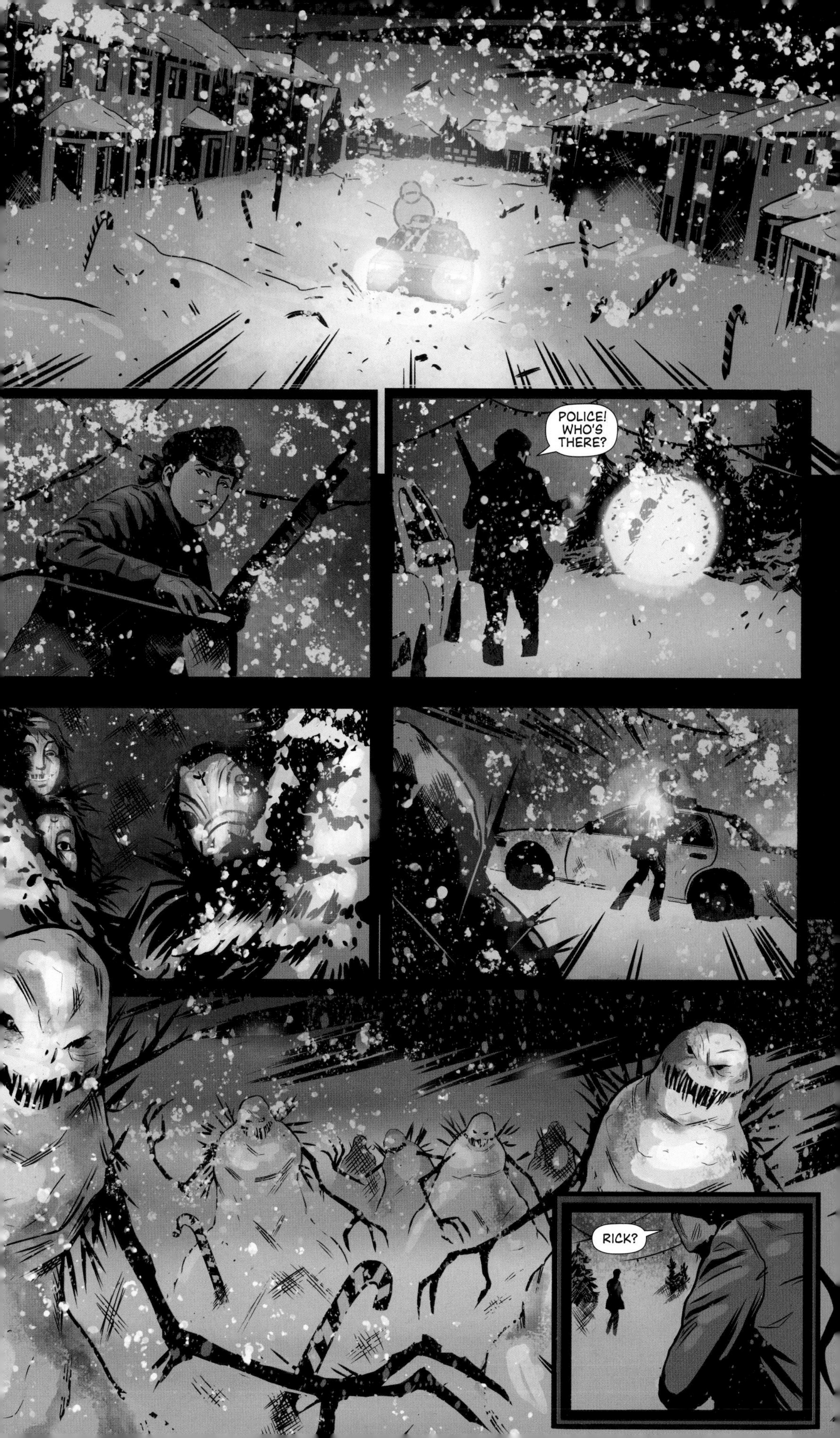
POLICE! WHO'S THERE?
RICK?

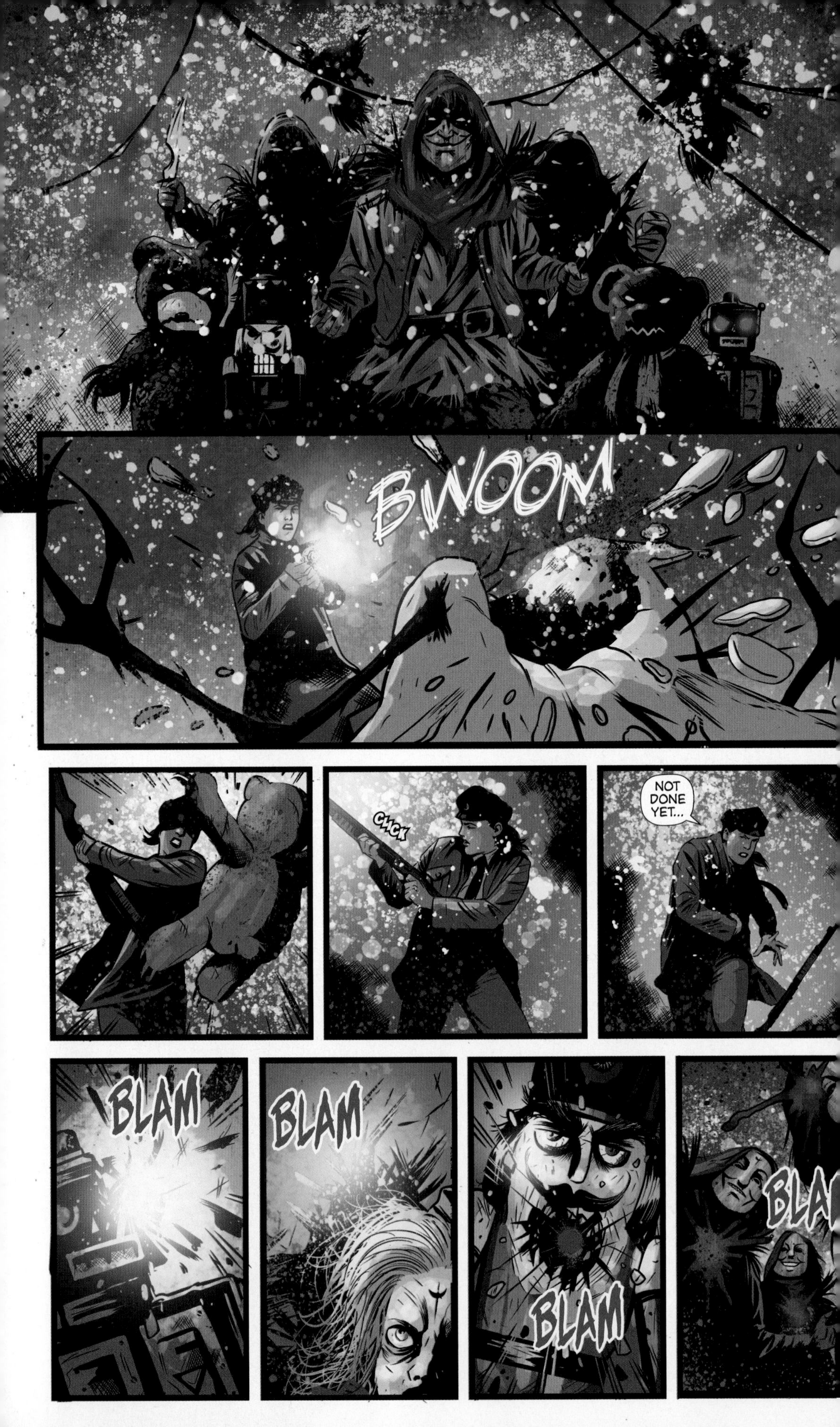
BWOOM
CLICK
NOT DONE YET...
BLAM
BLAM
BLAM

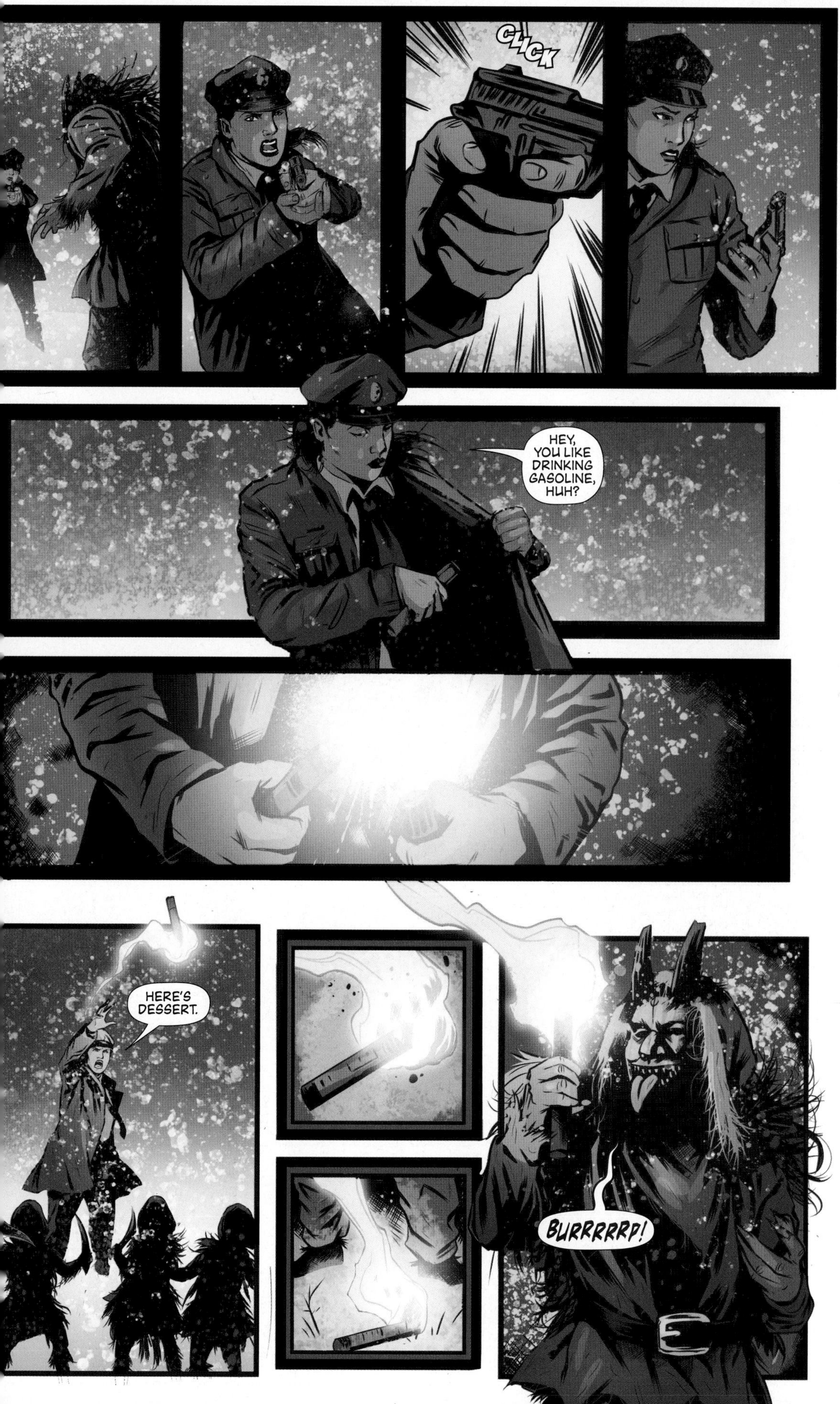
CLICK
HEY, YOU LIKE DRINKING GASOLINE, HUH?
HERE'S DESSERT.
BURRRRRP!

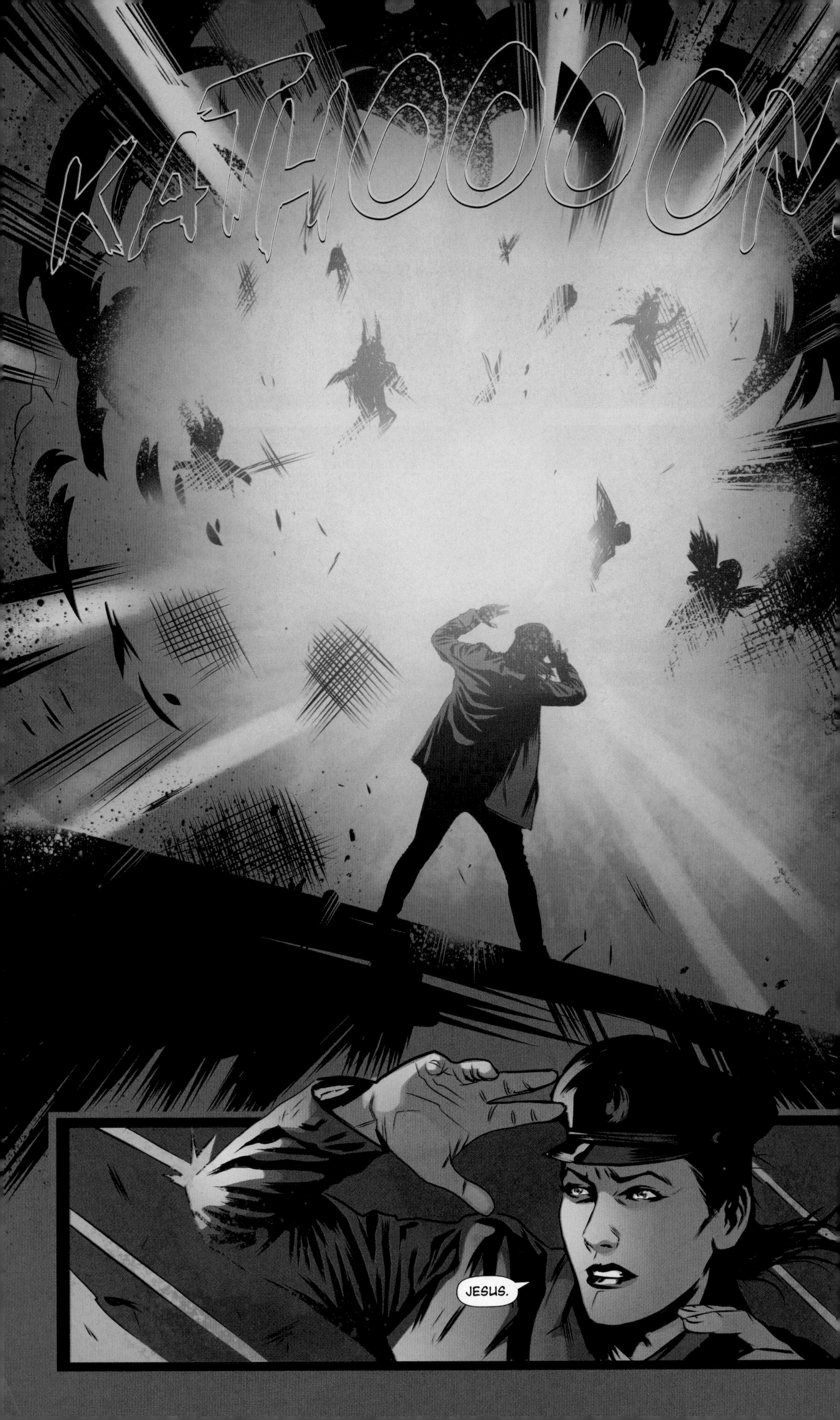
KATHOOOOM
JESUS.

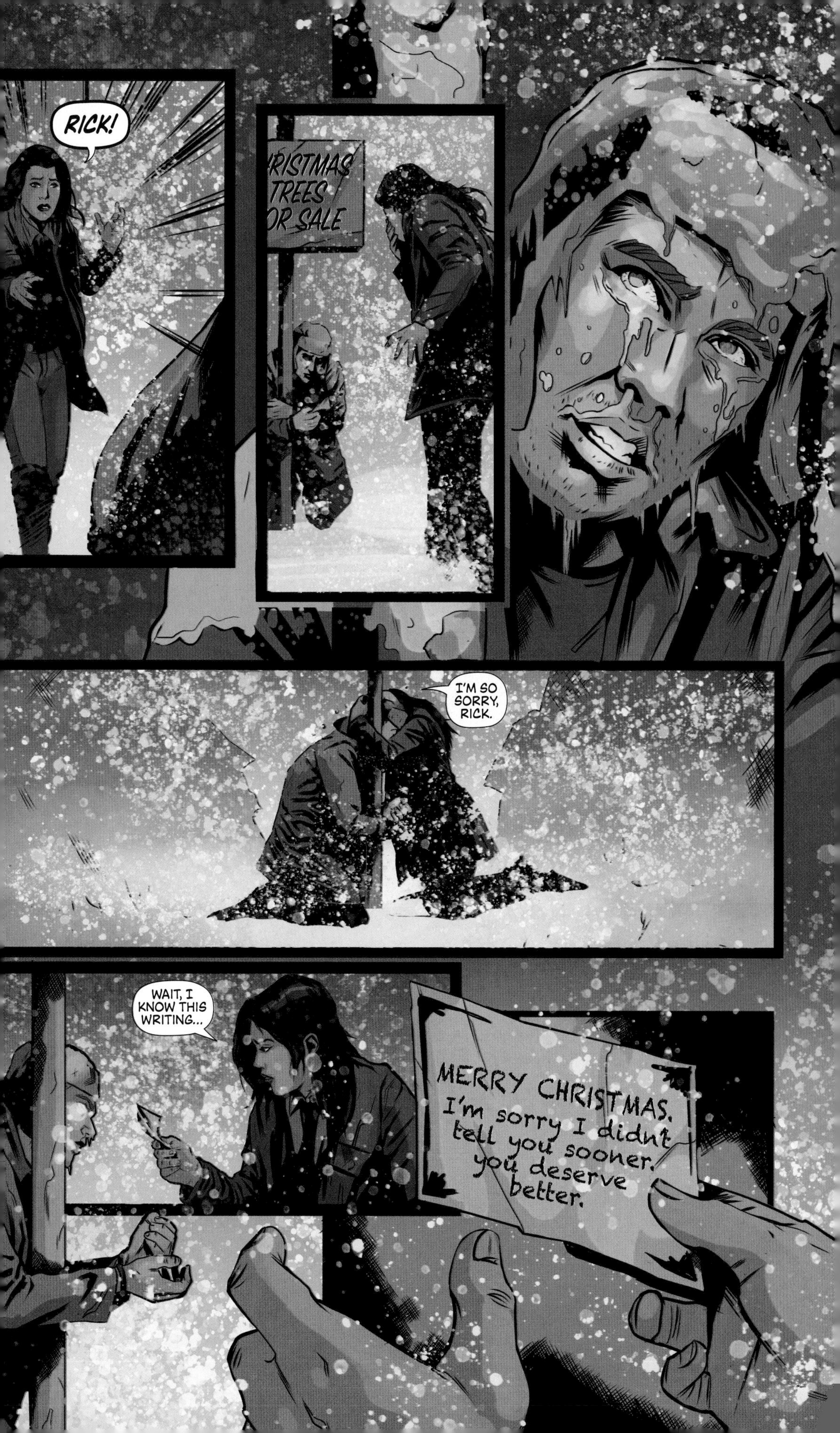
RICK!
CHRISTMAS TREES FOR SALE
I'M SO SORRY, RICK.
WAIT, I KNOW THIS WRITING...
MERRY CHRISTMAS.
I'm sorry I didnt tell you sooner. you deserve better.

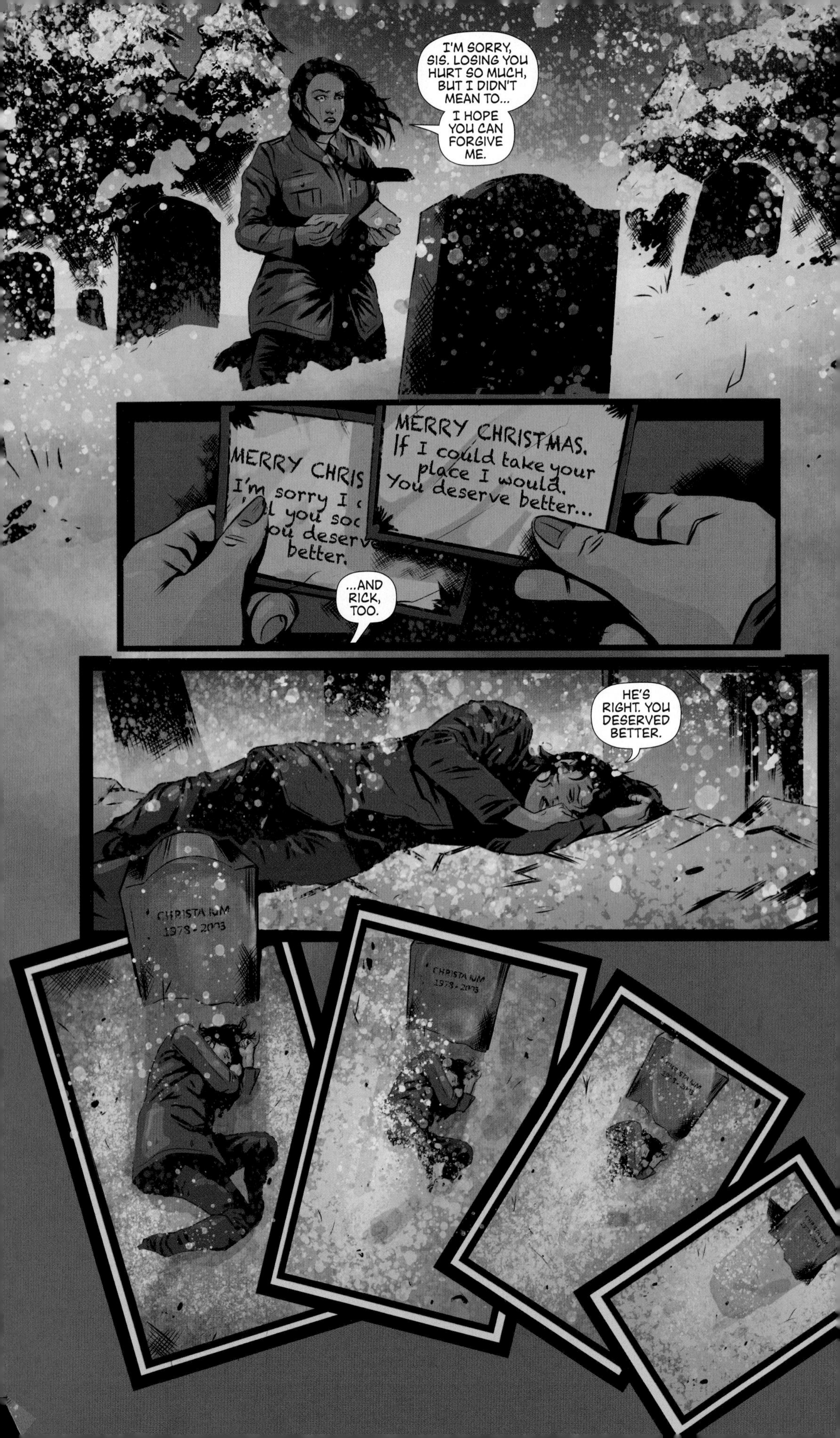
I'M SORRY, SIS. LOSING YOU HURT SO MUCH, BUT I DIDN'T MEAN TO...
I HOPE YOU CAN FORGIVE ME.
MERRY CHRIS I'm sorry I better.
MERRY CHRISTMAS. If I could take your place I would. You deserve better...
...AND RICK, TOO.
HE'S RIGHT. YOU DESERVED BETTER.
CHRISTA NM 1978 - 2013

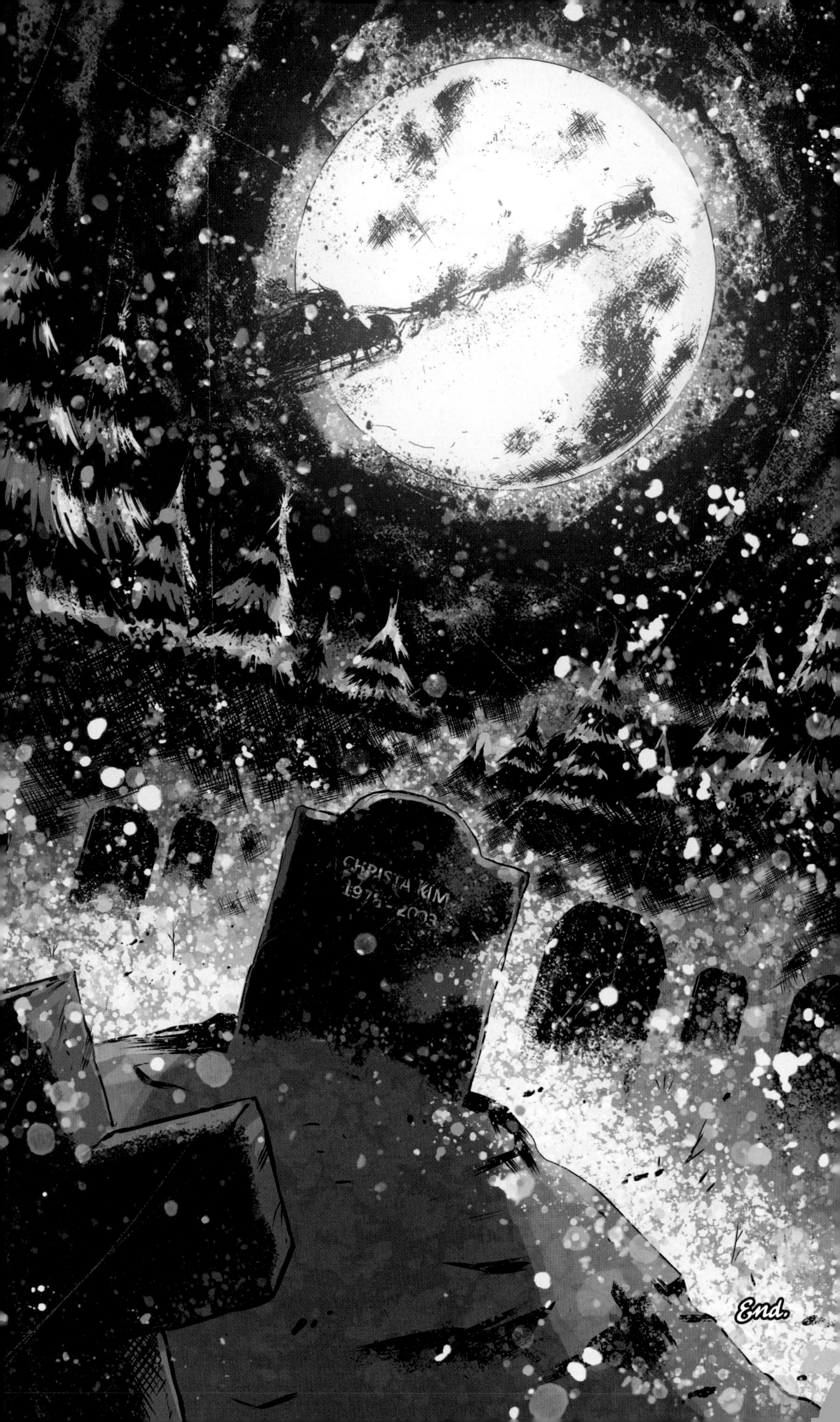
CHRISTA KIM
End.

III

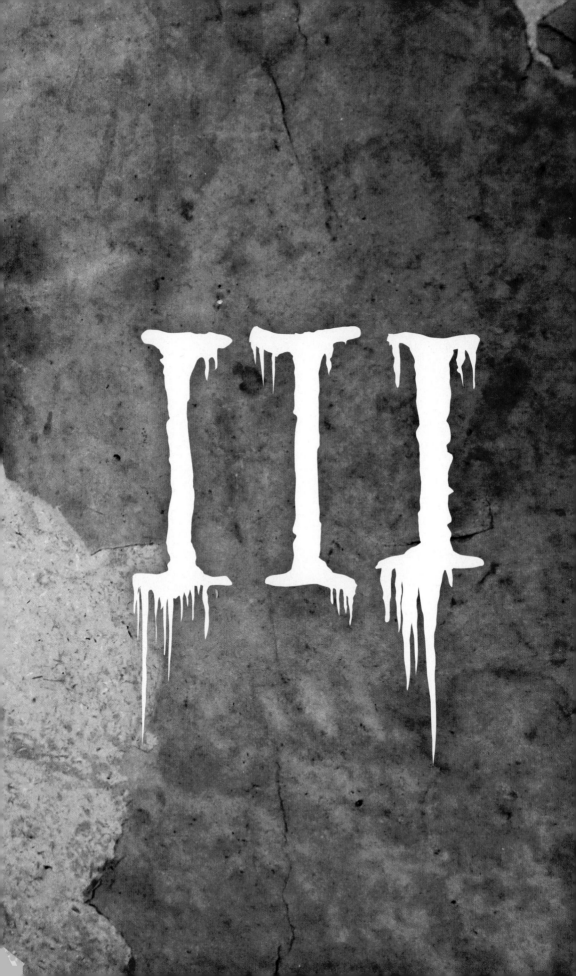

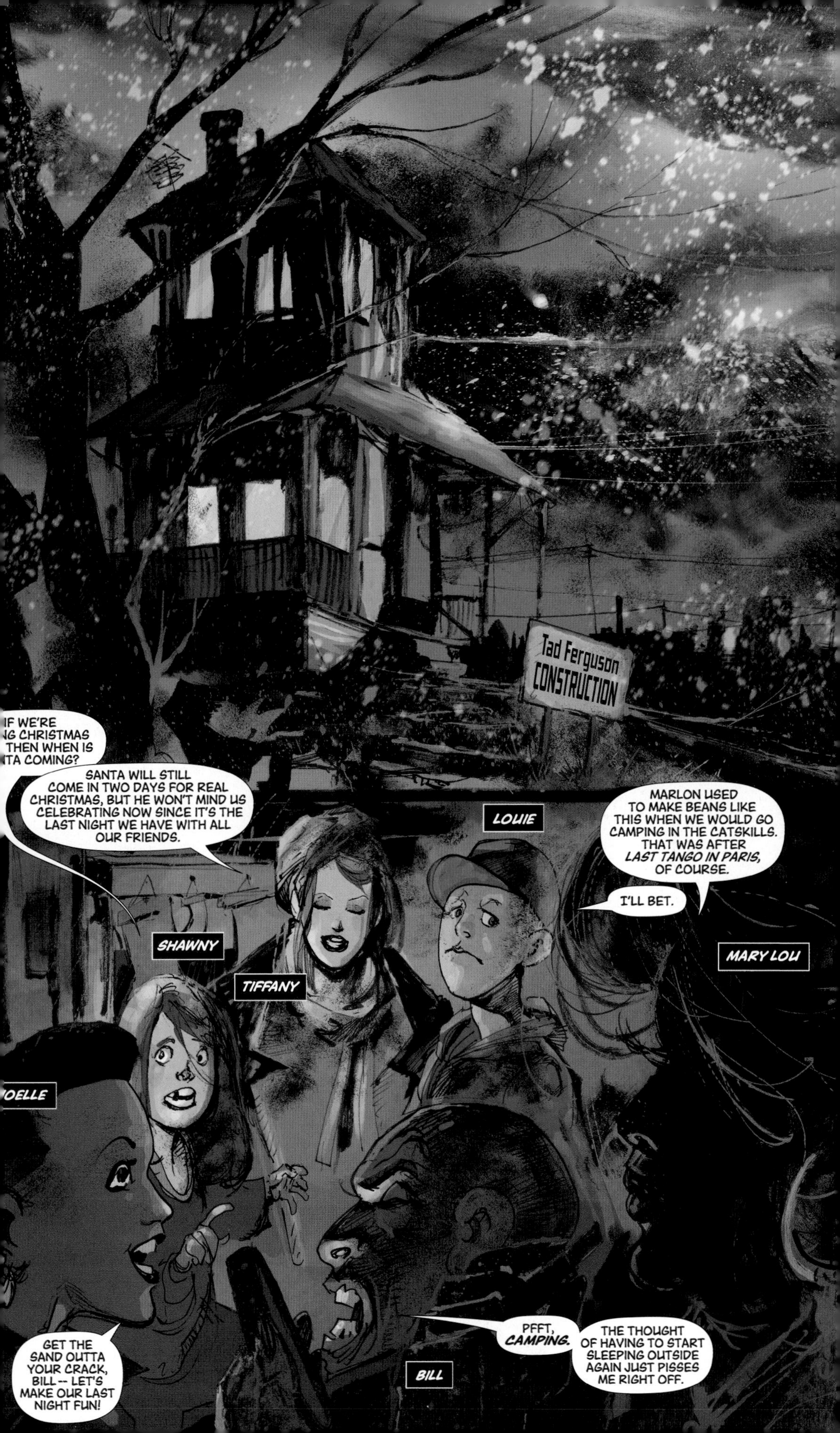
Tad Ferguson
CONSTRUCTION
IF WE'RE
NG CHRISTMAS
THEN WHEN IS
NTA COMING?
SANTA WILL STILL COME IN TWO DAYS FOR REAL CHRISTMAS, BUT HE WON'T MIND US CELEBRATING NOW SINCE IT'S THE LAST NIGHT WE HAVE WITH ALL OUR FRIENDS.
LOUIE
MARLON USED TO MAKE BEANS LIKE THIS WHEN WE WOULD GO CAMPING IN THE CATSKILLS. THAT WAS AFTER *LAST TANGO IN PARIS,* OF COURSE.
I'LL BET.
SHAWNY
MARY LOU
TIFFANY
OELLE
GET THE SAND OUTTA YOUR CRACK, BILL -- LET'S MAKE OUR LAST NIGHT FUN!
PFFT, *CAMPING.*
THE THOUGHT OF HAVING TO START SLEEPING OUTSIDE AGAIN JUST PISSES ME RIGHT OFF.
BILL

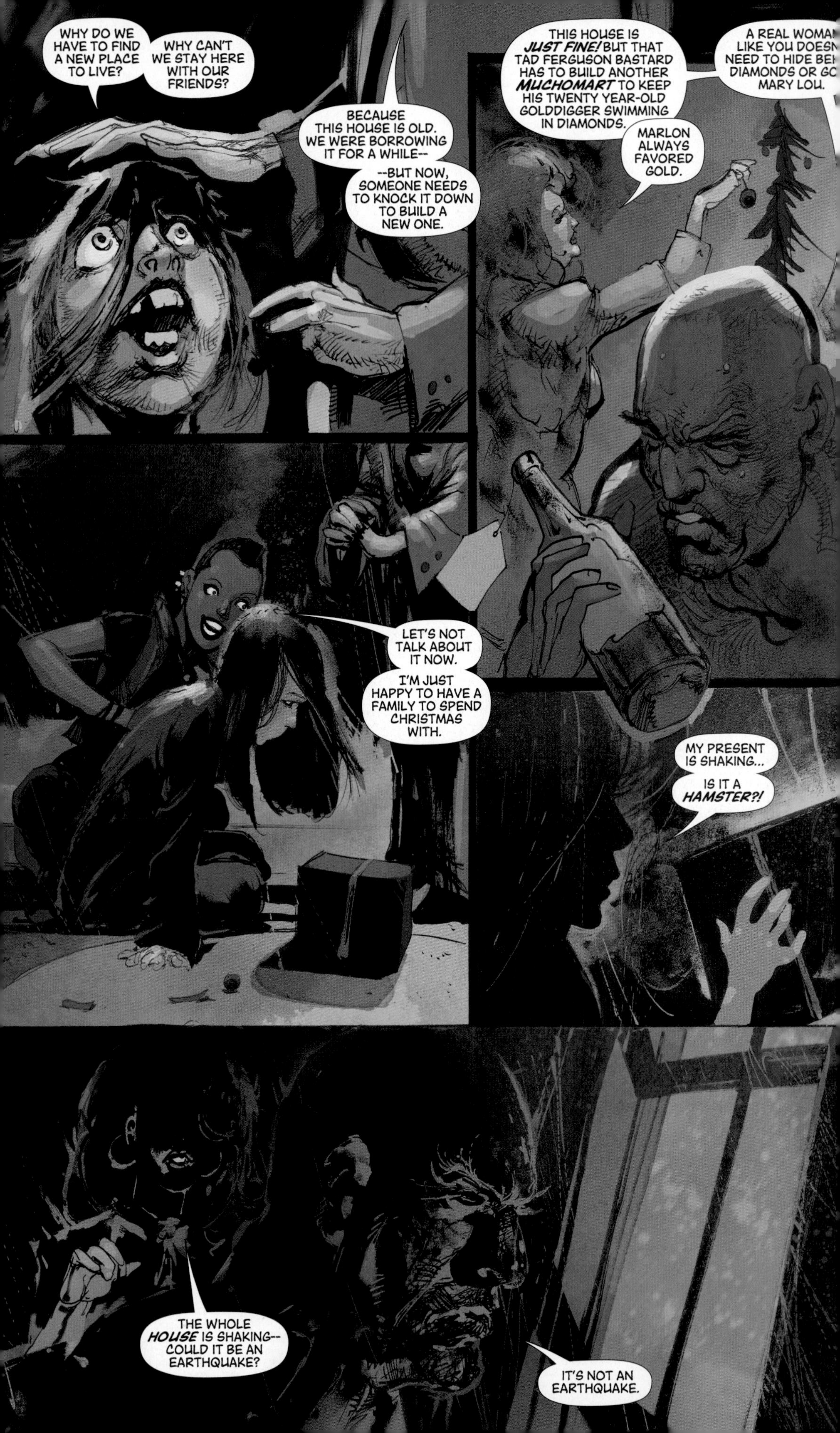
WHY DO WE HAVE TO FIND A NEW PLACE TO LIVE?
WHY CAN'T WE STAY HERE WITH OUR FRIENDS?
BECAUSE THIS HOUSE IS OLD. WE WERE BORROWING IT FOR A WHILE--
--BUT NOW, SOMEONE NEEDS TO KNOCK IT DOWN TO BUILD A NEW ONE.
THIS HOUSE IS *JUST FINE!* BUT THAT TAD FERGUSON BASTARD HAS TO BUILD ANOTHER *MUCHOMART* TO KEEP HIS TWENTY YEAR-OLD GOLDDIGGER SWIMMING IN DIAMONDS.
MARLON ALWAYS FAVORED GOLD.
LET'S NOT TALK ABOUT IT NOW.
I'M JUST HAPPY TO HAVE A FAMILY TO SPEND CHRISTMAS WITH.
MY PRESENT IS SHAKING...
IS IT A *HAMSTER?!*
THE WHOLE *HOUSE* IS SHAKING-- COULD IT BE AN EARTHQUAKE?
IT'S NOT AN EARTHQUAKE.

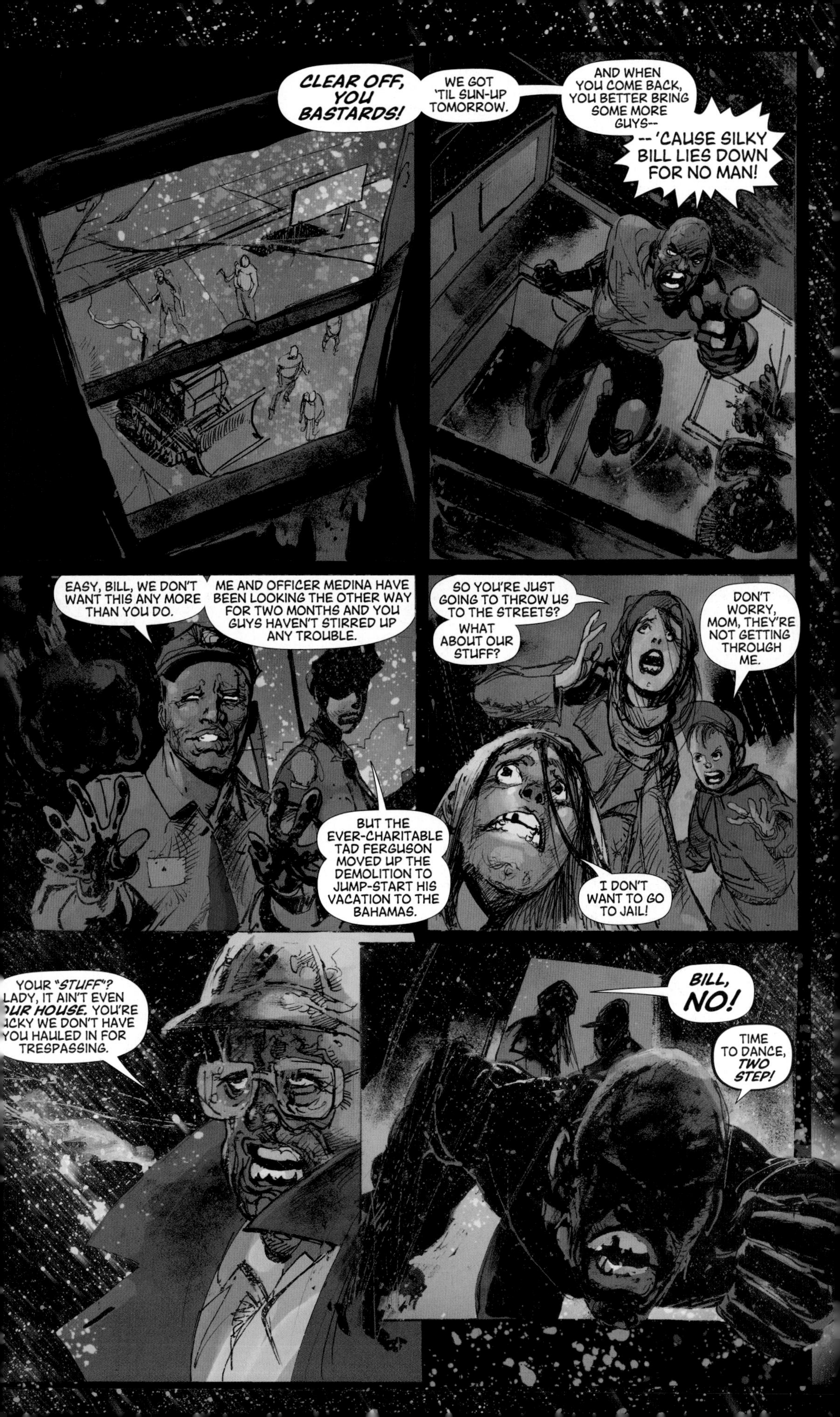

CLEAR OFF, YOU BASTARDS!
WE GOT 'TIL SUN-UP TOMORROW.
AND WHEN YOU COME BACK, YOU BETTER BRING SOME MORE GUYS--
-- 'CAUSE SILKY BILL LIES DOWN FOR NO MAN!
EASY, BILL, WE DON'T WANT THIS ANY MORE THAN YOU DO.
ME AND OFFICER MEDINA HAVE BEEN LOOKING THE OTHER WAY FOR TWO MONTHS AND YOU GUYS HAVEN'T STIRRED UP ANY TROUBLE.
BUT THE EVER-CHARITABLE TAD FERGUSON MOVED UP THE DEMOLITION TO JUMP-START HIS VACATION TO THE BAHAMAS.
SO YOU'RE JUST GOING TO THROW US TO THE STREETS?
WHAT ABOUT OUR STUFF?
DON'T WORRY, MOM, THEY'RE NOT GETTING THROUGH ME.
I DON'T WANT TO GO TO JAIL!
YOUR "STUFF"? LADY, IT AIN'T EVEN OUR HOUSE. YOU'RE LUCKY WE DON'T HAVE YOU HAULED IN FOR TRESPASSING.
BILL, NO!
TIME TO DANCE, TWO STEP!

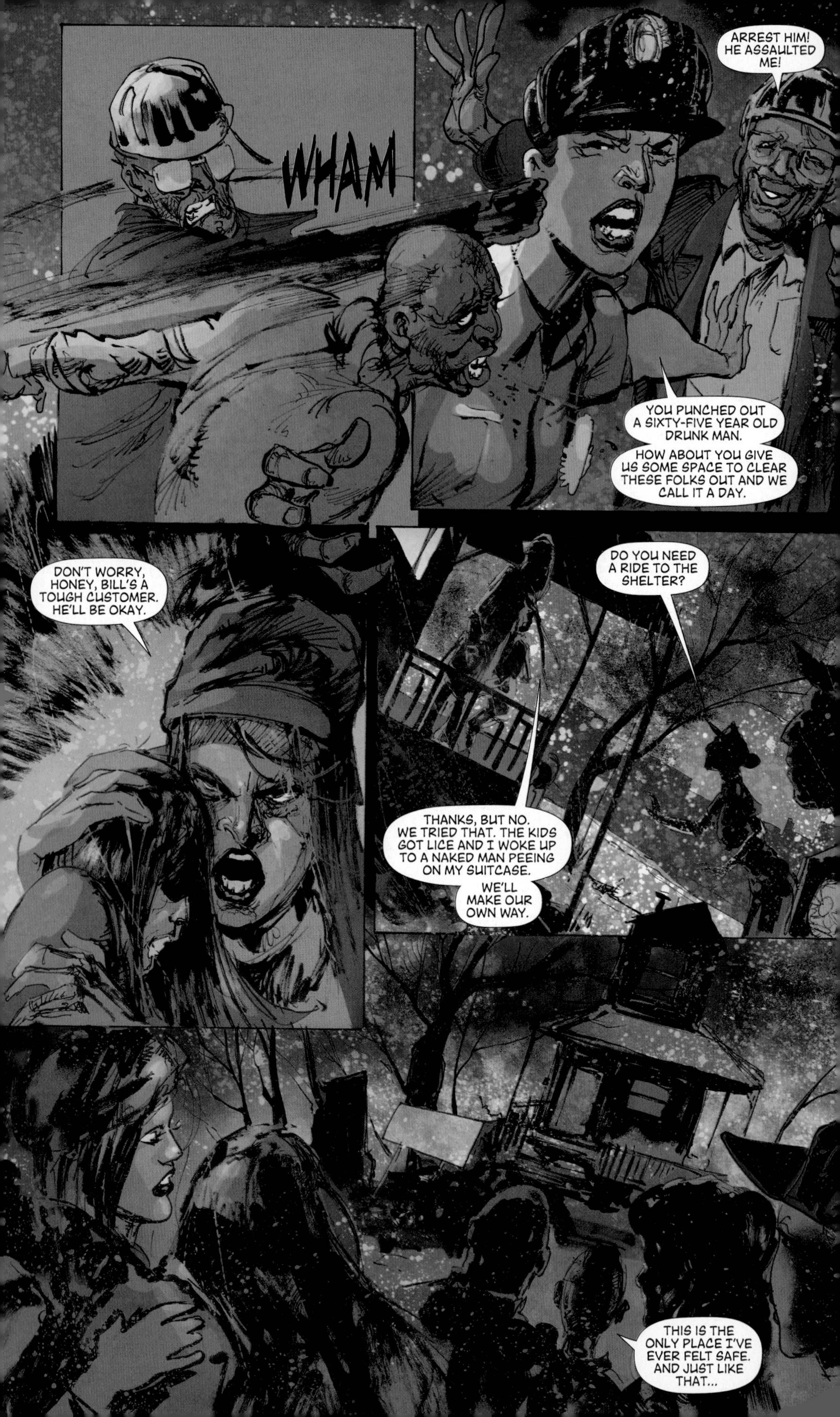
WHAM
ARREST HIM! HE ASSAULTED ME!
YOU PUNCHED OUT A SIXTY-FIVE YEAR OLD DRUNK MAN.
HOW ABOUT YOU GIVE US SOME SPACE TO CLEAR THESE FOLKS OUT AND WE CALL IT A DAY.
DON'T WORRY, HONEY, BILL'S A TOUGH CUSTOMER. HE'LL BE OKAY.
DO YOU NEED A RIDE TO THE SHELTER?
THANKS, BUT NO. WE TRIED THAT. THE KIDS GOT LICE AND I WOKE UP TO A NAKED MAN PEEING ON MY SUITCASE.
WE'LL MAKE OUR OWN WAY.
THIS IS THE ONLY PLACE I'VE EVER FELT SAFE. AND JUST LIKE THAT...

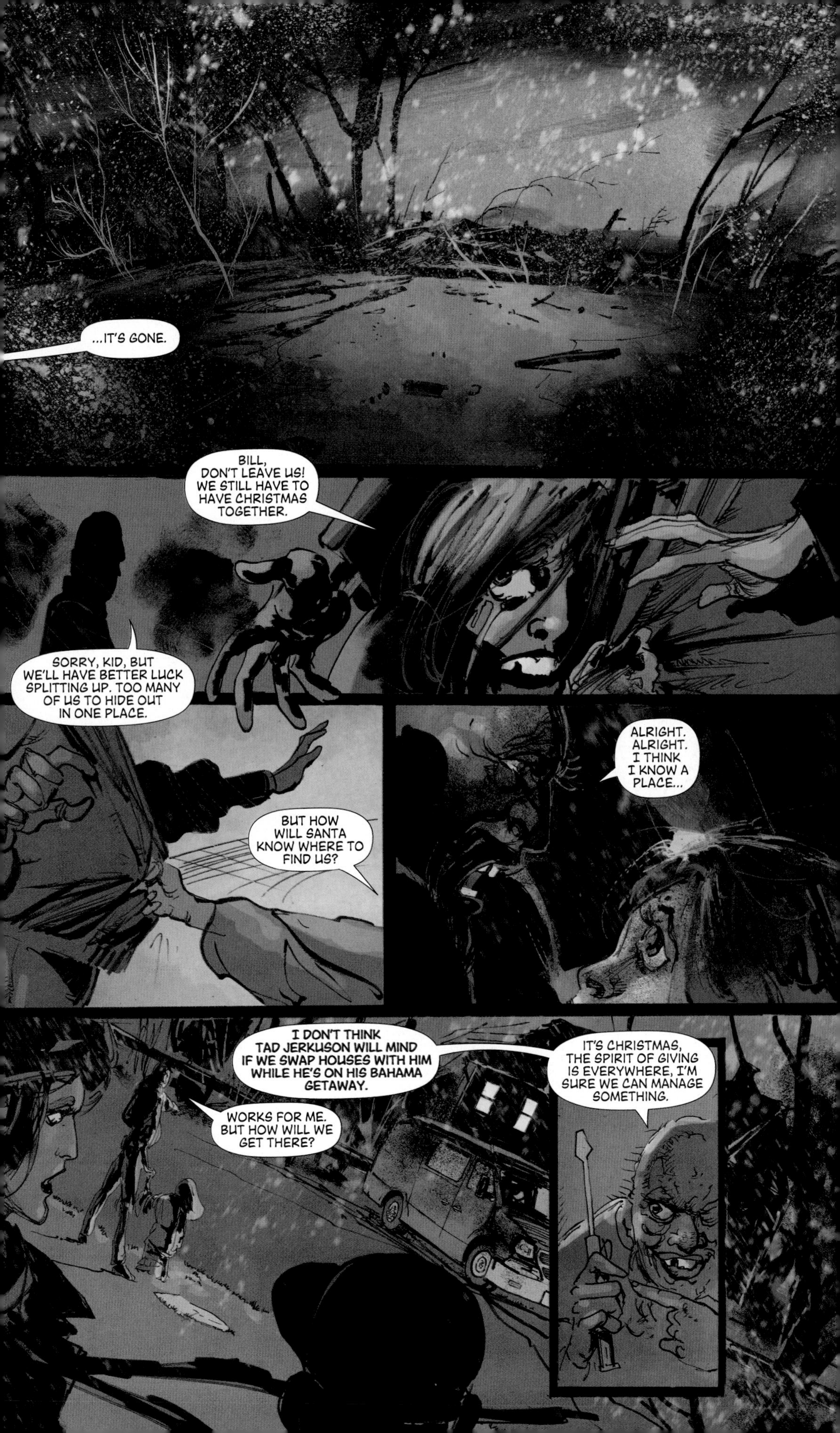
...IT'S GONE.
BILL, DON'T LEAVE US! WE STILL HAVE TO HAVE CHRISTMAS TOGETHER.
SORRY, KID, BUT WE'LL HAVE BETTER LUCK SPLITTING UP. TOO MANY OF US TO HIDE OUT IN ONE PLACE.
BUT HOW WILL SANTA KNOW WHERE TO FIND US?
ALRIGHT. ALRIGHT. I THINK I KNOW A PLACE...
I DON'T THINK TAD JERKUSON WILL MIND IF WE SWAP HOUSES WITH HIM WHILE HE'S ON HIS BAHAMA GETAWAY.
WORKS FOR ME. BUT HOW WILL WE GET THERE?
IT'S CHRISTMAS, THE SPIRIT OF GIVING IS EVERYWHERE, I'M SURE WE CAN MANAGE SOMETHING.

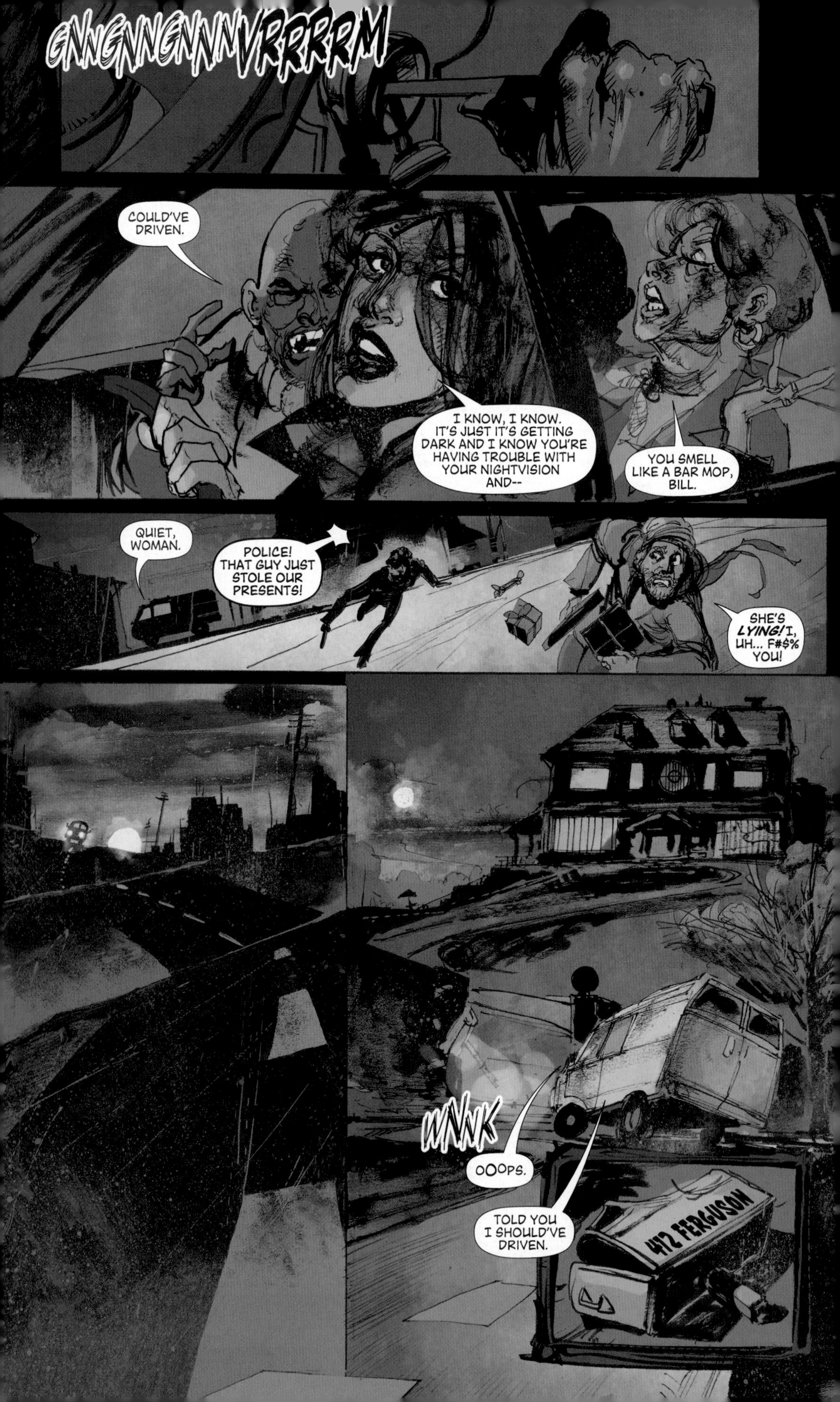
GNNGNNGNNNVRRRRM
COULD'VE DRIVEN.
I KNOW, I KNOW. IT'S JUST IT'S GETTING DARK AND I KNOW YOU'RE HAVING TROUBLE WITH YOUR NIGHTVISION AND--
YOU SMELL LIKE A BAR MOP, BILL.
QUIET, WOMAN.
POLICE! THAT GUY JUST STOLE OUR PRESENTS!
SHE'S *LYING!* I, UH... F#$% YOU!
WNNK
OOOPS.
TOLD YOU I SHOULD'VE DRIVEN.
412 FERGUSON

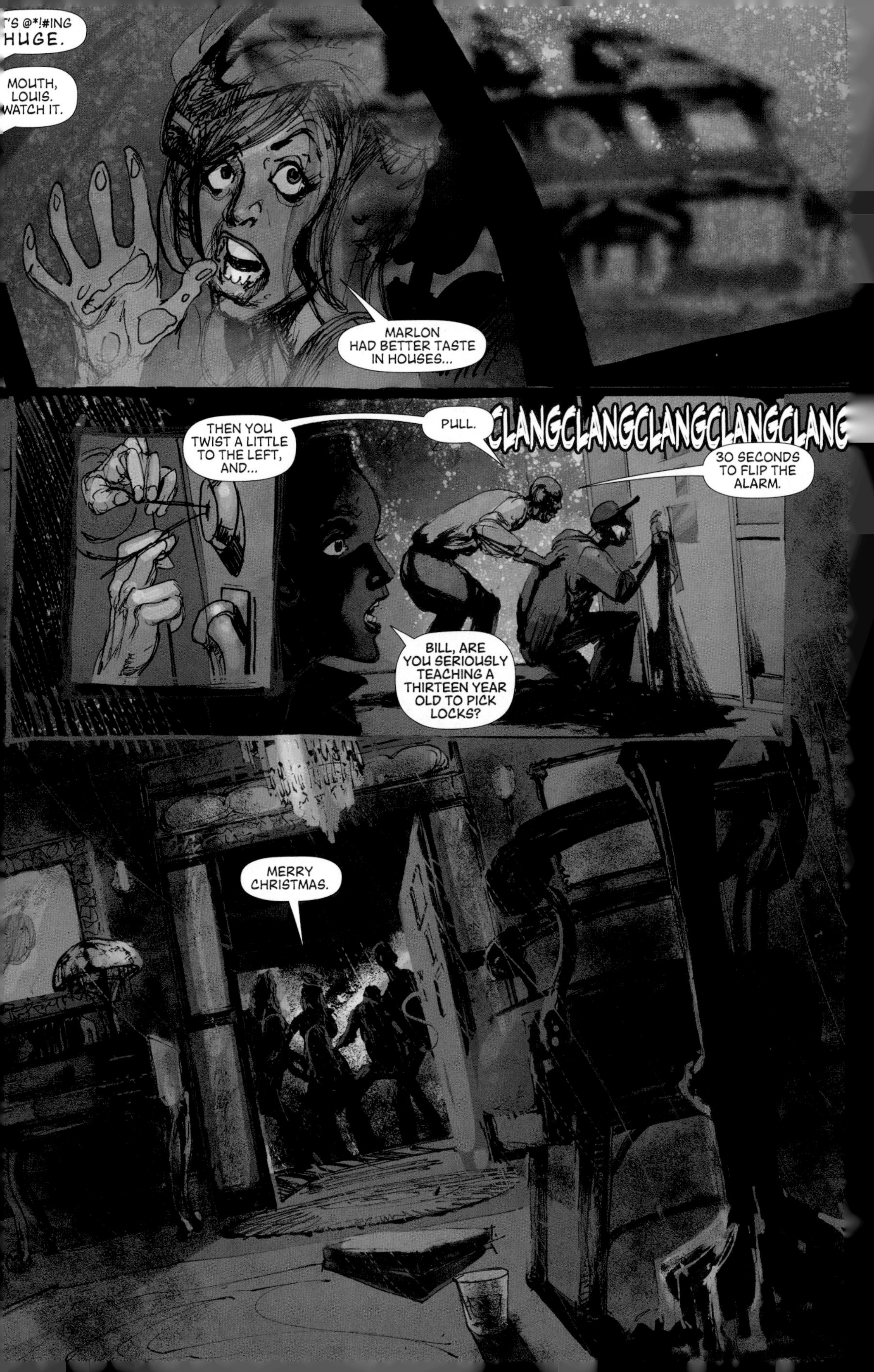
'T'S @*!#ING HUGE.
MOUTH, LOUIS. WATCH IT.
MARLON HAD BETTER TASTE IN HOUSES...
THEN YOU TWIST A LITTLE TO THE LEFT, AND...
PULL.
CLANGCLANGCLANGCLANGCLANG
30 SECONDS TO FLIP THE ALARM.
BILL, ARE YOU SERIOUSLY TEACHING A THIRTEEN YEAR OLD TO PICK LOCKS?
MERRY CHRISTMAS.

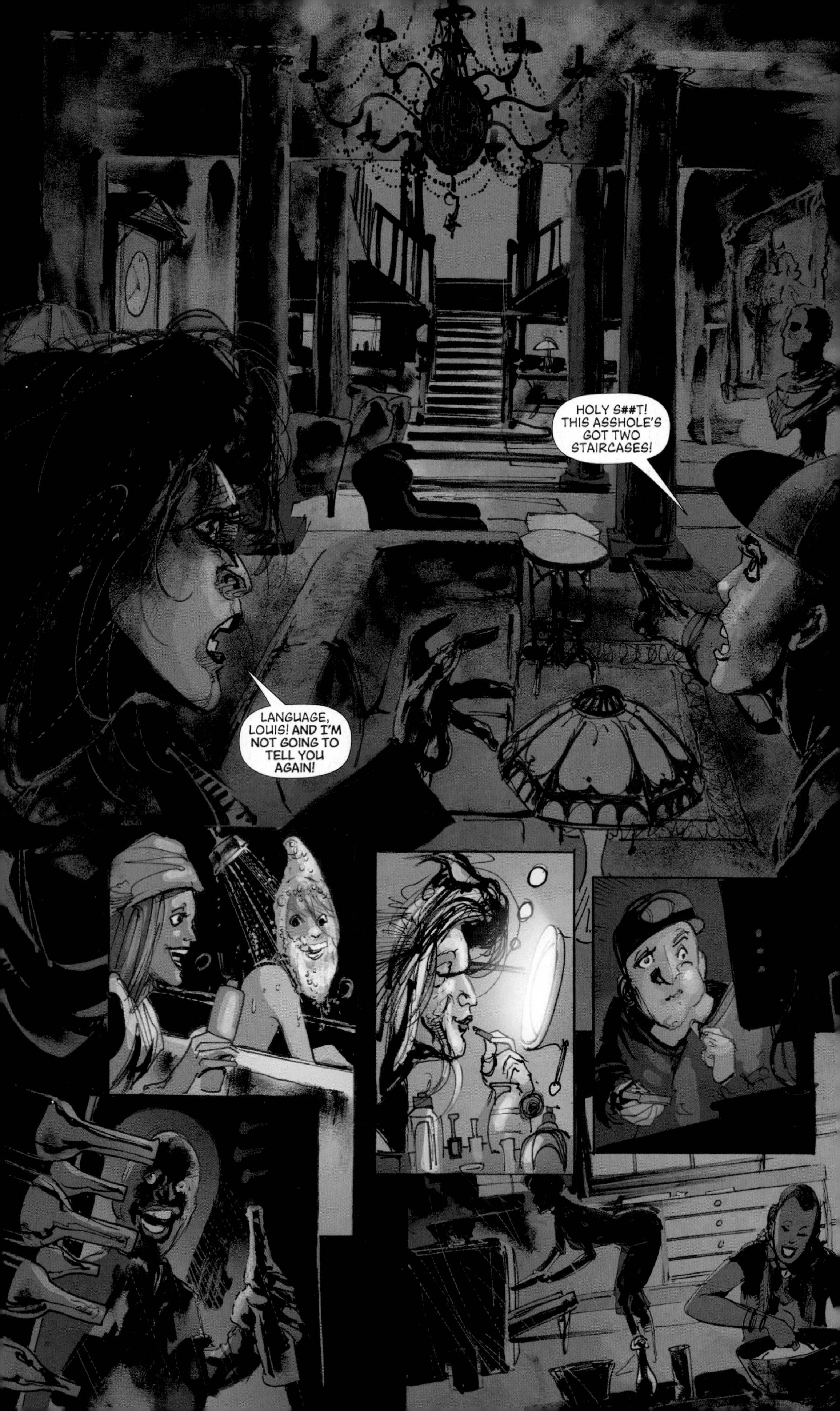
HOLY S##T! THIS ASSHOLE'S GOT TWO STAIRCASES!
LANGUAGE, LOUIS! AND I'M NOT GOING TO TELL YOU AGAIN!

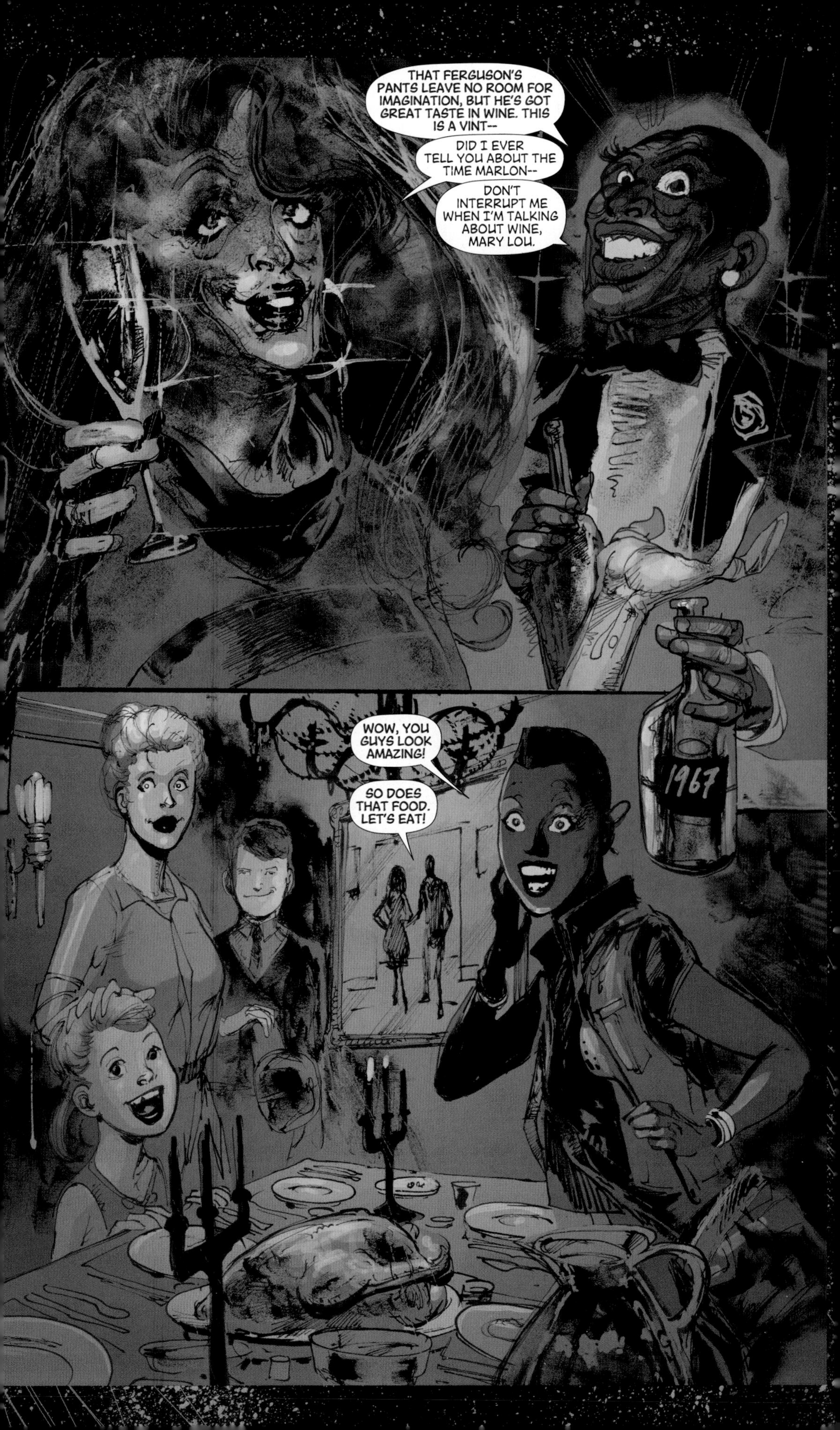
THAT FERGUSON'S PANTS LEAVE NO ROOM FOR IMAGINATION, BUT HE'S GOT GREAT TASTE IN WINE. THIS IS A VINT--
DID I EVER TELL YOU ABOUT THE TIME MARLON--
DON'T INTERRUPT ME WHEN I'M TALKING ABOUT WINE, MARY LOU.
1967
WOW, YOU GUYS LOOK AMAZING!
SO DOES THAT FOOD. LET'S EAT!

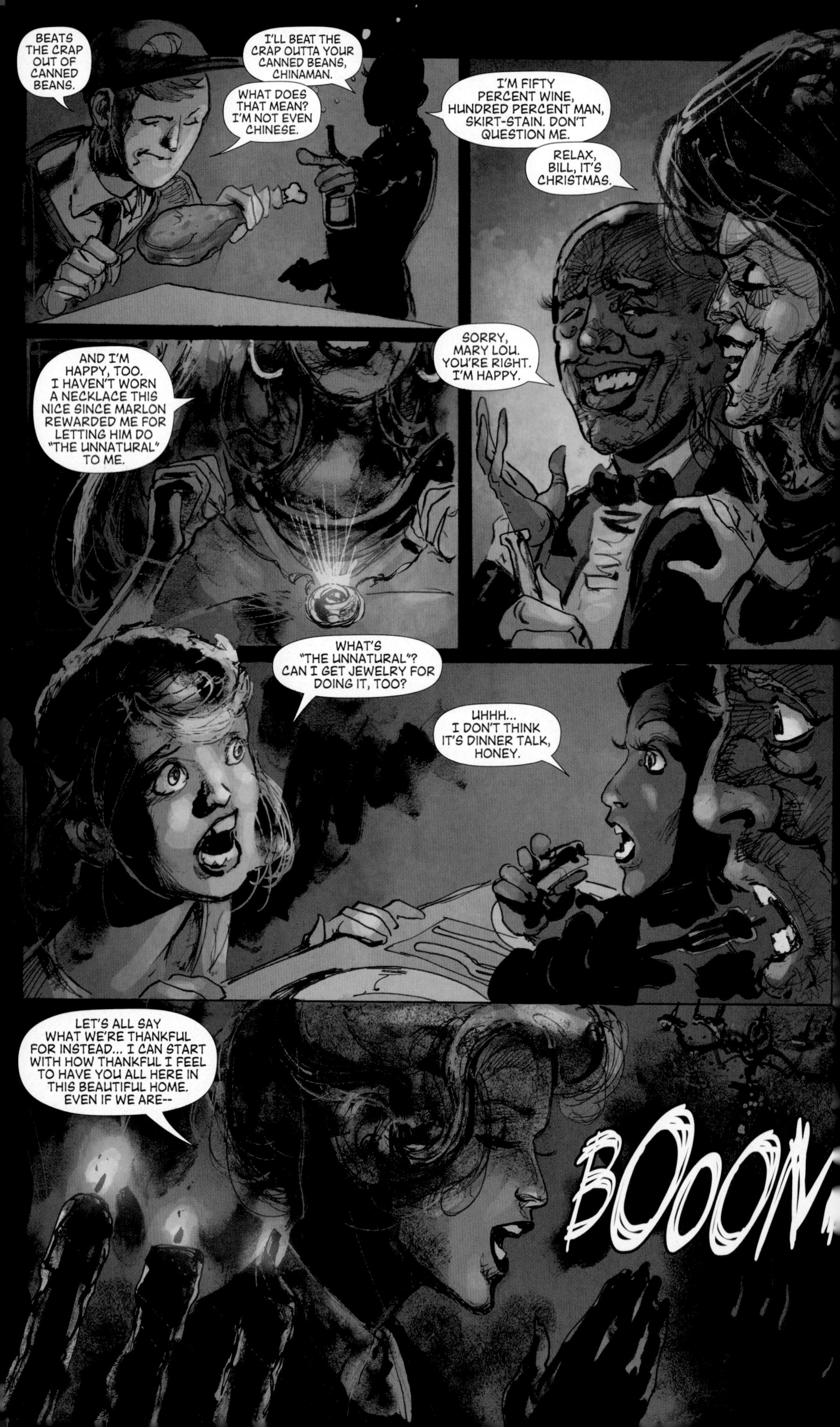
BEATS THE CRAP OUT OF CANNED BEANS.
I'LL BEAT THE CRAP OUTTA YOUR CANNED BEANS, CHINAMAN.
WHAT DOES THAT MEAN? I'M NOT EVEN CHINESE.
I'M FIFTY PERCENT WINE, HUNDRED PERCENT MAN, SKIRT-STAIN. DON'T QUESTION ME.
RELAX, BILL, IT'S CHRISTMAS.
SORRY, MARY LOU. YOU'RE RIGHT. I'M HAPPY.
AND I'M HAPPY, TOO. I HAVEN'T WORN A NECKLACE THIS NICE SINCE MARLON REWARDED ME FOR LETTING HIM DO "THE UNNATURAL" TO ME.
WHAT'S "THE UNNATURAL"? CAN I GET JEWELRY FOR DOING IT, TOO?
UHHH... I DON'T THINK IT'S DINNER TALK, HONEY.
LET'S ALL SAY WHAT WE'RE THANKFUL FOR INSTEAD... I CAN START WITH HOW THANKFUL I FEEL TO HAVE YOU ALL HERE IN THIS BEAUTIFUL HOME. EVEN IF WE ARE--
BOOOM

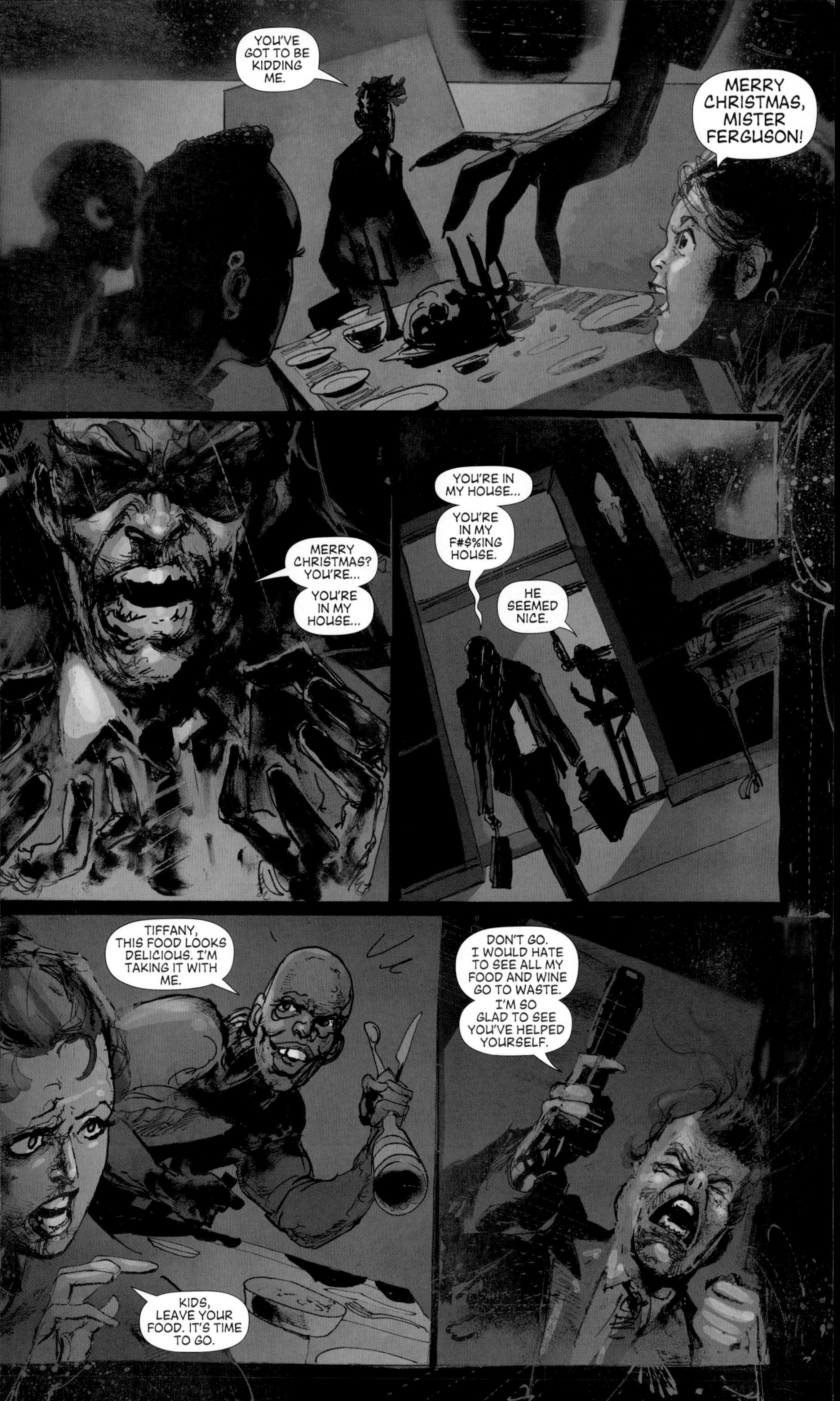
YOU'VE GOT TO BE KIDDING ME.
MERRY CHRISTMAS, MISTER FERGUSON!
MERRY CHRISTMAS? YOU'RE...
YOU'RE IN MY HOUSE...
YOU'RE IN MY HOUSE...
YOU'RE IN MY F#$%ING HOUSE.
HE SEEMED NICE.
TIFFANY, THIS FOOD LOOKS DELICIOUS. I'M TAKING IT WITH ME.
KIDS, LEAVE YOUR FOOD. IT'S TIME TO GO.
DON'T GO. I WOULD HATE TO SEE ALL MY FOOD AND WINE GO TO WASTE.
I'M SO GLAD TO SEE YOU'VE HELPED YOURSELF.

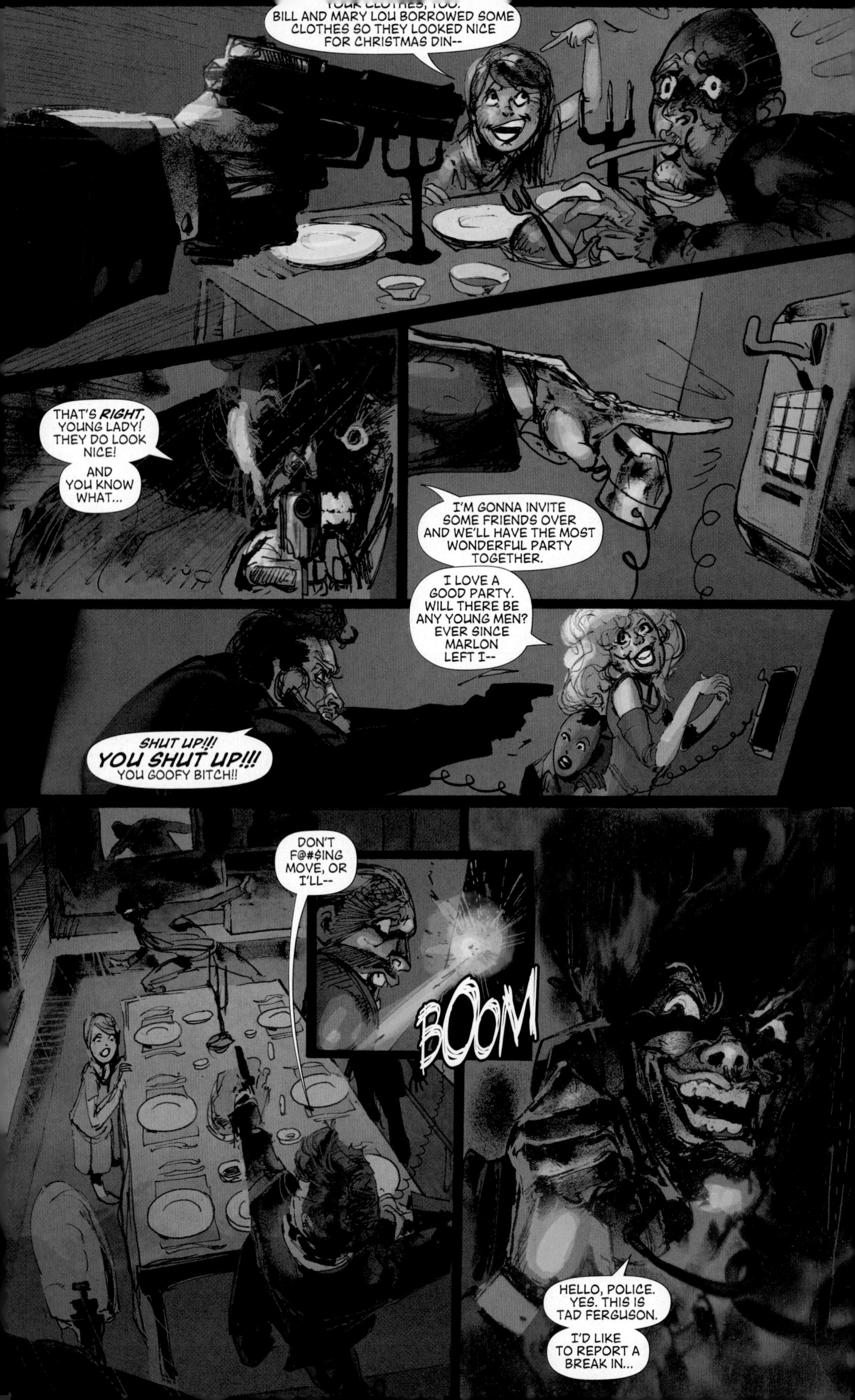
BILL AND MARY LOU BORROWED SOME CLOTHES SO THEY LOOKED NICE FOR CHRISTMAS DIN--
THAT'S *RIGHT,* YOUNG LADY! THEY DO LOOK NICE!
AND YOU KNOW WHAT...
I'M GONNA INVITE SOME FRIENDS OVER AND WE'LL HAVE THE MOST WONDERFUL PARTY TOGETHER.
I LOVE A GOOD PARTY. WILL THERE BE ANY YOUNG MEN? EVER SINCE MARLON LEFT I--
SHUT UP!!! **YOU SHUT UP!!!** YOU GOOFY BITCH!!
DON'T F@#$ING MOVE, OR I'LL--
BOOM
HELLO, POLICE. YES. THIS IS TAD FERGUSON.
I'D LIKE TO REPORT A BREAK IN...

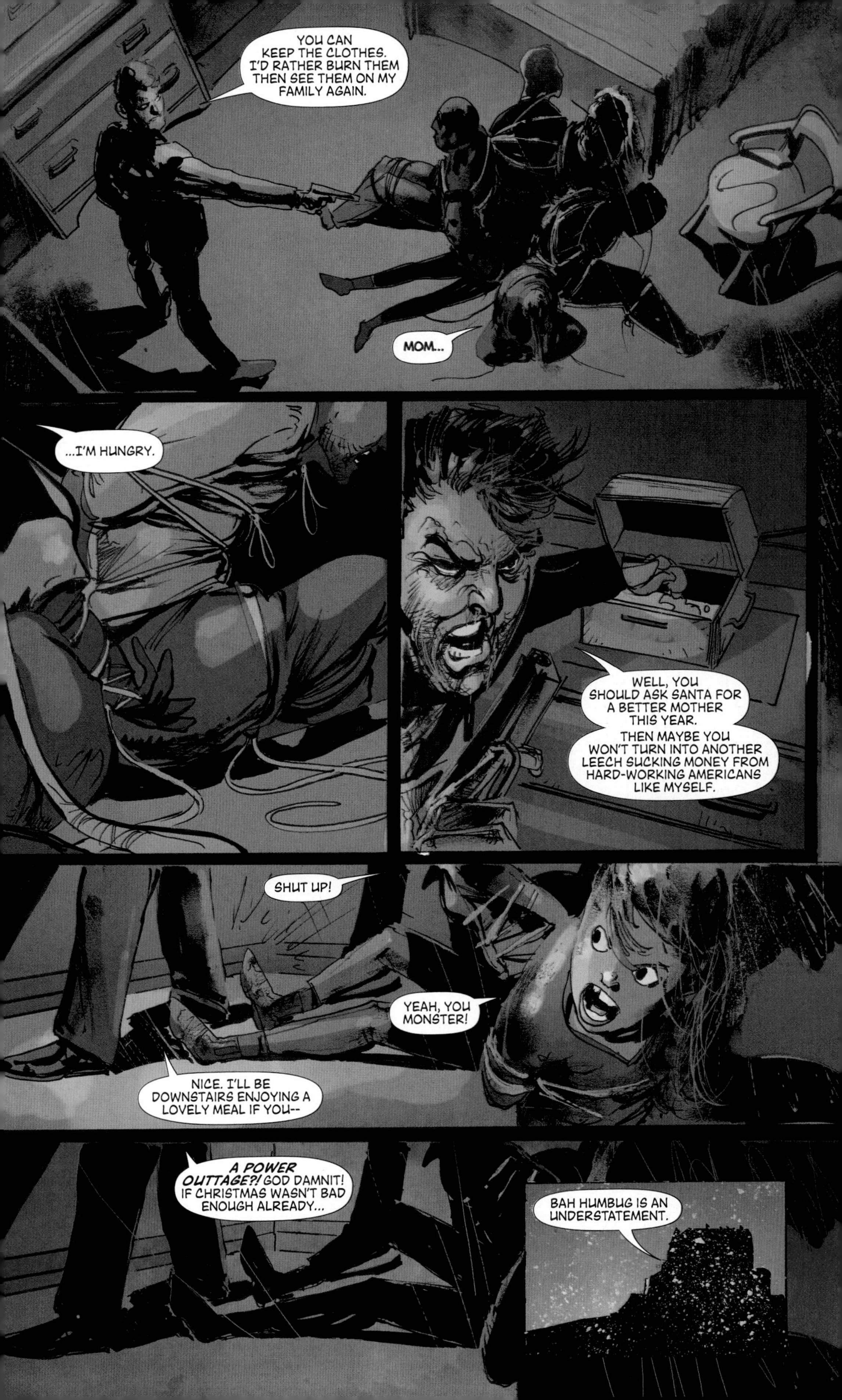
YOU CAN KEEP THE CLOTHES. I'D RATHER BURN THEM THEN SEE THEM ON MY FAMILY AGAIN.
MOM...
...I'M HUNGRY.
WELL, YOU SHOULD ASK SANTA FOR A BETTER MOTHER THIS YEAR.
THEN MAYBE YOU WON'T TURN INTO ANOTHER LEECH SUCKING MONEY FROM HARD-WORKING AMERICANS LIKE MYSELF.
SHUT UP!
YEAH, YOU MONSTER!
NICE. I'LL BE DOWNSTAIRS ENJOYING A LOVELY MEAL IF YOU--
A POWER OUTTAGE?! GOD DAMNIT! IF CHRISTMAS WASN'T BAD ENOUGH ALREADY...
BAH HUMBUG IS AN UNDERSTATEMENT.

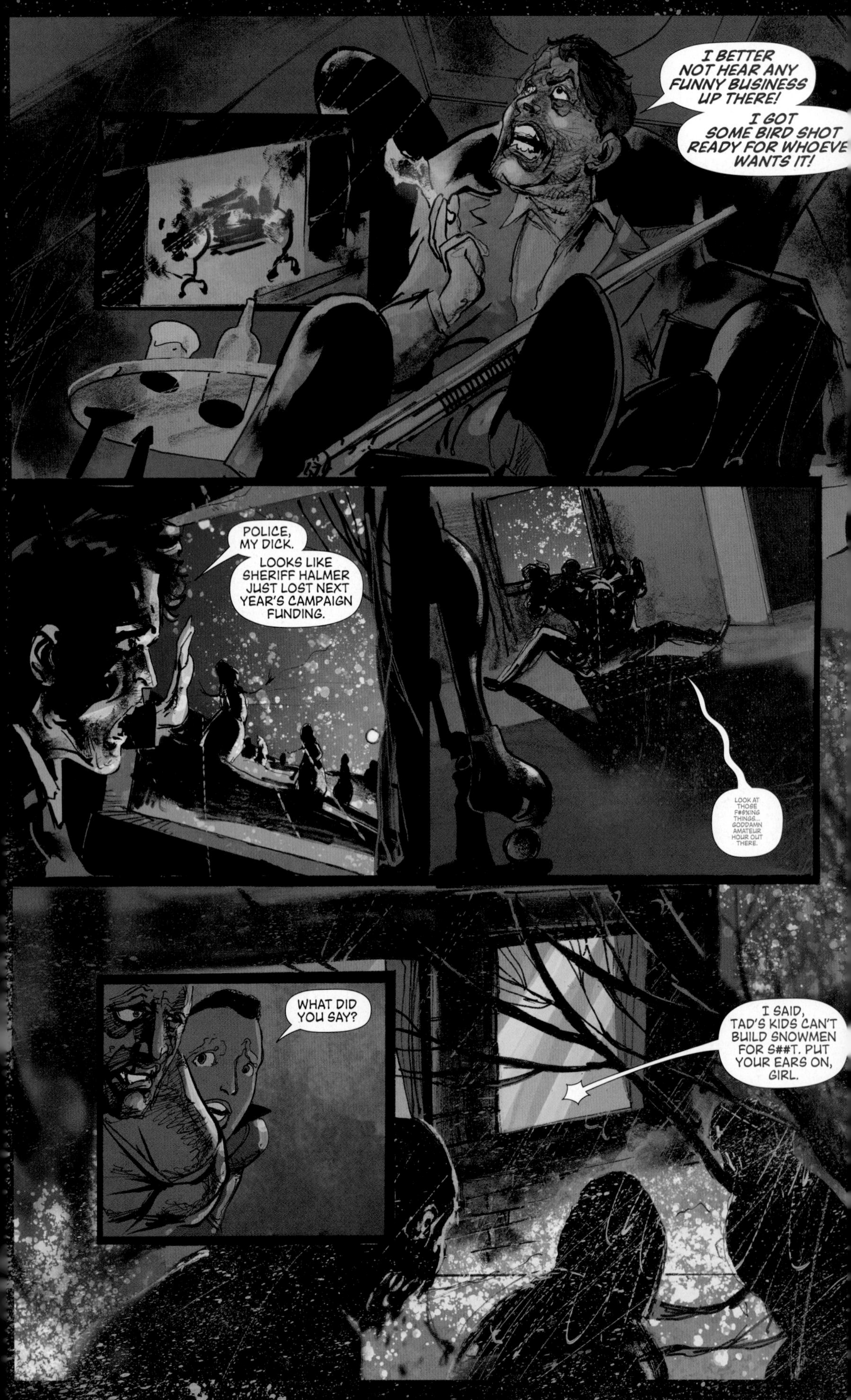
I BETTER NOT HEAR ANY FUNNY BUSINESS UP THERE!
I GOT SOME BIRD SHOT READY FOR WHOEVE WANTS IT!
POLICE, MY DICK.
LOOKS LIKE SHERIFF HALMER JUST LOST NEXT YEAR'S CAMPAIGN FUNDING.
LOOK AT THOSE F#$%ING THINGS... GODDAMN AMATEUR HOUR OUT THERE.
WHAT DID YOU SAY?
I SAID, TAD'S KIDS CAN'T BUILD SNOWMEN FOR S##T. PUT YOUR EARS ON, GIRL.

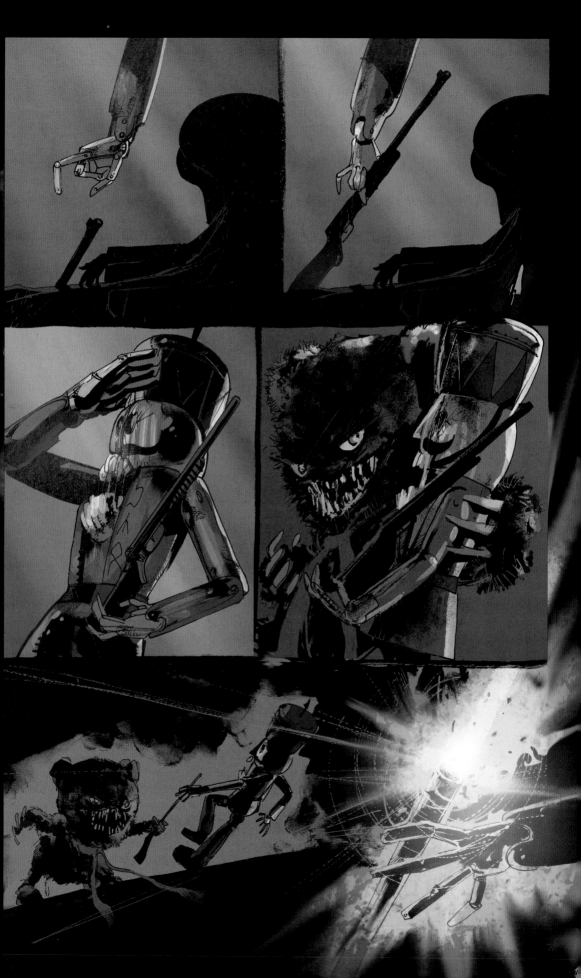

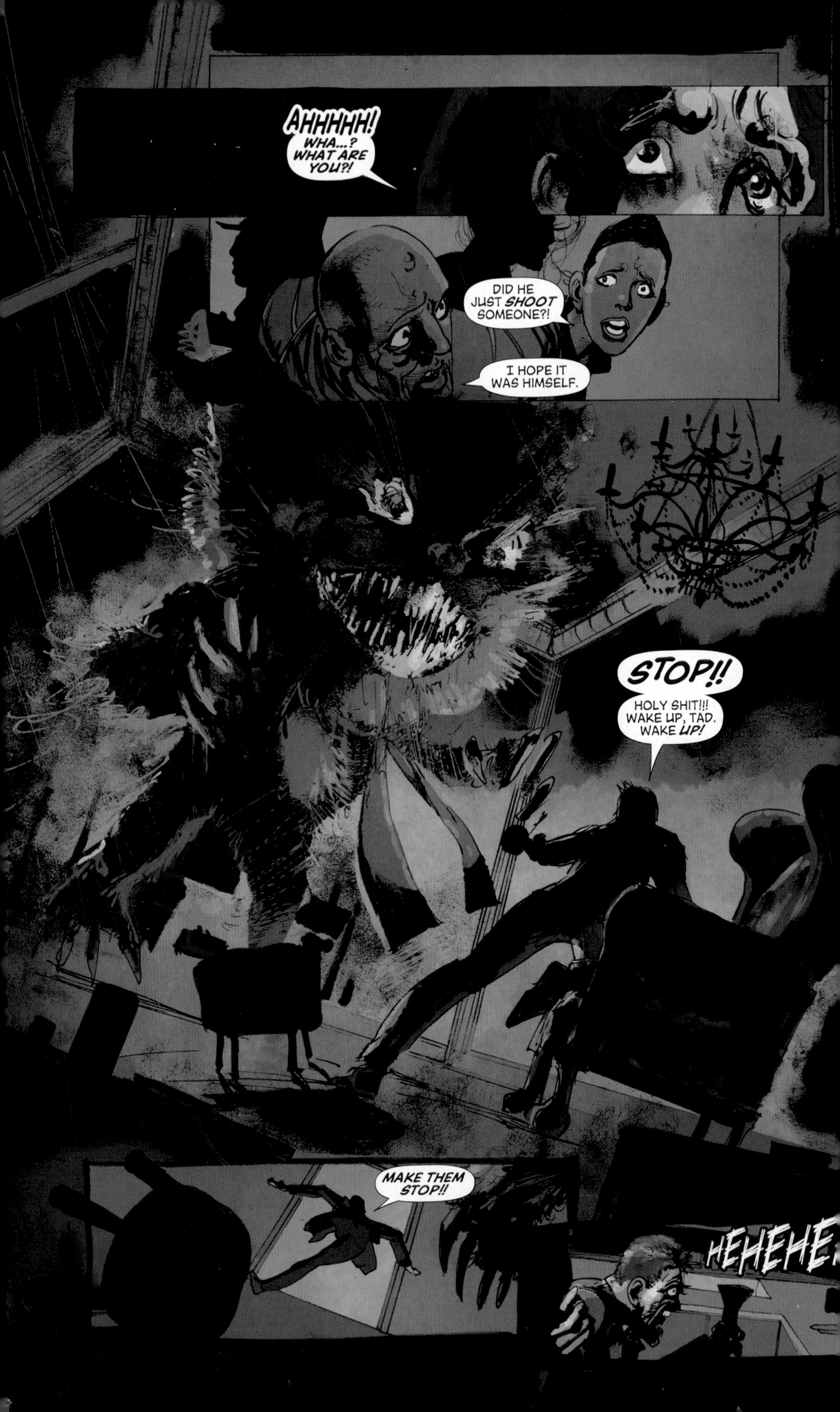
AHHHHH!
WHA...? WHAT ARE YOU?!
DID HE JUST SHOOT SOMEONE?!
I HOPE IT WAS HIMSELF.
STOP!!
HOLY SHIT!!! WAKE UP, TAD. WAKE UP!
MAKE THEM STOP!!
HEHEHE

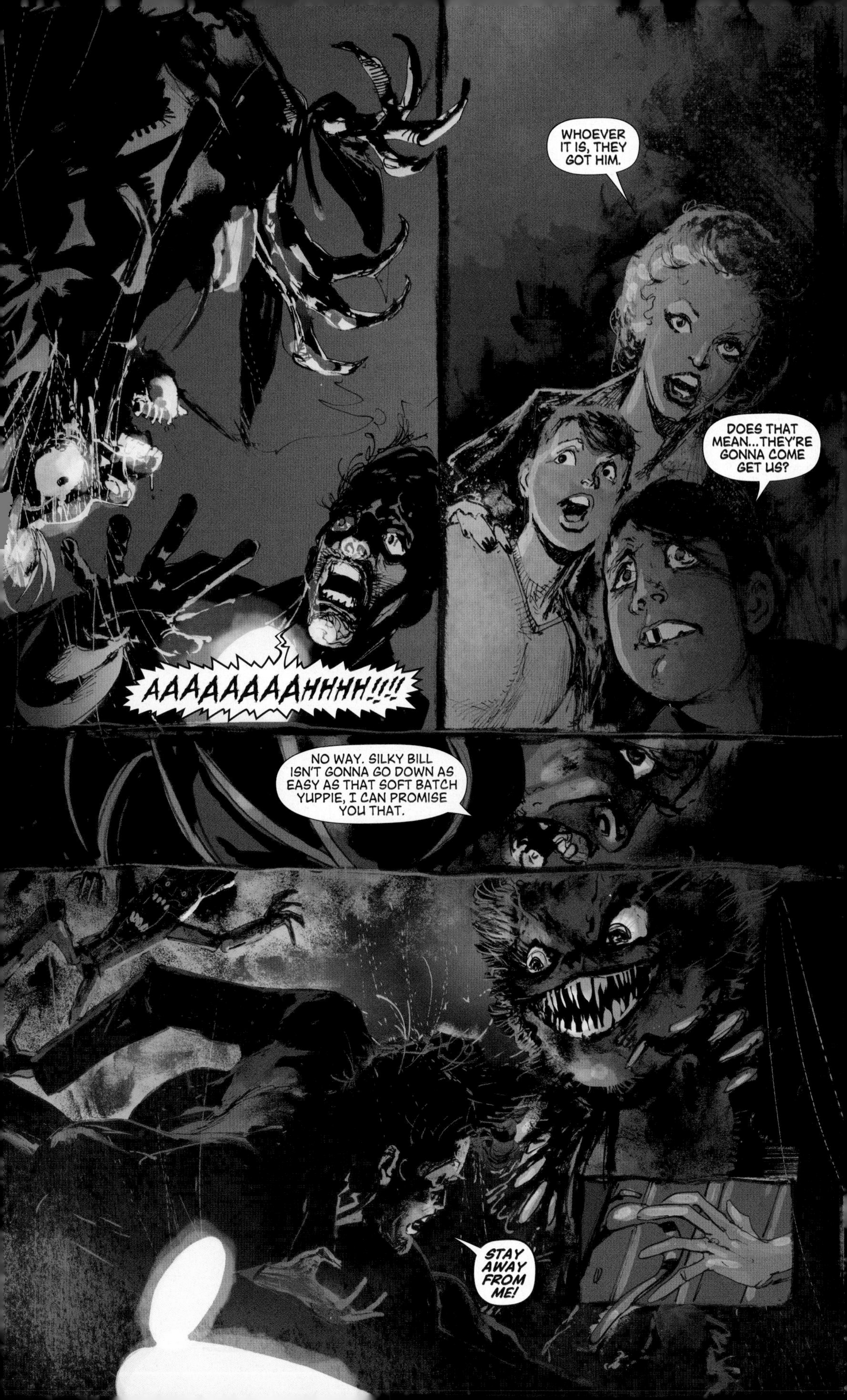
AAAAAAAAHHHH!!!!
WHOEVER IT IS, THEY GOT HIM.
DOES THAT MEAN...THEY'RE GONNA COME GET US?
NO WAY. SILKY BILL ISN'T GONNA GO DOWN AS EASY AS THAT SOFT BATCH YUPPIE, I CAN PROMISE YOU THAT.
STAY AWAY FROM ME!

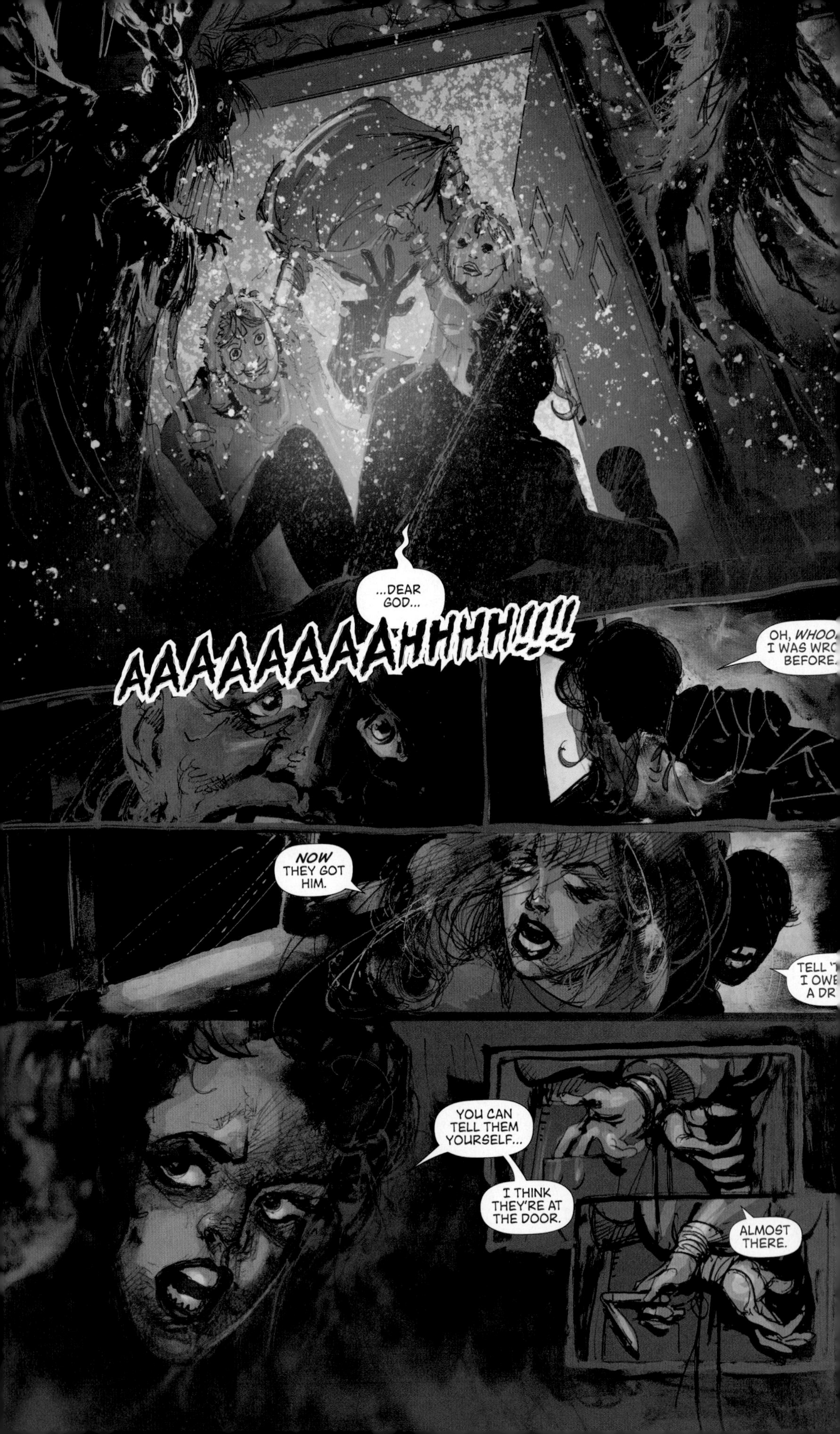

...DEAR GOD...
AAAAAAAAAHHHH!!!!
OH, *WHOO*
I WAS WRO
BEFORE.
NOW THEY GOT HIM.
TELL 'T
I OWE
A DR
YOU CAN TELL THEM YOURSELF...
I THINK THEY'RE AT THE DOOR.
ALMOST THERE.

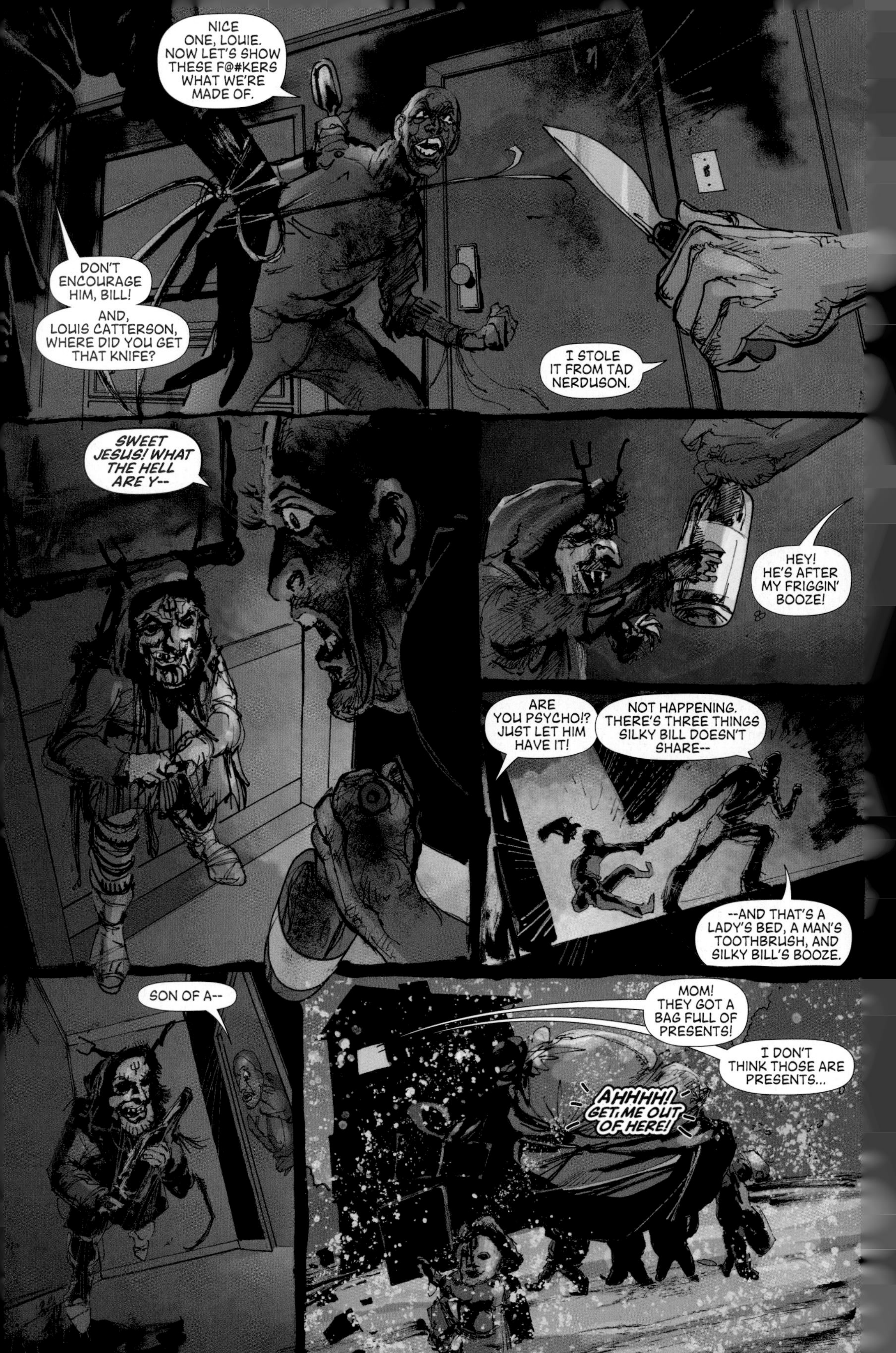
NICE ONE, LOUIE. NOW LET'S SHOW THESE F@#KERS WHAT WE'RE MADE OF.
DON'T ENCOURAGE HIM, BILL!
AND, LOUIS CATTERSON, WHERE DID YOU GET THAT KNIFE?
I STOLE IT FROM TAD NERDUSON.
SWEET JESUS! WHAT THE HELL ARE Y--
HEY! HE'S AFTER MY FRIGGIN' BOOZE!
ARE YOU PSYCHO!? JUST LET HIM HAVE IT!
NOT HAPPENING. THERE'S THREE THINGS SILKY BILL DOESN'T SHARE--
--AND THAT'S A LADY'S BED, A MAN'S TOOTHBRUSH, AND SILKY BILL'S BOOZE.
SON OF A--
MOM! THEY GOT A BAG FULL OF PRESENTS!
I DON'T THINK THOSE ARE PRESENTS...
AHHHH! GET ME OUT OF HERE!

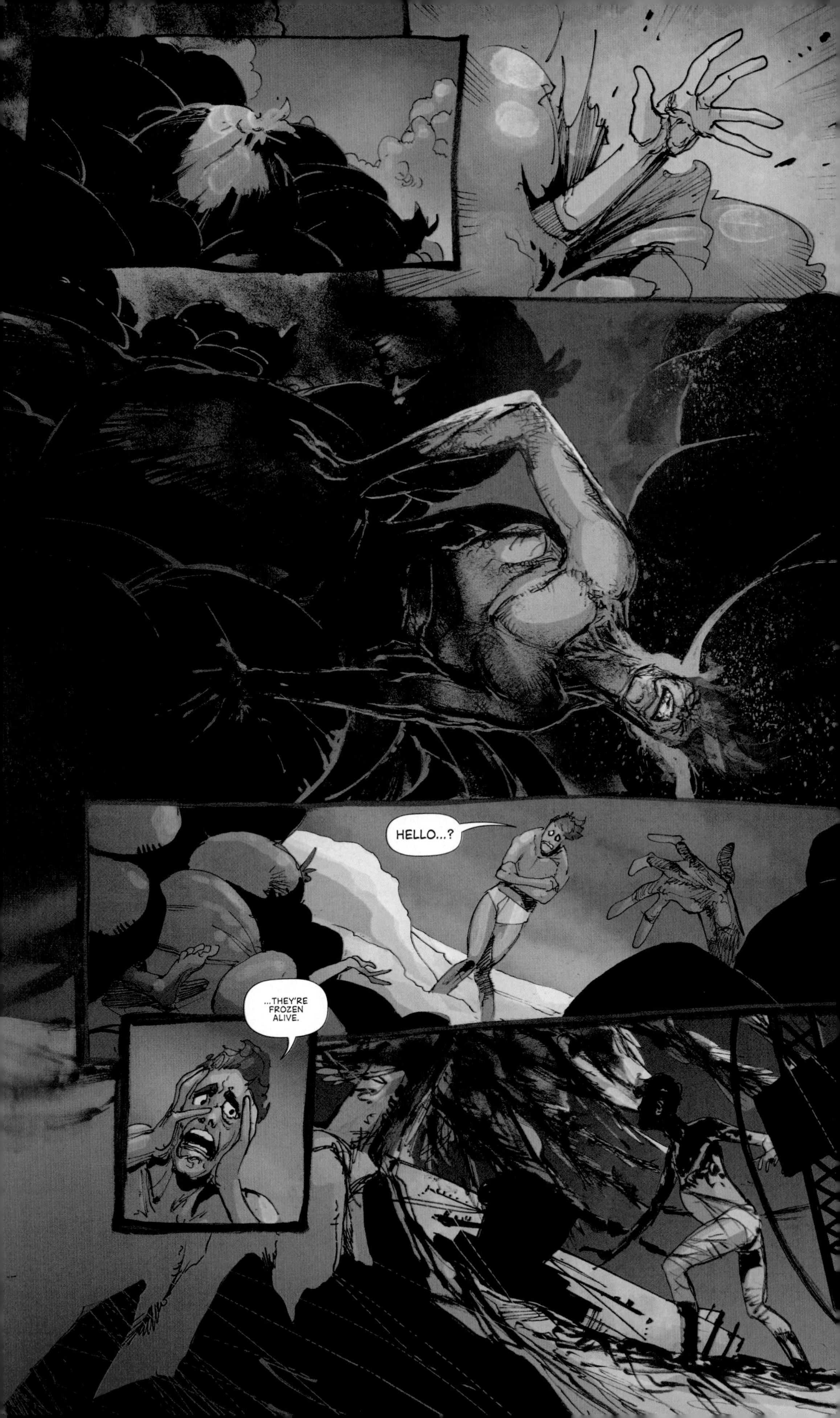
HELLO...?
...THEY'RE FROZEN ALIVE.

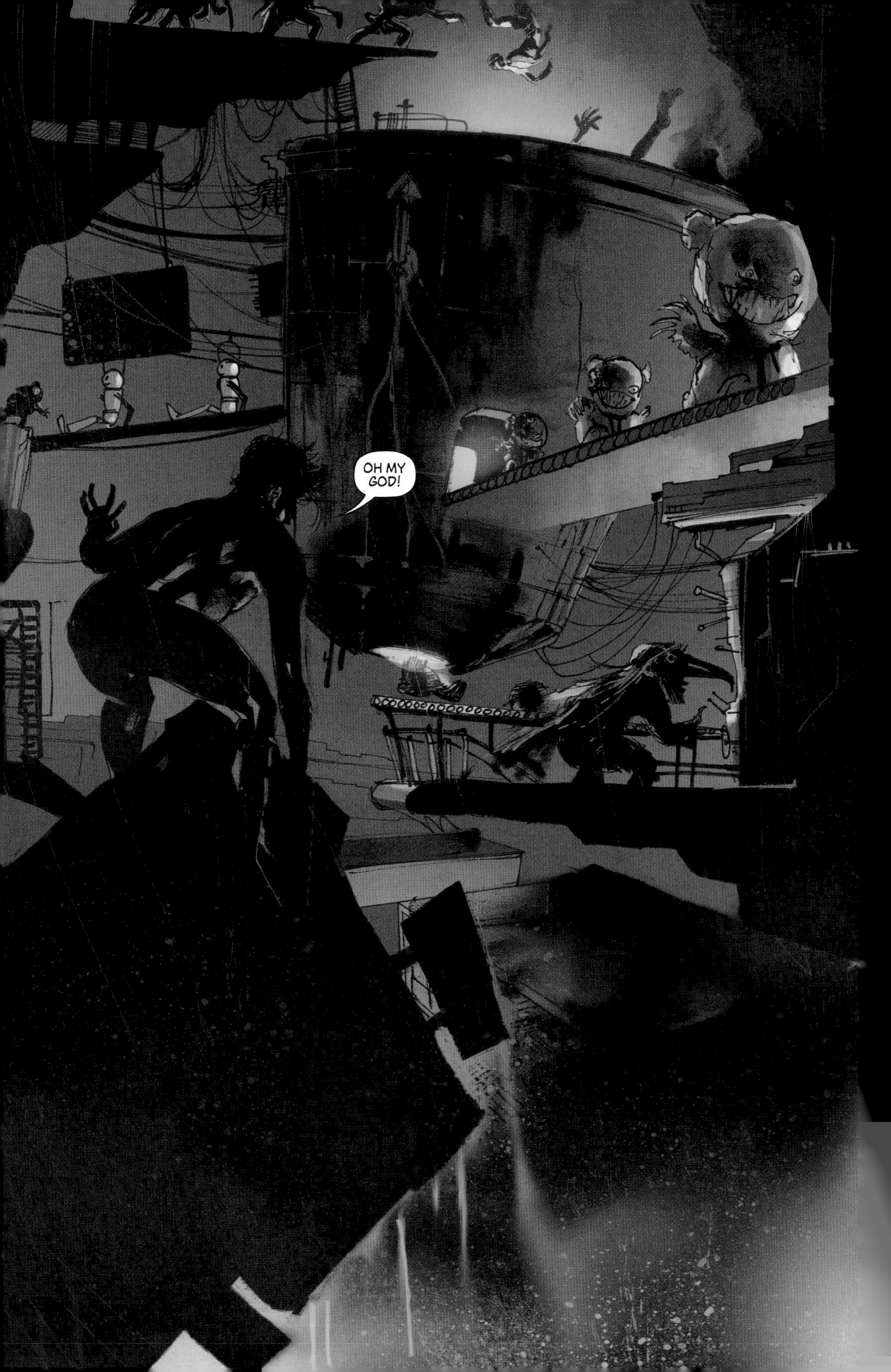
OH MY GOD!

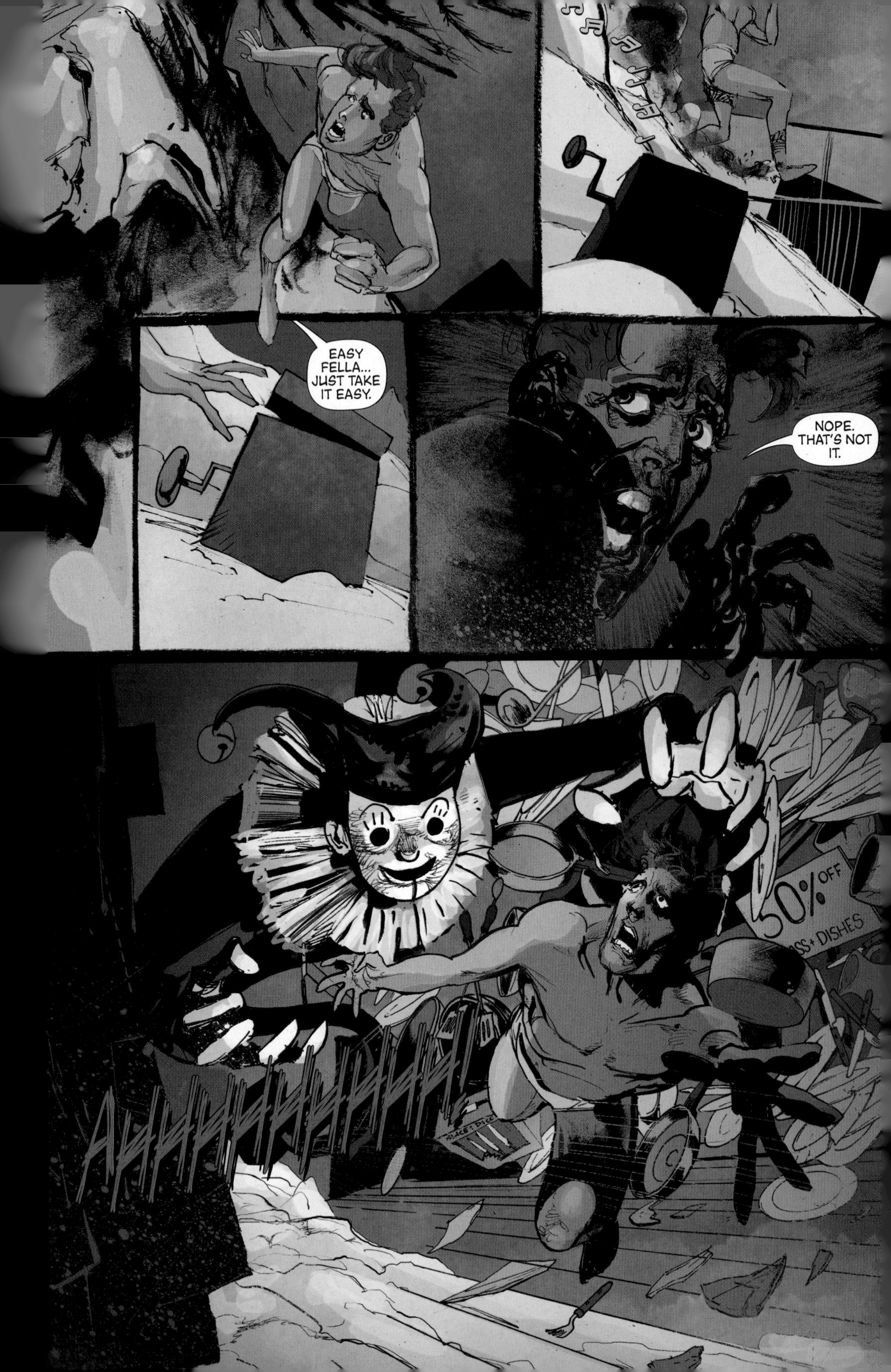
EASY FELLA... JUST TAKE IT EASY.
NOPE. THAT'S NOT IT.
50% OFF

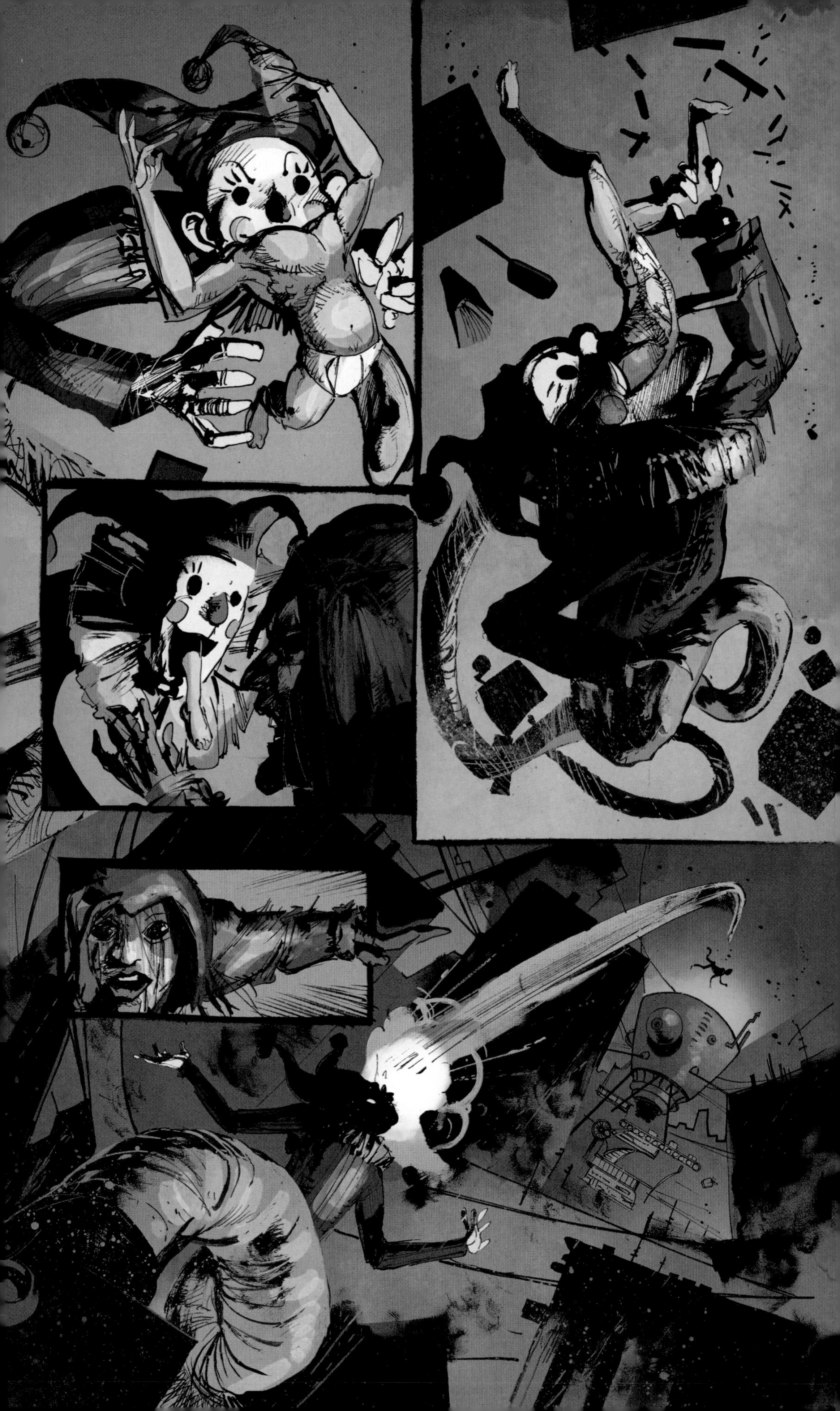

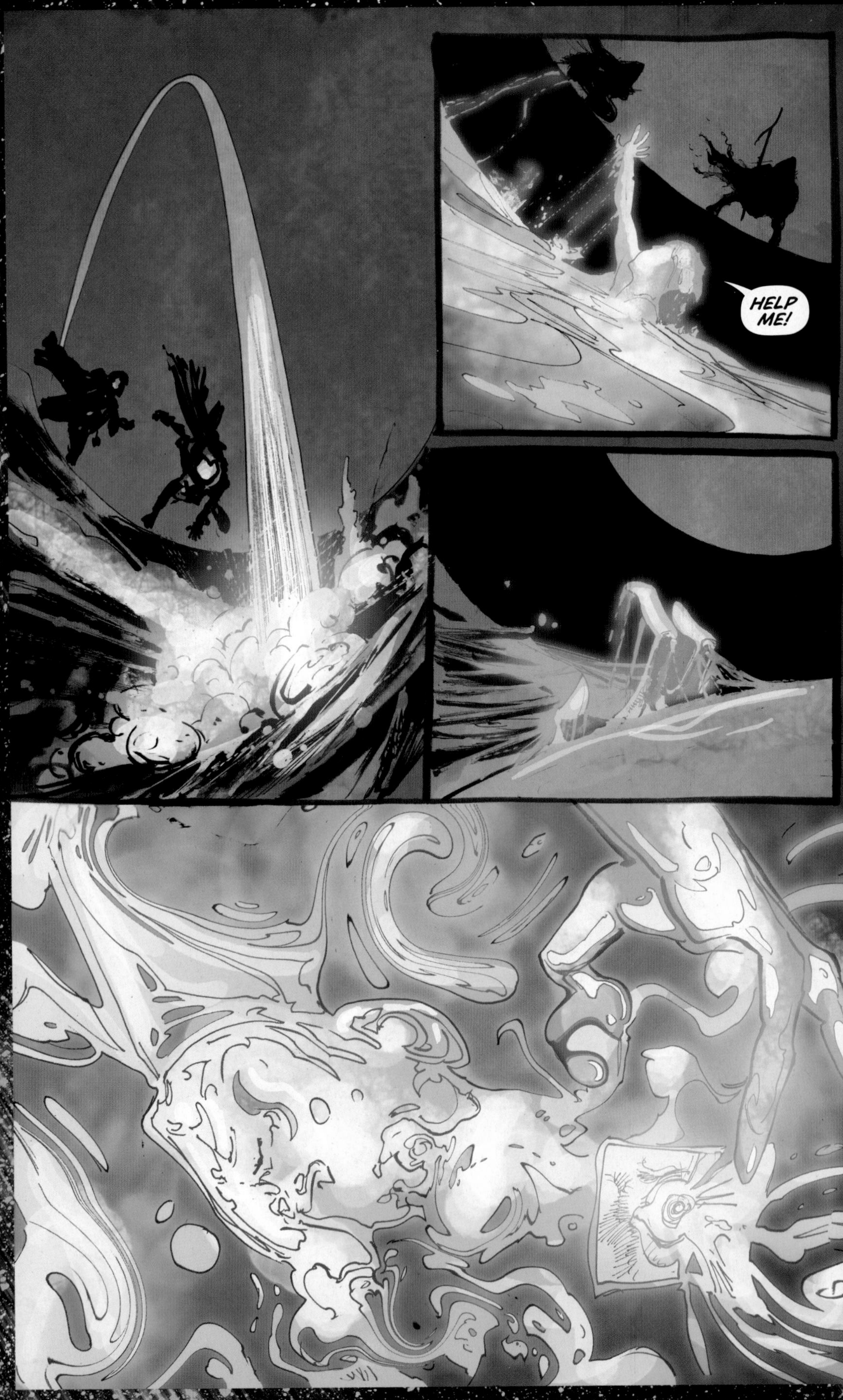
HELP ME!

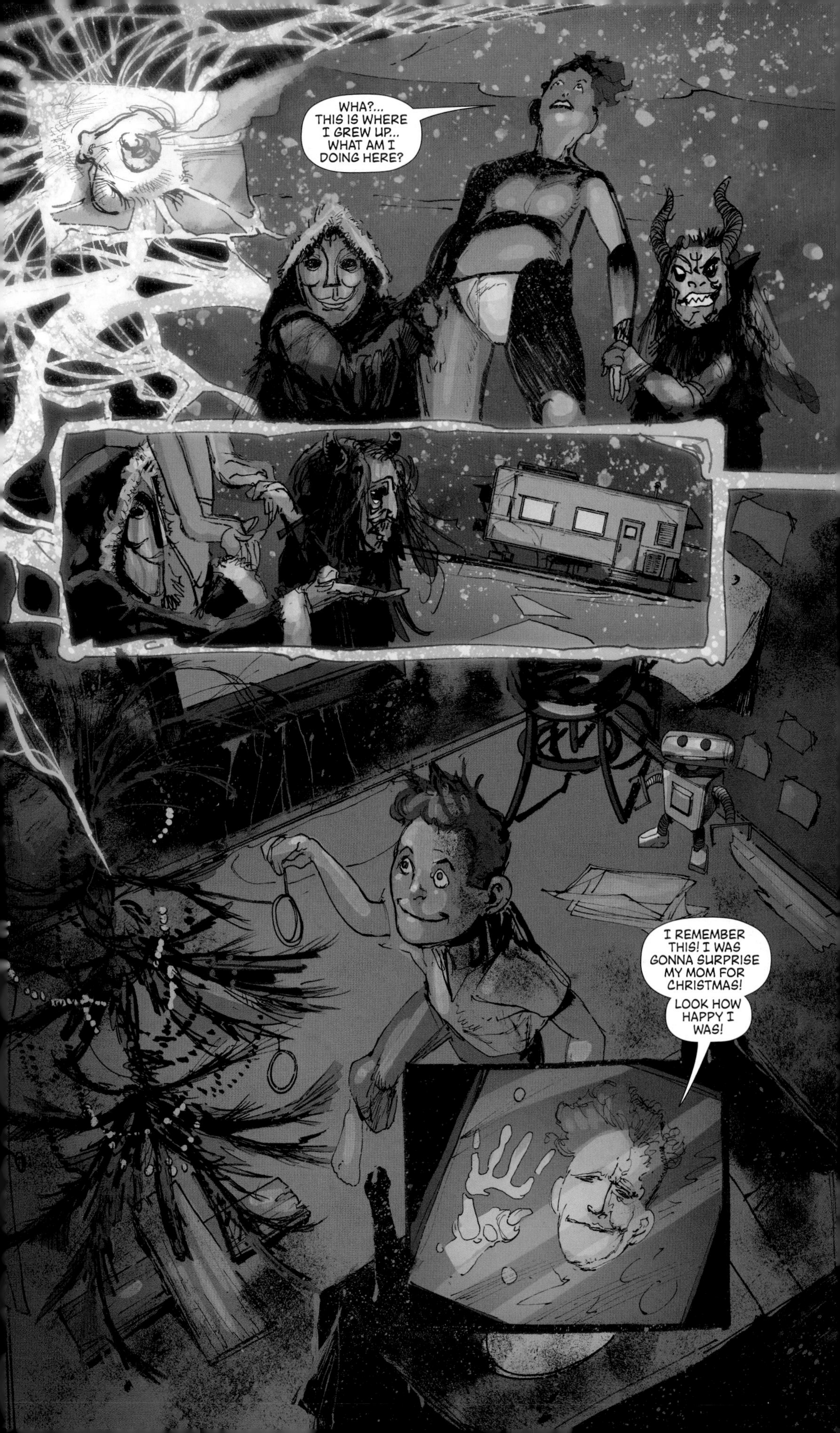
WHA?... THIS IS WHERE I GREW UP... WHAT AM I DOING HERE?
I REMEMBER THIS! I WAS GONNA SURPRISE MY MOM FOR CHRISTMAS!
LOOK HOW HAPPY I WAS!

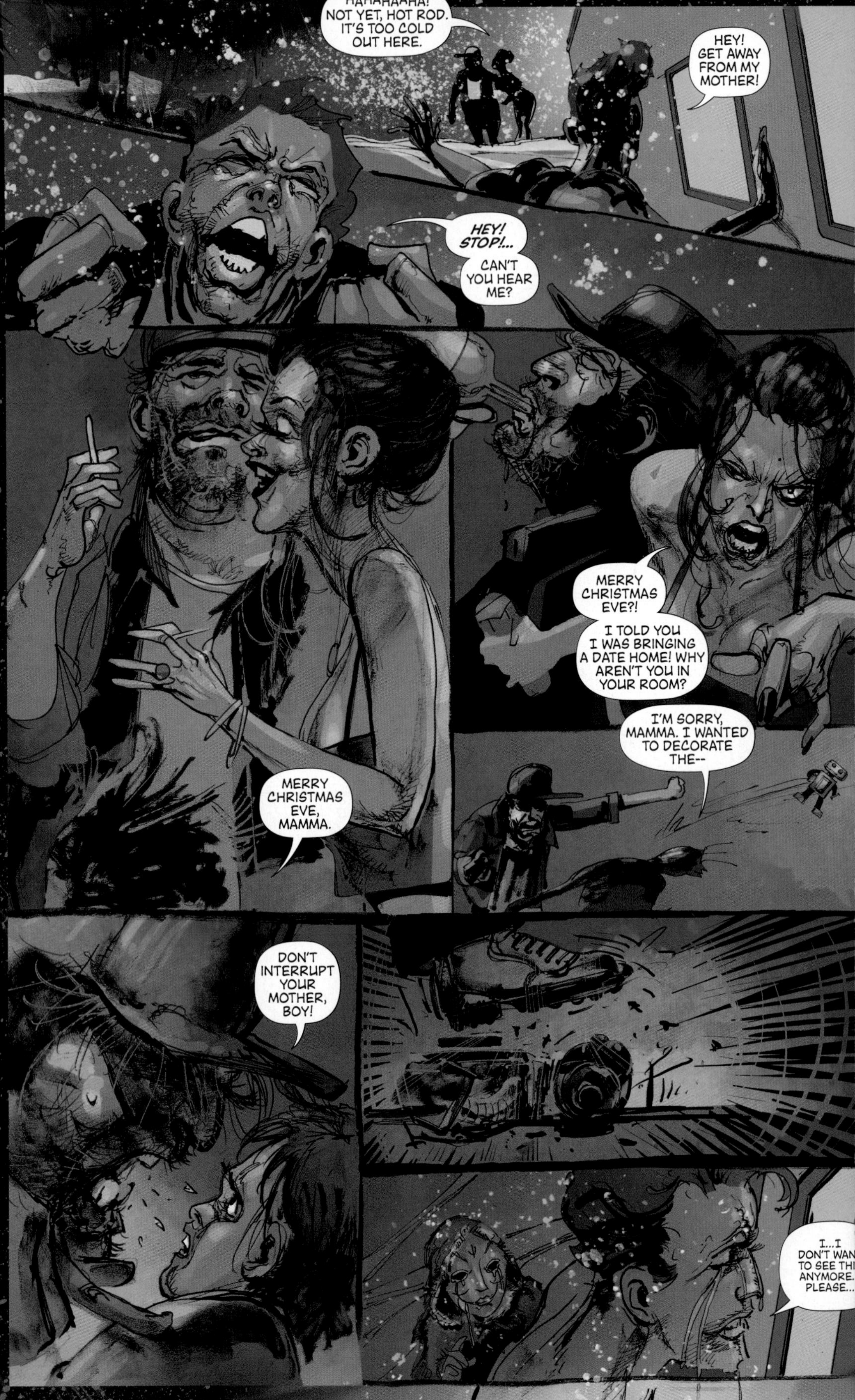
HAHAHAAHA! NOT YET, HOT ROD. IT'S TOO COLD OUT HERE.
HEY! GET AWAY FROM MY MOTHER!
HEY! STOP!...
CAN'T YOU HEAR ME?
MERRY CHRISTMAS EVE, MAMMA.
MERRY CHRISTMAS EVE?!
I TOLD YOU I WAS BRINGING A DATE HOME! WHY AREN'T YOU IN YOUR ROOM?
I'M SORRY, MAMMA. I WANTED TO DECORATE THE--
DON'T INTERRUPT YOUR MOTHER, BOY!
I...I DON'T WAN TO SEE THI ANYMORE. PLEASE...

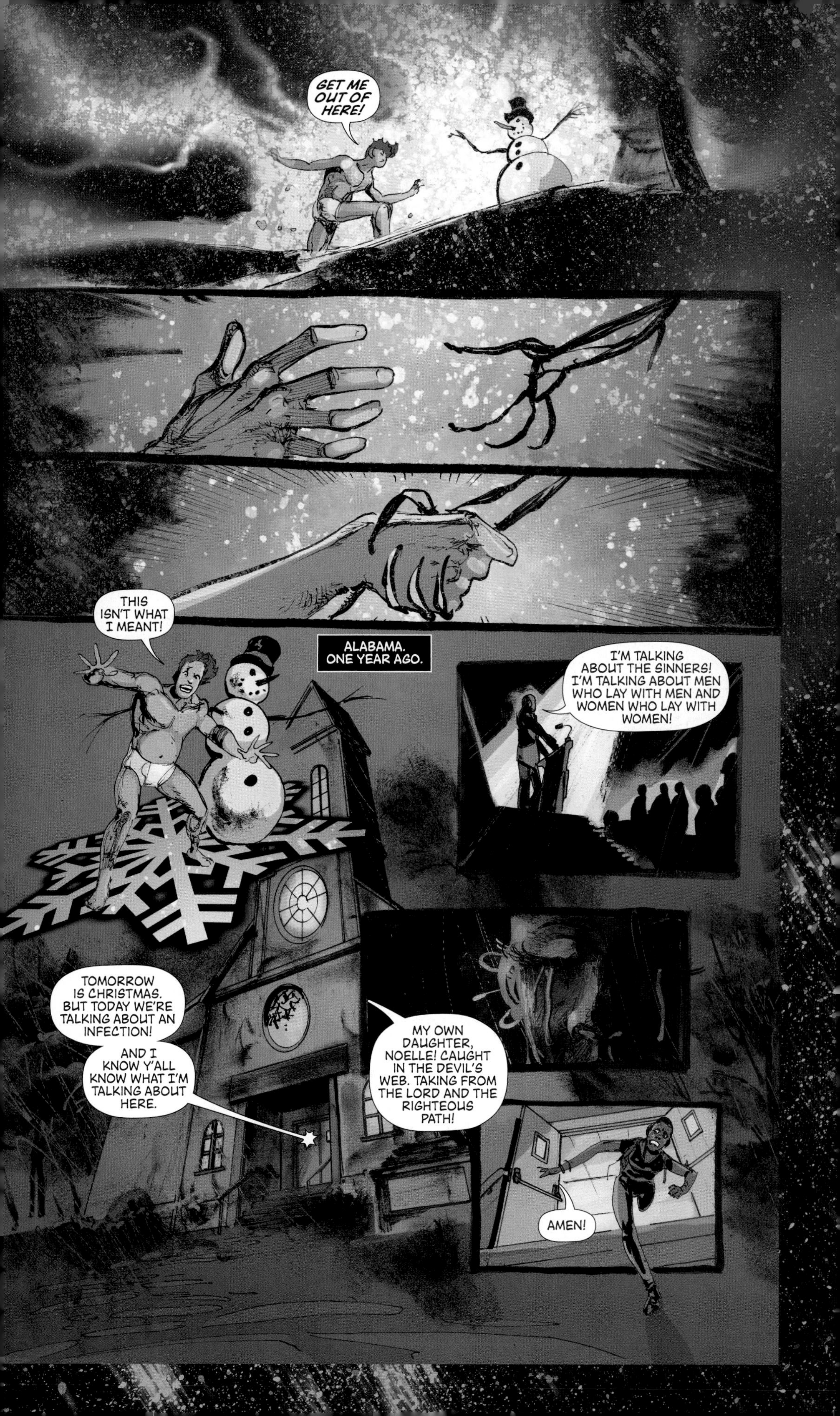
GET ME OUT OF HERE!
THIS ISN'T WHAT I MEANT!
ALABAMA. ONE YEAR AGO.
I'M TALKING ABOUT THE SINNERS! I'M TALKING ABOUT MEN WHO LAY WITH MEN AND WOMEN WHO LAY WITH WOMEN!
TOMORROW IS CHRISTMAS. BUT TODAY WE'RE TALKING ABOUT AN INFECTION!
AND I KNOW Y'ALL KNOW WHAT I'M TALKING ABOUT HERE.
MY OWN DAUGHTER, NOELLE! CAUGHT IN THE DEVIL'S WEB. TAKING FROM THE LORD AND THE RIGHTEOUS PATH!
AMEN!

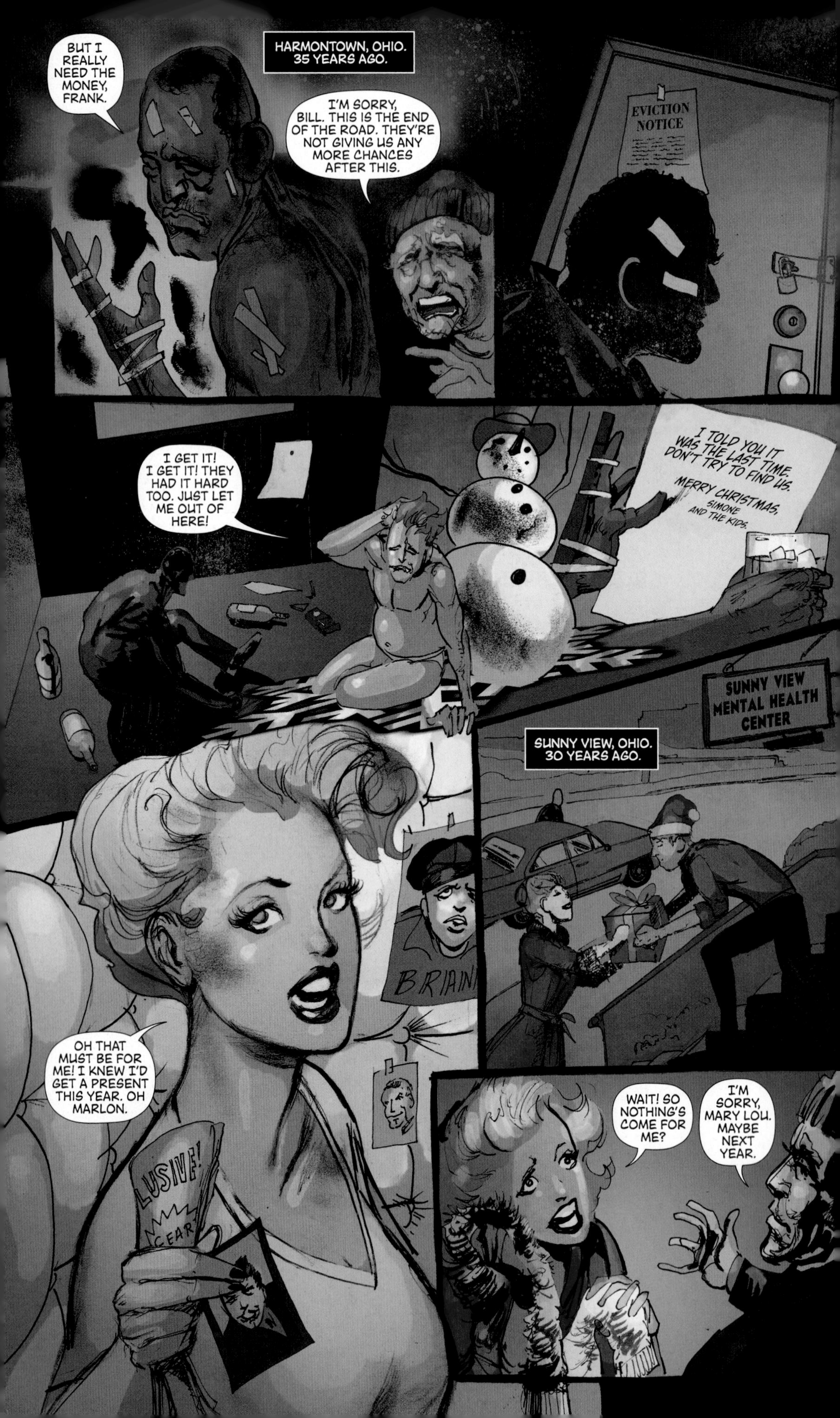
HARMONTOWN, OHIO. 35 YEARS AGO.
BUT I REALLY NEED THE MONEY, FRANK.
I'M SORRY, BILL. THIS IS THE END OF THE ROAD. THEY'RE NOT GIVING US ANY MORE CHANCES AFTER THIS.
EVICTION NOTICE
I GET IT! I GET IT! THEY HAD IT HARD TOO. JUST LET ME OUT OF HERE!
I TOLD YOU IT WAS THE LAST TIME. DON'T TRY TO FIND US.
MERRY CHRISTMAS, SIMONE AND THE KIDS.
SUNNY VIEW MENTAL HEALTH CENTER
SUNNY VIEW, OHIO. 30 YEARS AGO.
BRIAN
OH THAT MUST BE FOR ME! I KNEW I'D GET A PRESENT THIS YEAR. OH MARLON.
WAIT! SO NOTHING'S COME FOR ME?
I'M SORRY, MARY LOU. MAYBE NEXT YEAR.

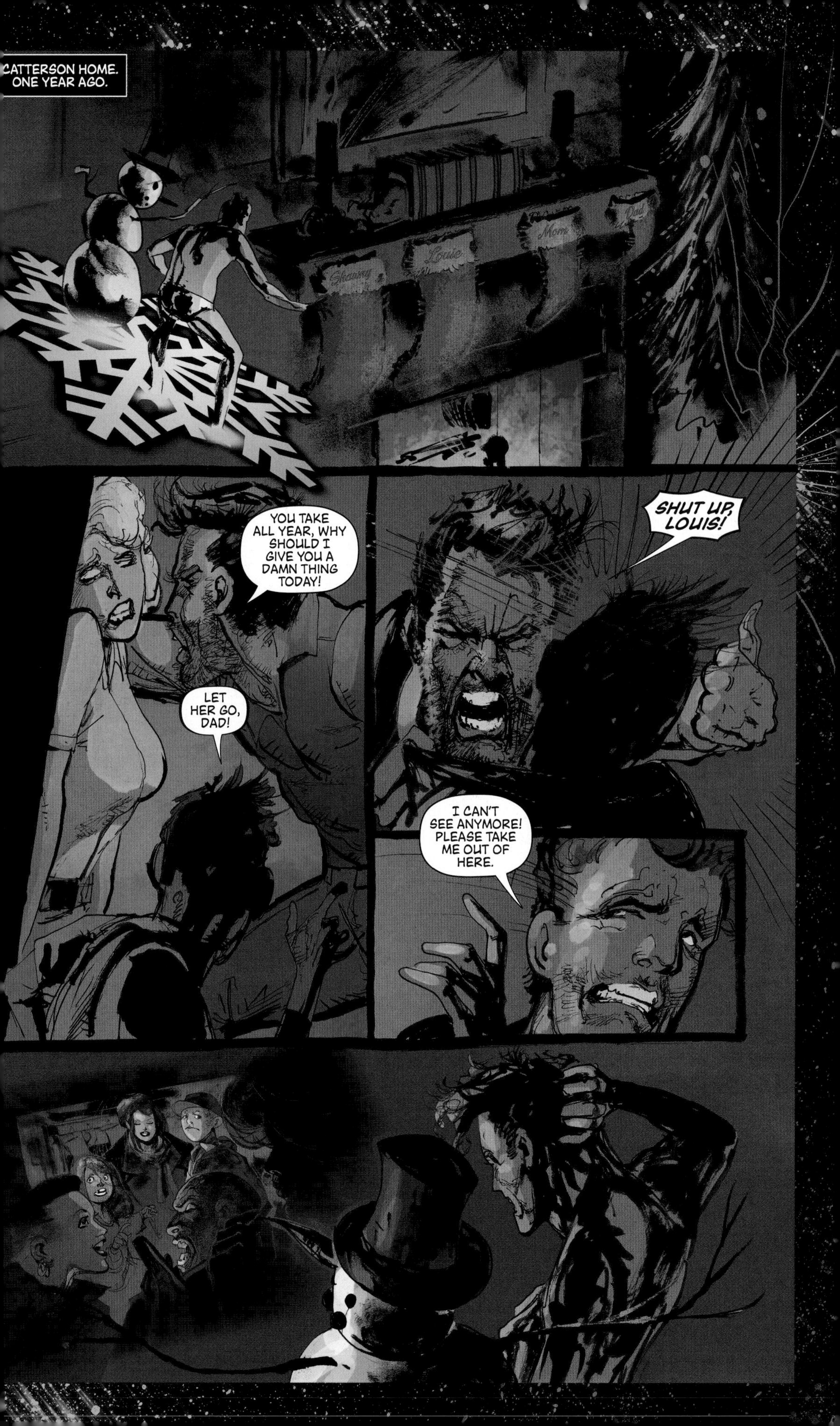
CATTERSON HOME. ONE YEAR AGO.
Shawny
Louie
Mom
Dad
YOU TAKE ALL YEAR, WHY SHOULD I GIVE YOU A DAMN THING TODAY!
LET HER GO, DAD!
SHUT UP, LOUIS!
I CAN'T SEE ANYMORE! PLEASE TAKE ME OUT OF HERE.

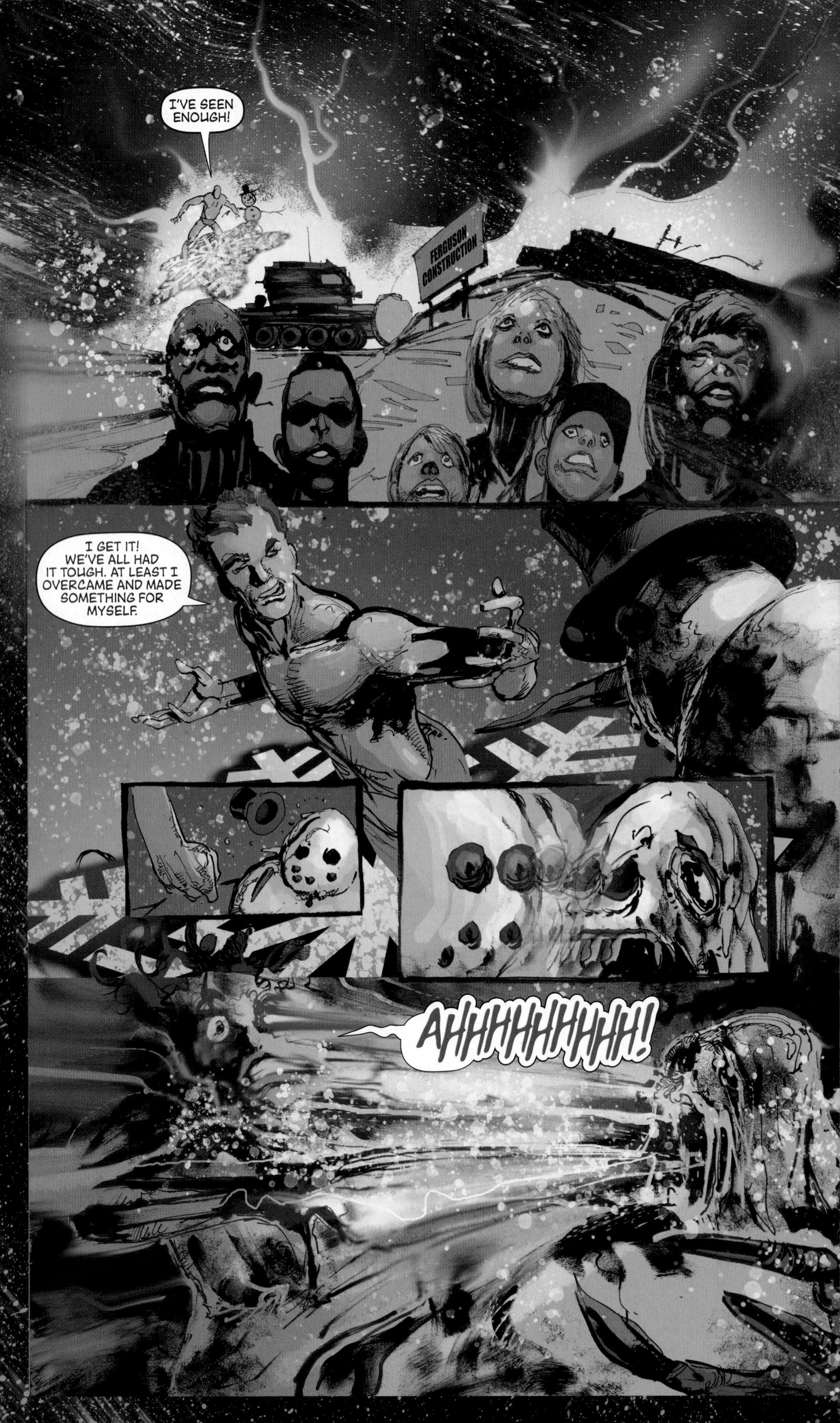
I'VE SEEN ENOUGH!
FERGUSON CONSTRUCTION
I GET IT! WE'VE ALL HAD IT TOUGH. AT LEAST I OVERCAME AND MADE SOMETHING FOR MYSELF.
AHHHHHHHHH!

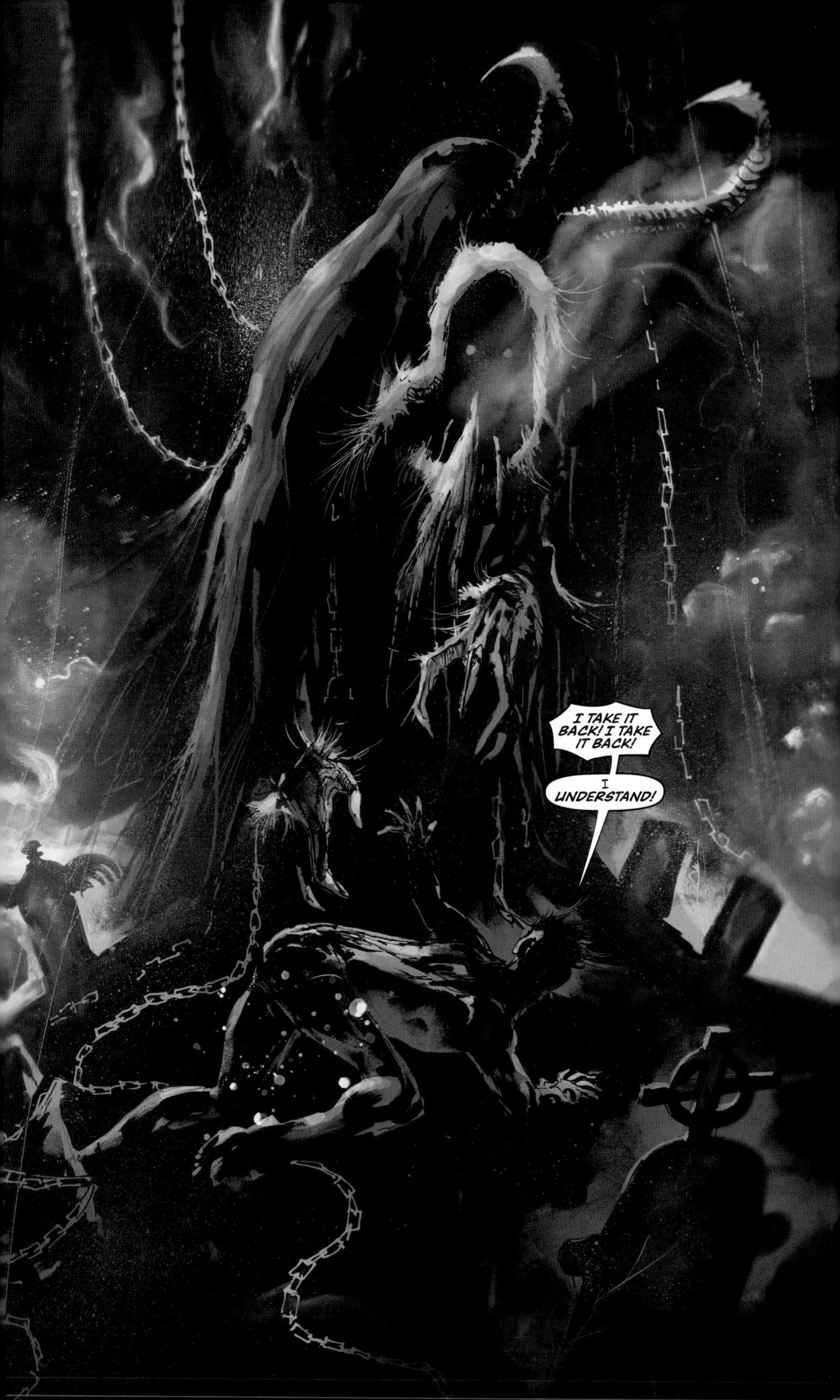
I TAKE IT BACK! I TAKE IT BACK!
I UNDERSTAND!

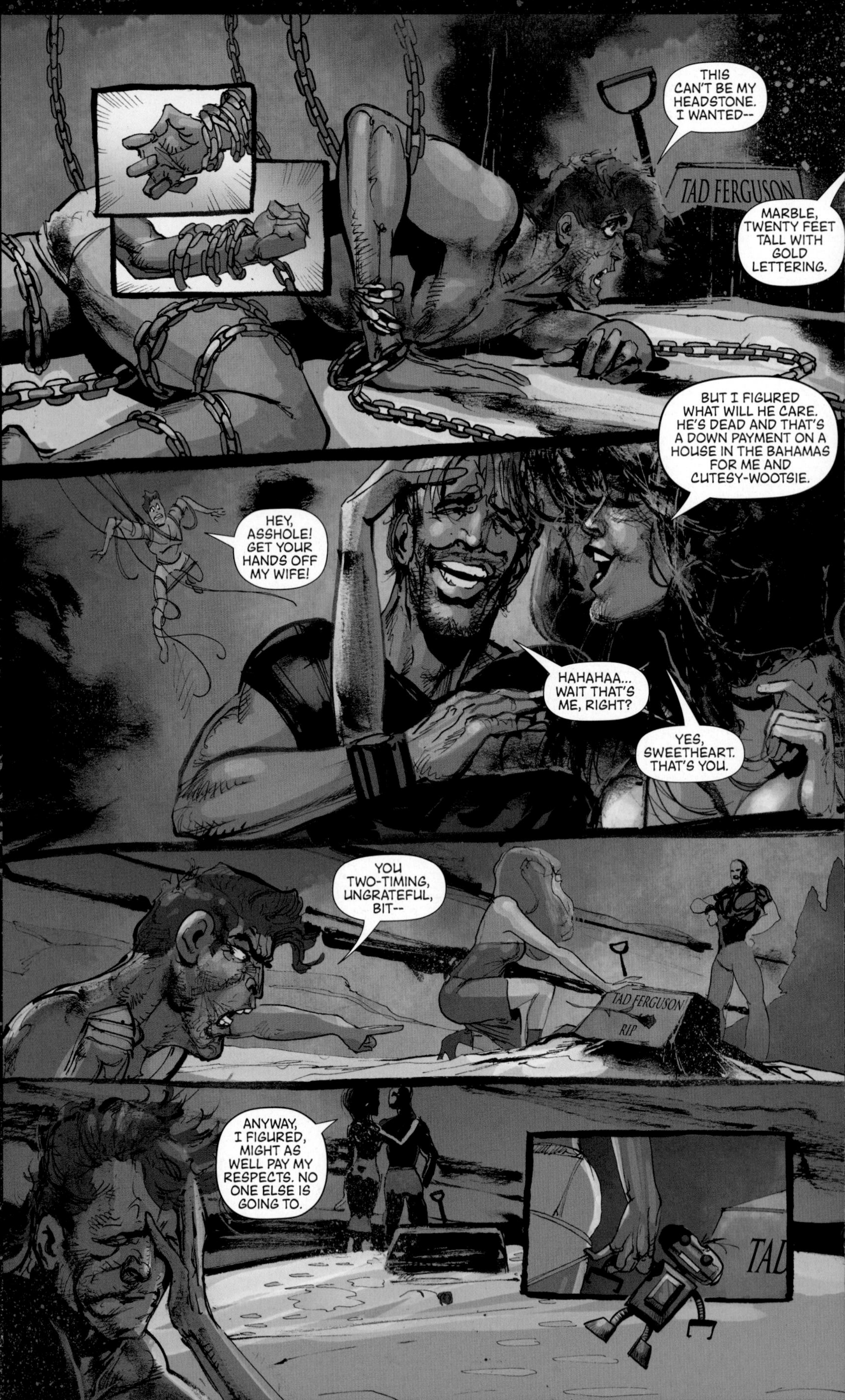
THIS CAN'T BE MY HEADSTONE. I WANTED--
TAD FERGUSON
MARBLE, TWENTY FEET TALL WITH GOLD LETTERING.
BUT I FIGURED WHAT WILL HE CARE. HE'S DEAD AND THAT'S A DOWN PAYMENT ON A HOUSE IN THE BAHAMAS FOR ME AND CUTESY-WOOTSIE.
HEY, ASSHOLE! GET YOUR HANDS OFF MY WIFE!
HAHAHAA... WAIT THAT'S ME, RIGHT?
YES, SWEETHEART. THAT'S YOU.
YOU TWO-TIMING, UNGRATEFUL, BIT--
TAD FERGUSON
RIP
ANYWAY, I FIGURED, MIGHT AS WELL PAY MY RESPECTS. NO ONE ELSE IS GOING TO.
TAD

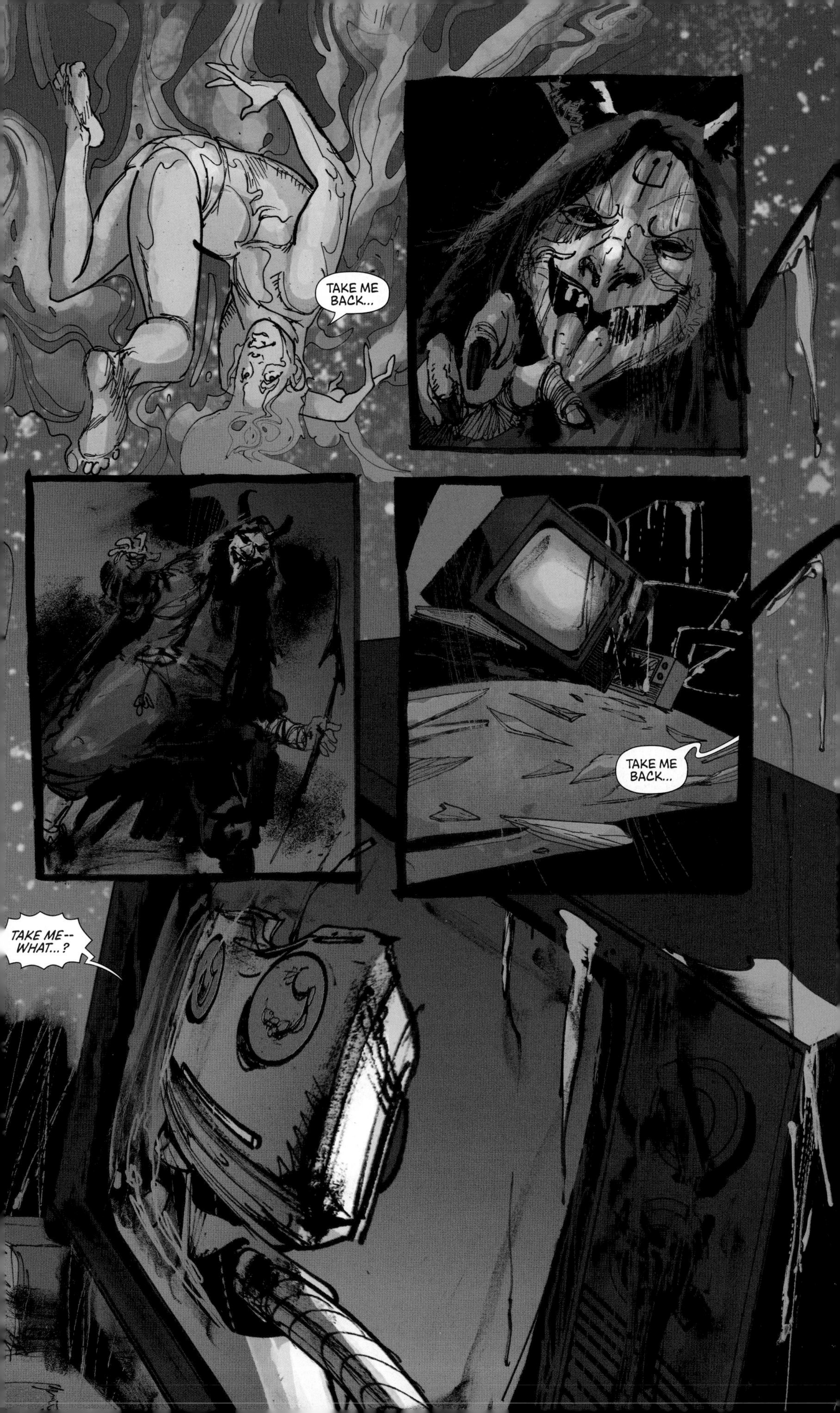
TAKE ME BACK...
TAKE ME BACK...
TAKE ME-- WHAT...?

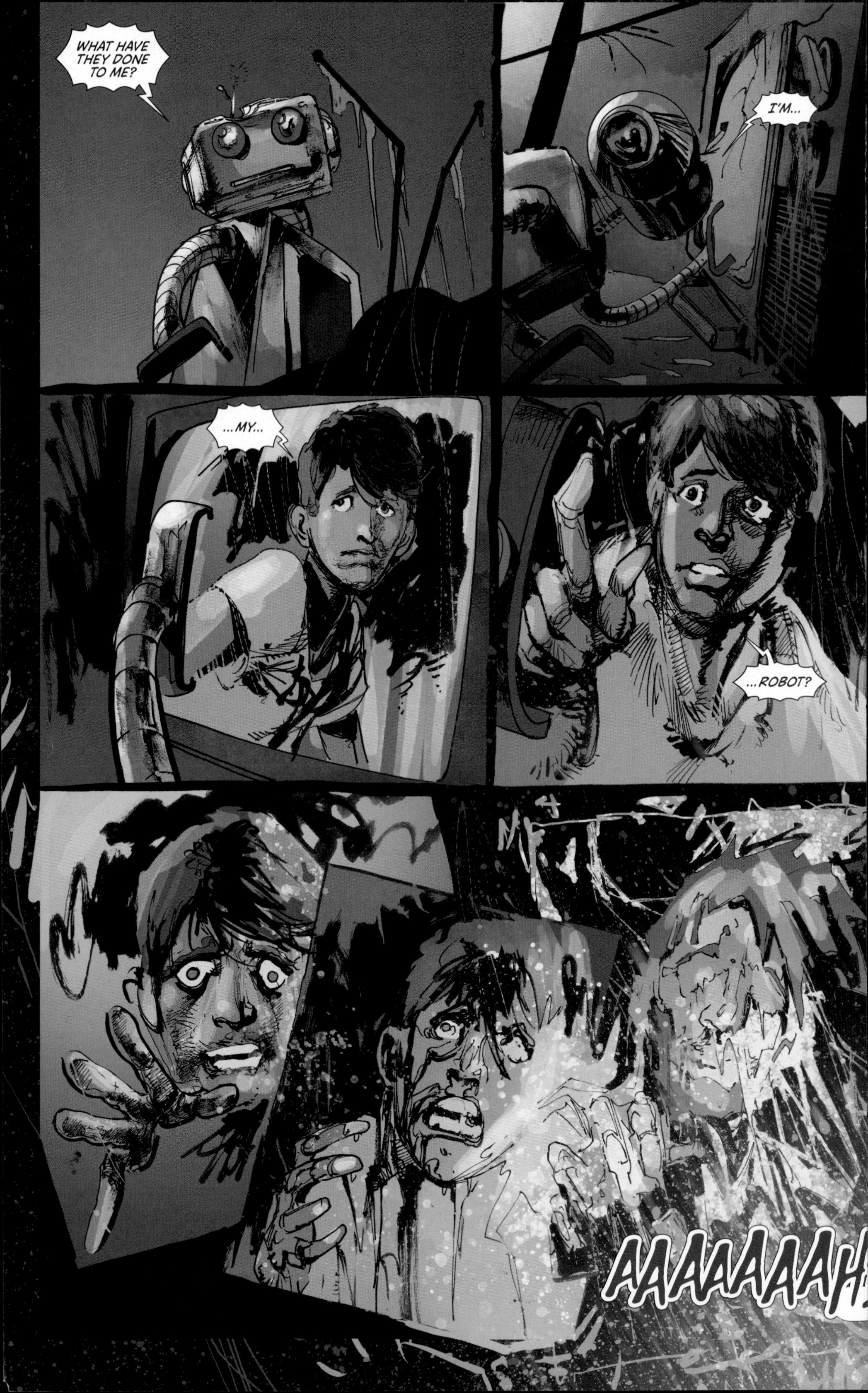
WHAT HAVE THEY DONE TO ME?
I'M...
...MY...
...ROBOT?
AAAAAAAH!

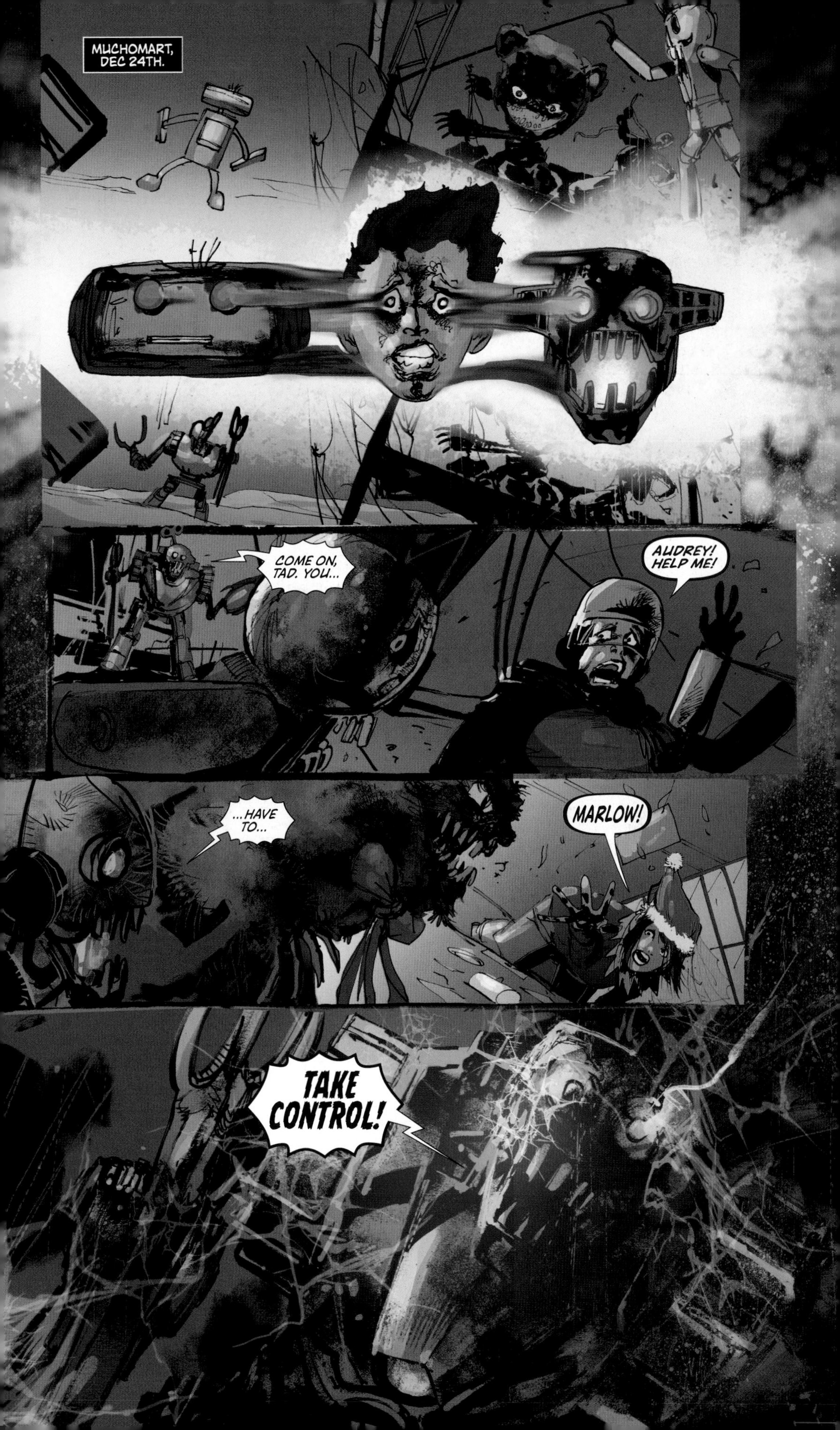

MUCHOMART, DEC 24TH.
COME ON, TAD. YOU...
AUDREY! HELP ME!
...HAVE TO...
MARLOW!
TAKE CONTROL!

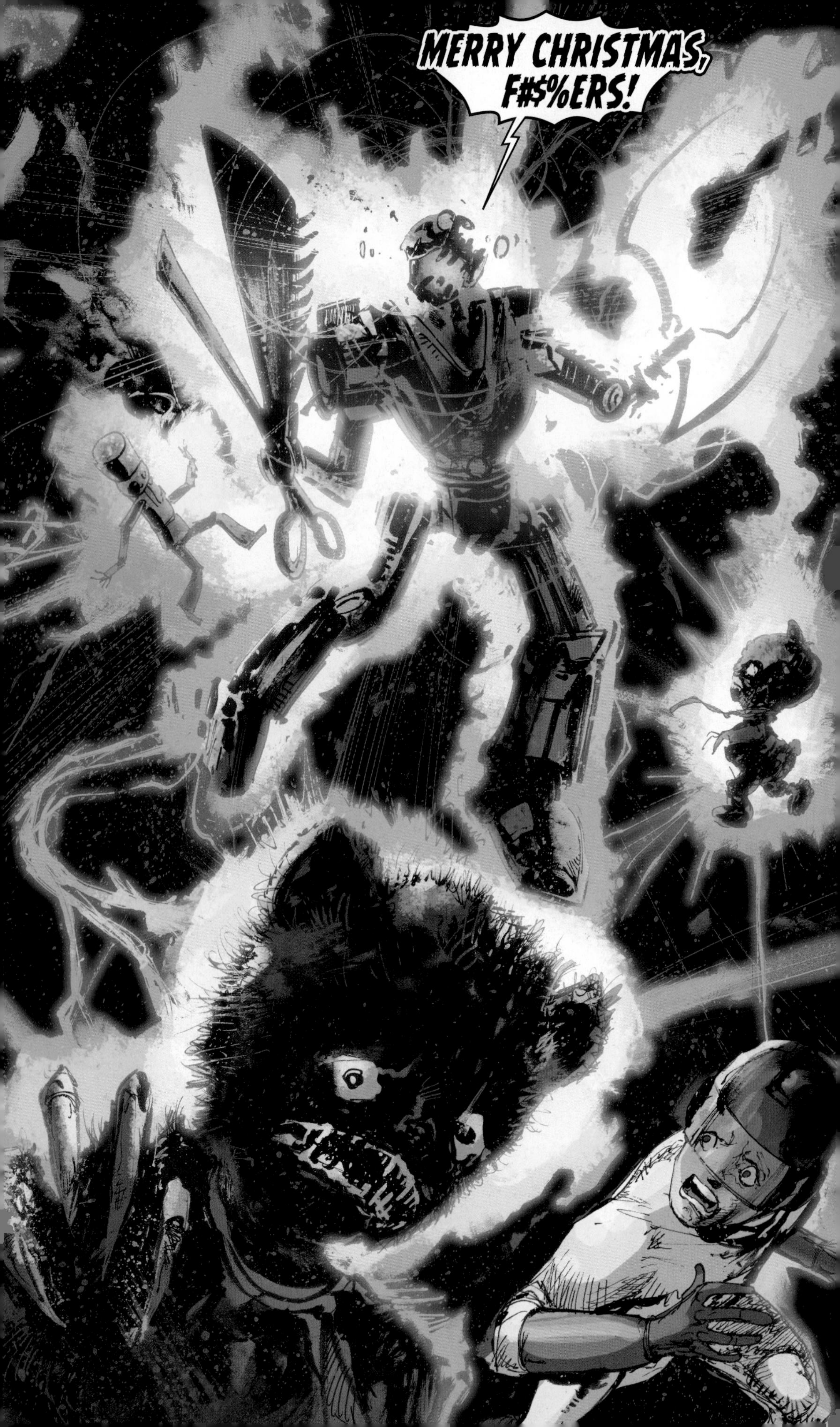
MERRY CHRISTMAS, F#$%ERS!

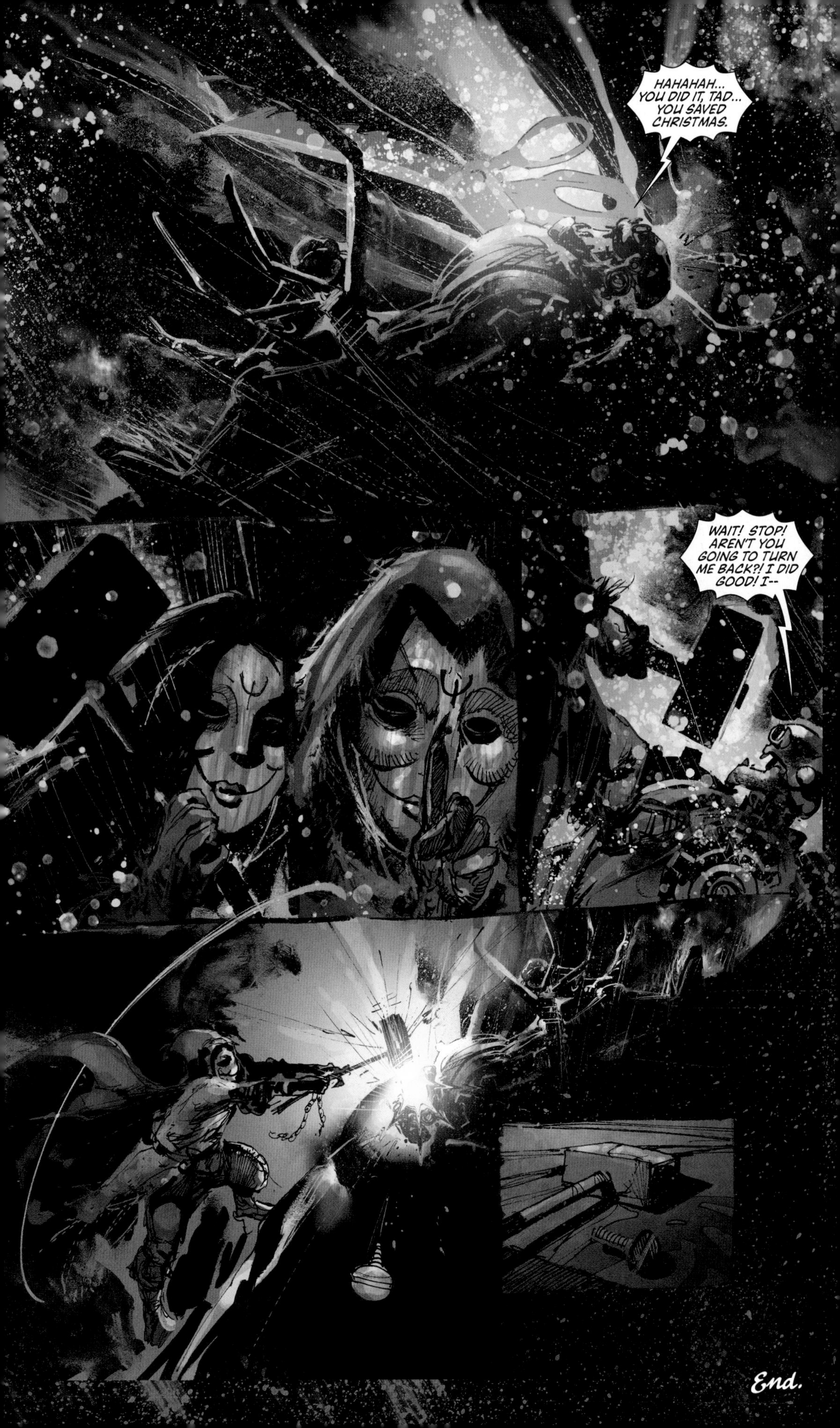
HAHAHAH... YOU DID IT, TAD... YOU SAVED CHRISTMAS.
WAIT! STOP! AREN'T YOU GOING TO TURN ME BACK?! I DID GOOD! I--
End.

IV

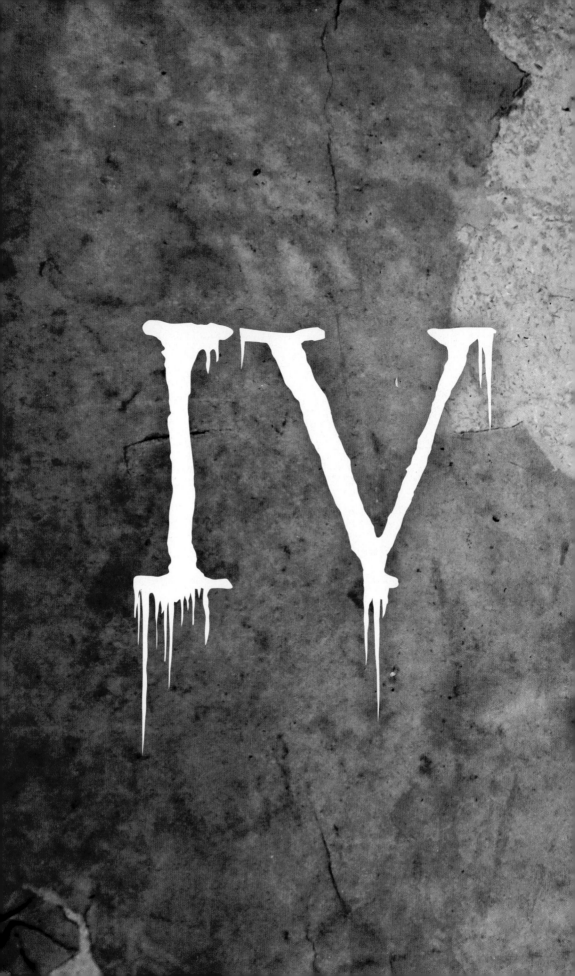

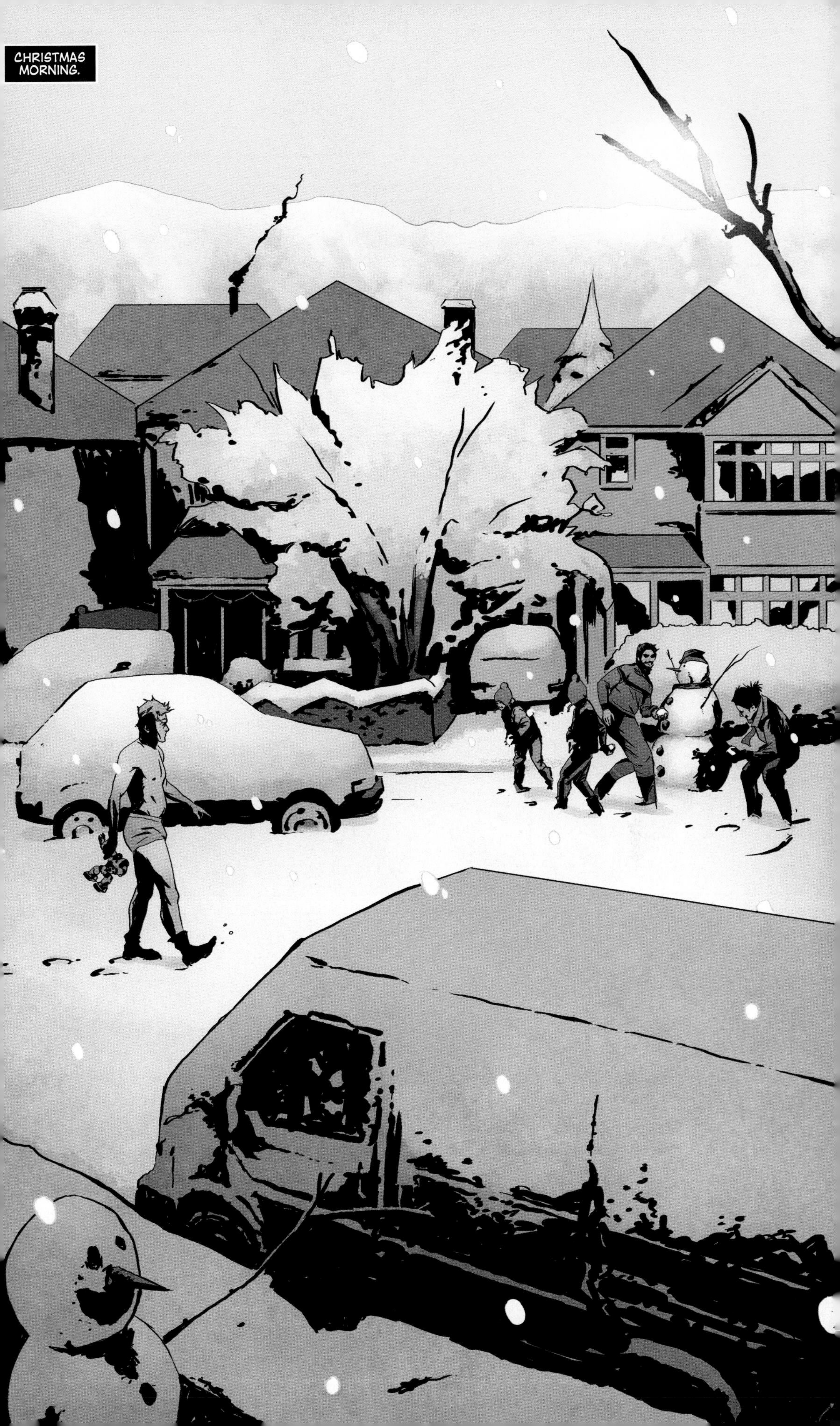
CHRISTMAS MORNING.

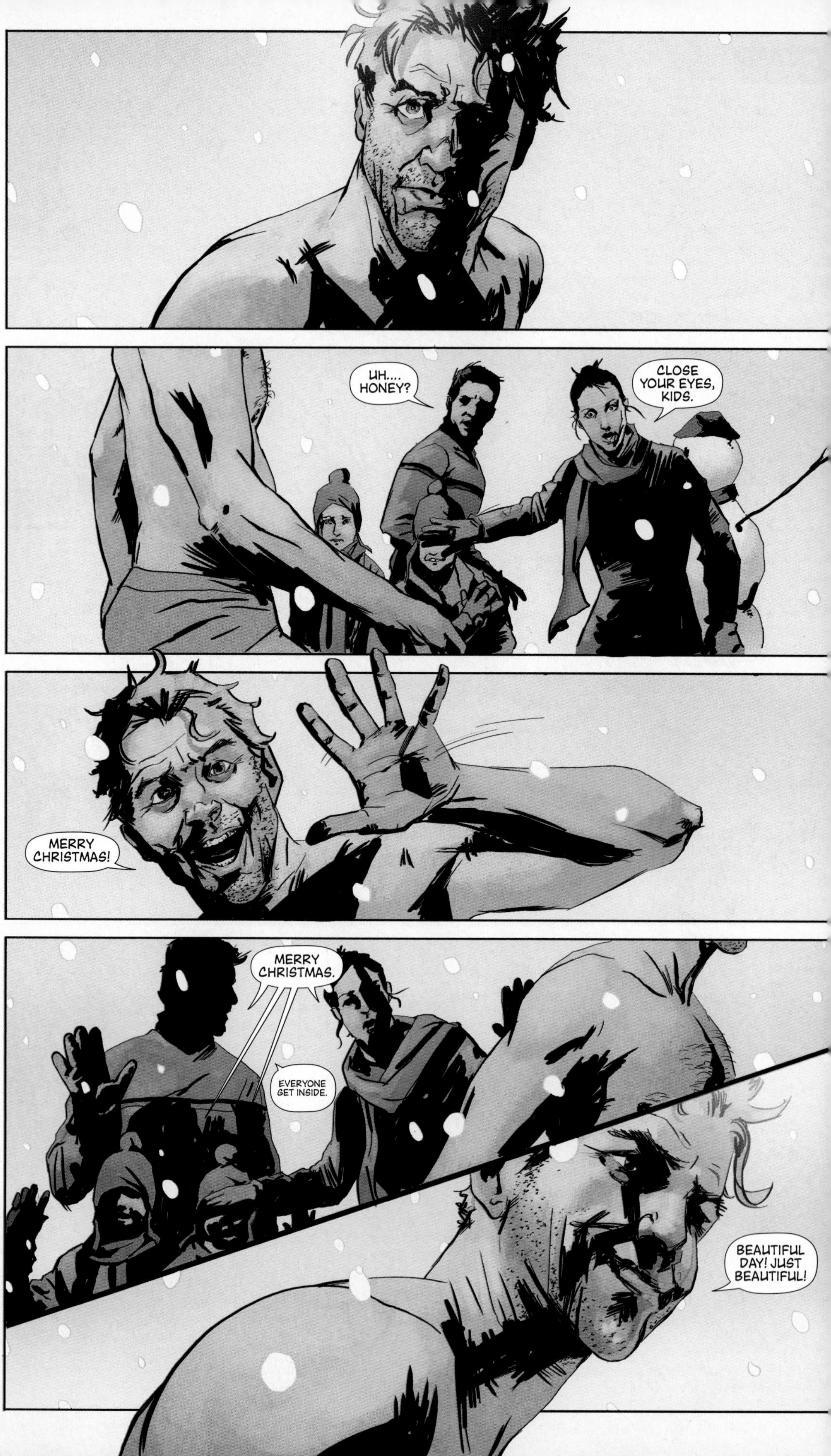
UH.... HONEY?
CLOSE YOUR EYES, KIDS.
MERRY CHRISTMAS!
MERRY CHRISTMAS.
EVERYONE GET INSIDE.
BEAUTIFUL DAY! JUST BEAUTIFUL!

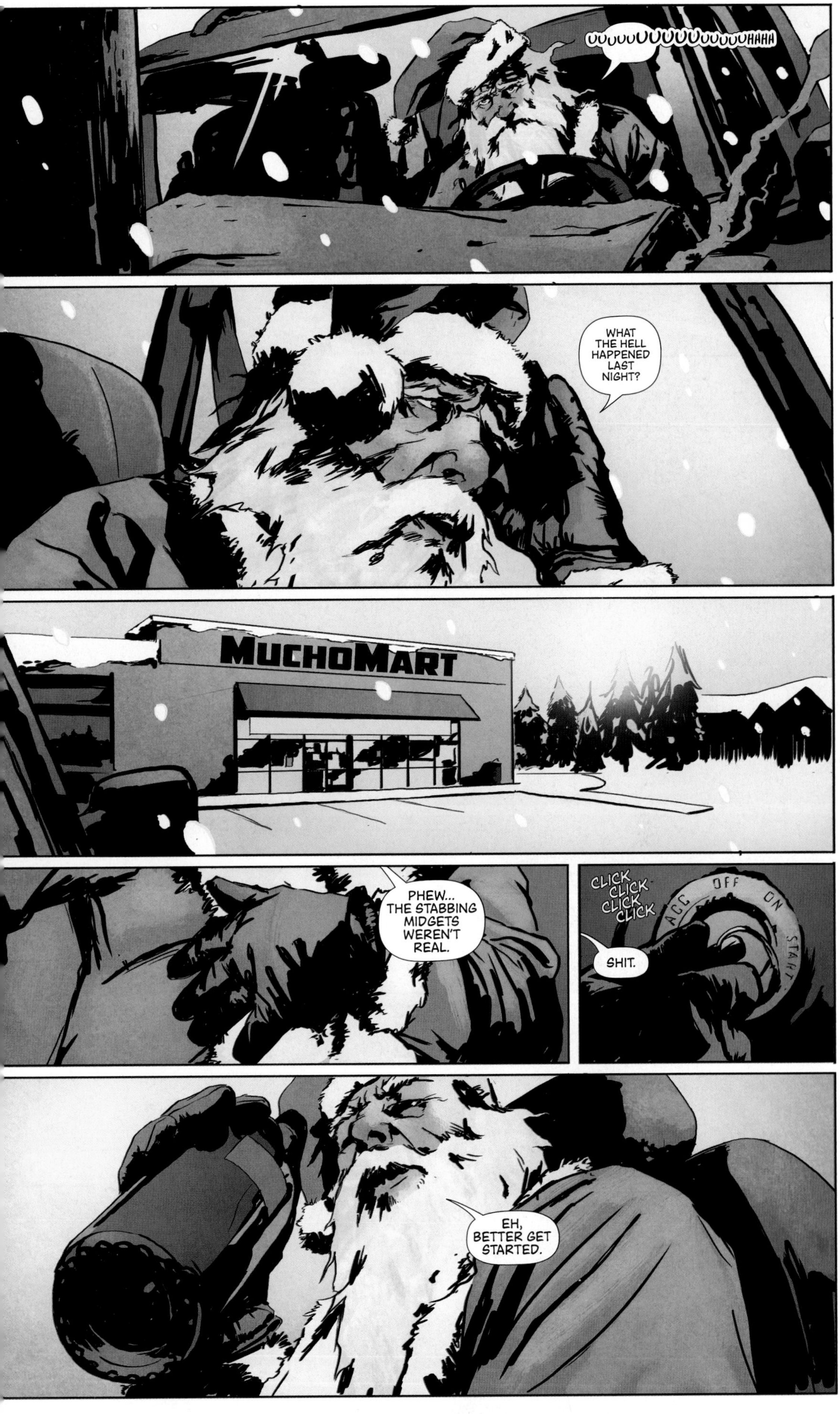
UUUUUUUUUUUUUUUHHHH
WHAT THE HELL HAPPENED LAST NIGHT?
MUCHOMART
PHEW... THE STABBING MIDGETS WEREN'T REAL.
CLICK CLICK CLICK CLICK
ACC OFF ON START
SHIT.
EH, BETTER GET STARTED.

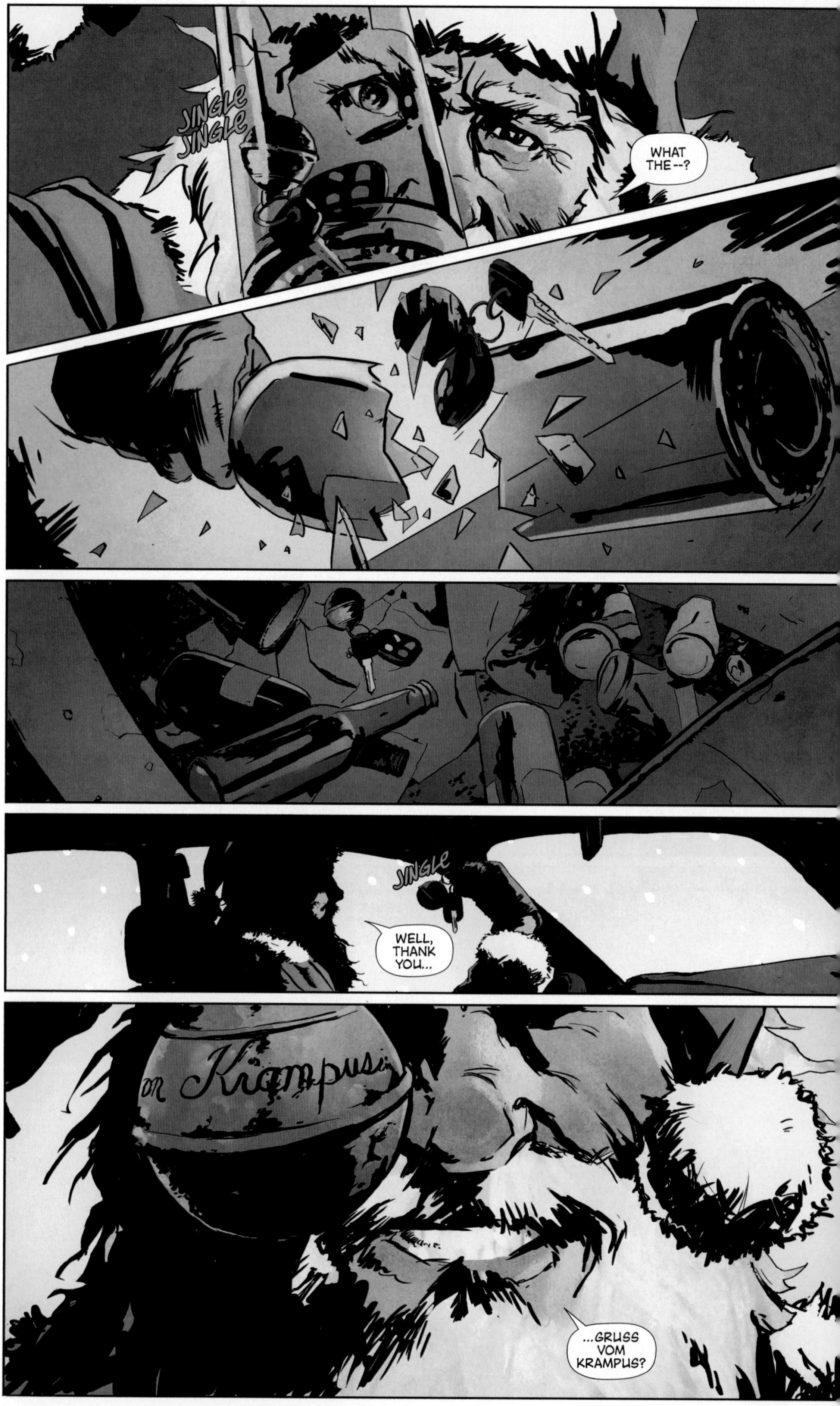
JINGLE JINGLE
WHAT THE--?
JINGLE
WELL, THANK YOU...
on Krampus
...GRUSS VOM KRAMPUS?

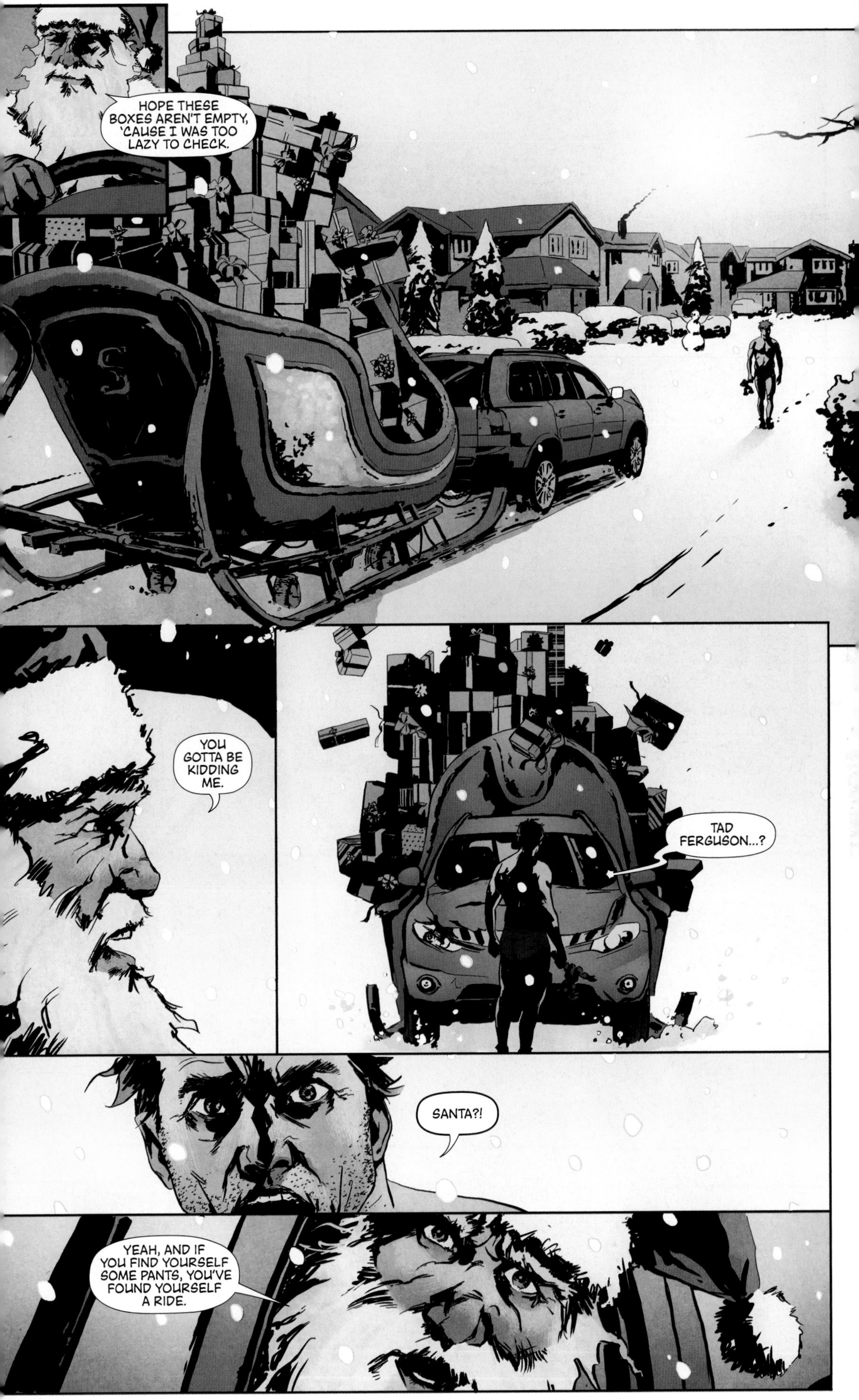
HOPE THESE BOXES AREN'T EMPTY, 'CAUSE I WAS TOO LAZY TO CHECK.
YOU GOTTA BE KIDDING ME.
TAD FERGUSON...?
SANTA?!
YEAH, AND IF YOU FIND YOURSELF SOME PANTS, YOU'VE FOUND YOURSELF A RIDE.

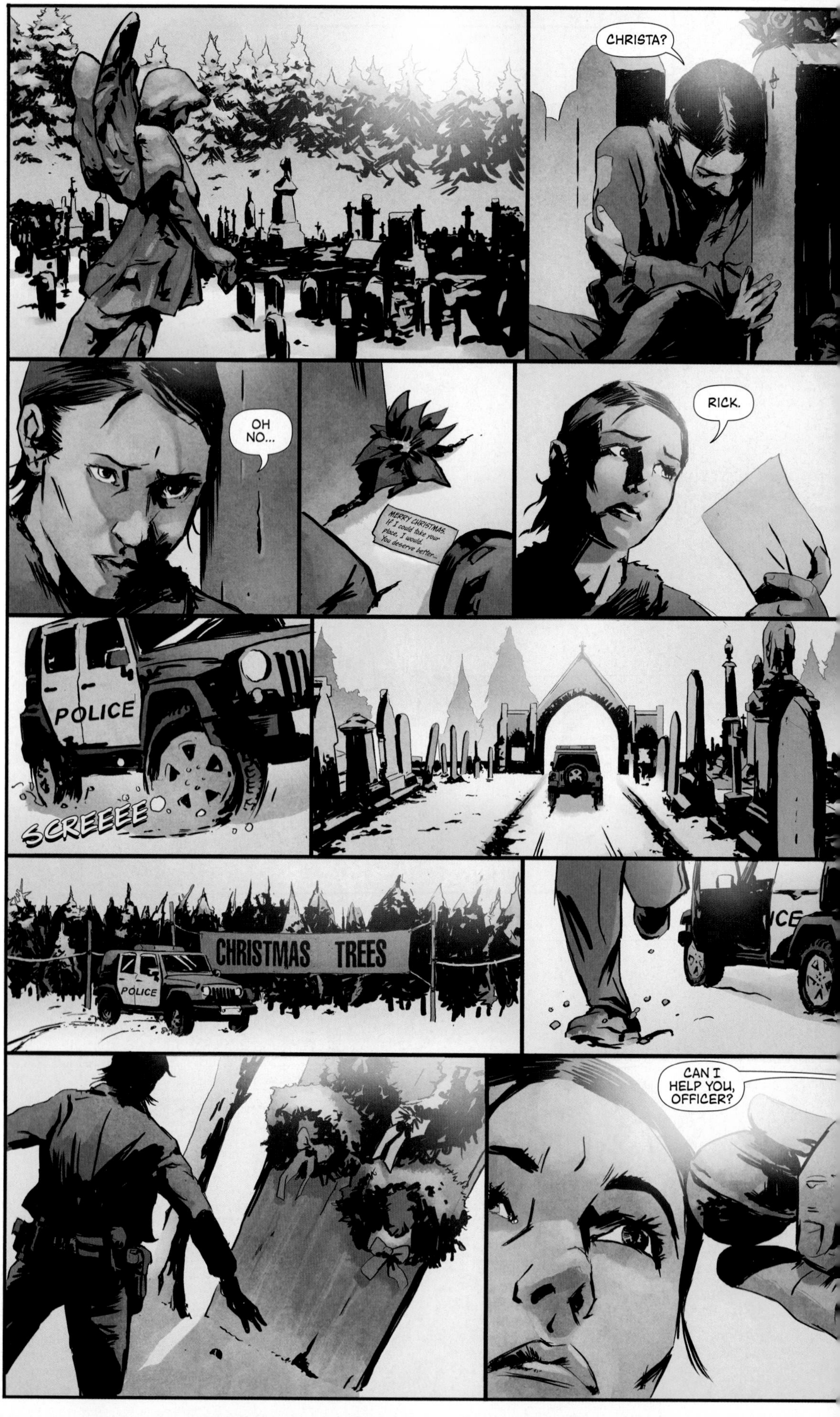
CHRISTA?
OH NO...
MERRY CHRISTMAS. If I could take your place, I would. You deserve better...
RICK.
POLICE
SCREEEEE
CHRISTMAS TREES
POLICE
CAN I HELP YOU, OFFICER?

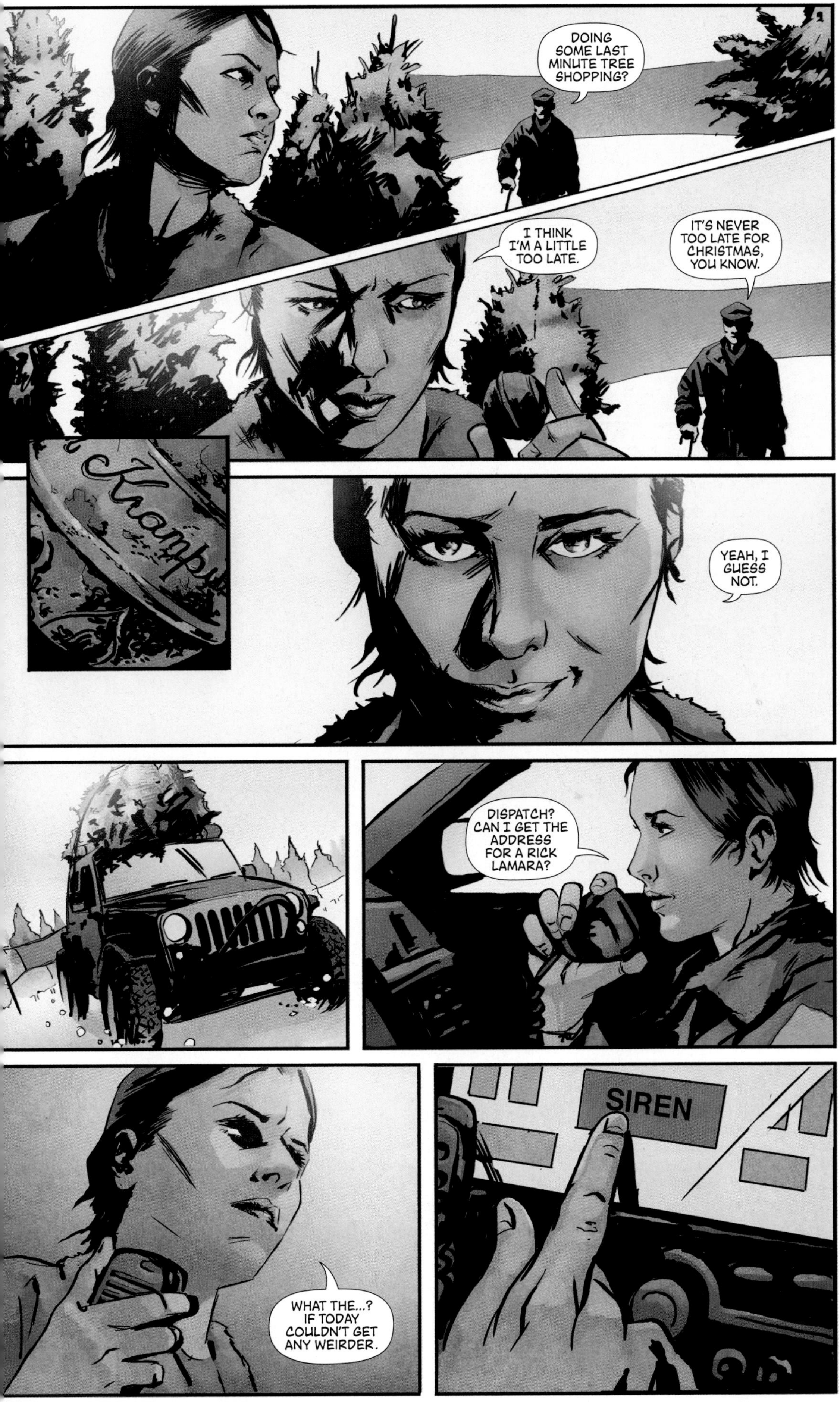
DOING SOME LAST MINUTE TREE SHOPPING?
I THINK I'M A LITTLE TOO LATE.
IT'S NEVER TOO LATE FOR CHRISTMAS, YOU KNOW.
Krampus
YEAH, I GUESS NOT.
DISPATCH? CAN I GET THE ADDRESS FOR A RICK LAMARA?
WHAT THE...? IF TODAY COULDN'T GET ANY WEIRDER.
SIREN

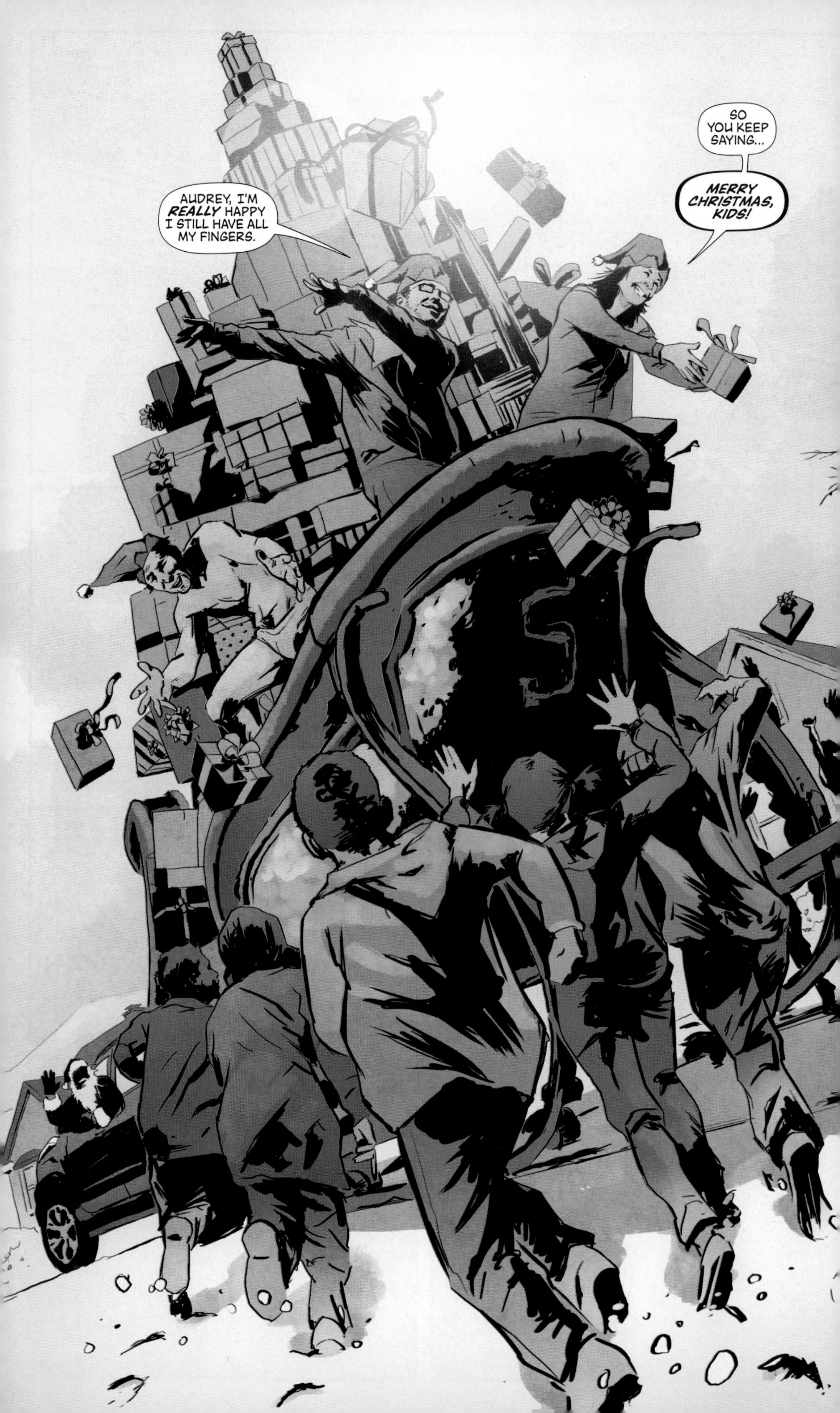
AUDREY, I'M *REALLY* HAPPY I STILL HAVE ALL MY FINGERS.
SO YOU KEEP SAYING...
MERRY CHRISTMAS, KIDS!

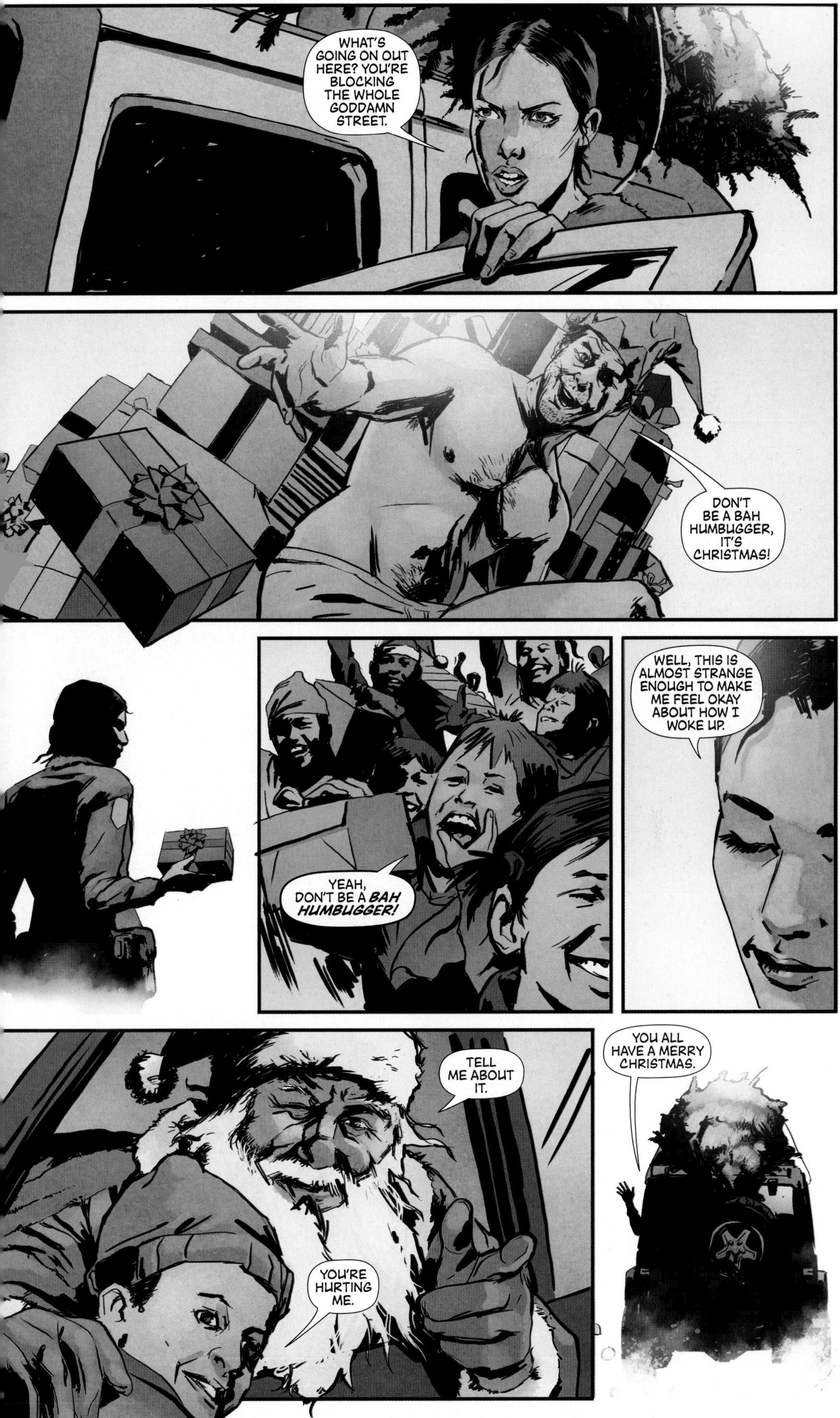
WHAT'S GOING ON OUT HERE? YOU'RE BLOCKING THE WHOLE GODDAMN STREET.
DON'T BE A BAH HUMBUGGER, IT'S CHRISTMAS!
YEAH, DON'T BE A *BAH HUMBUGGER!*
WELL, THIS IS ALMOST STRANGE ENOUGH TO MAKE ME FEEL OKAY ABOUT HOW I WOKE UP.
TELL ME ABOUT IT.
YOU'RE HURTING ME.
YOU ALL HAVE A MERRY CHRISTMAS.

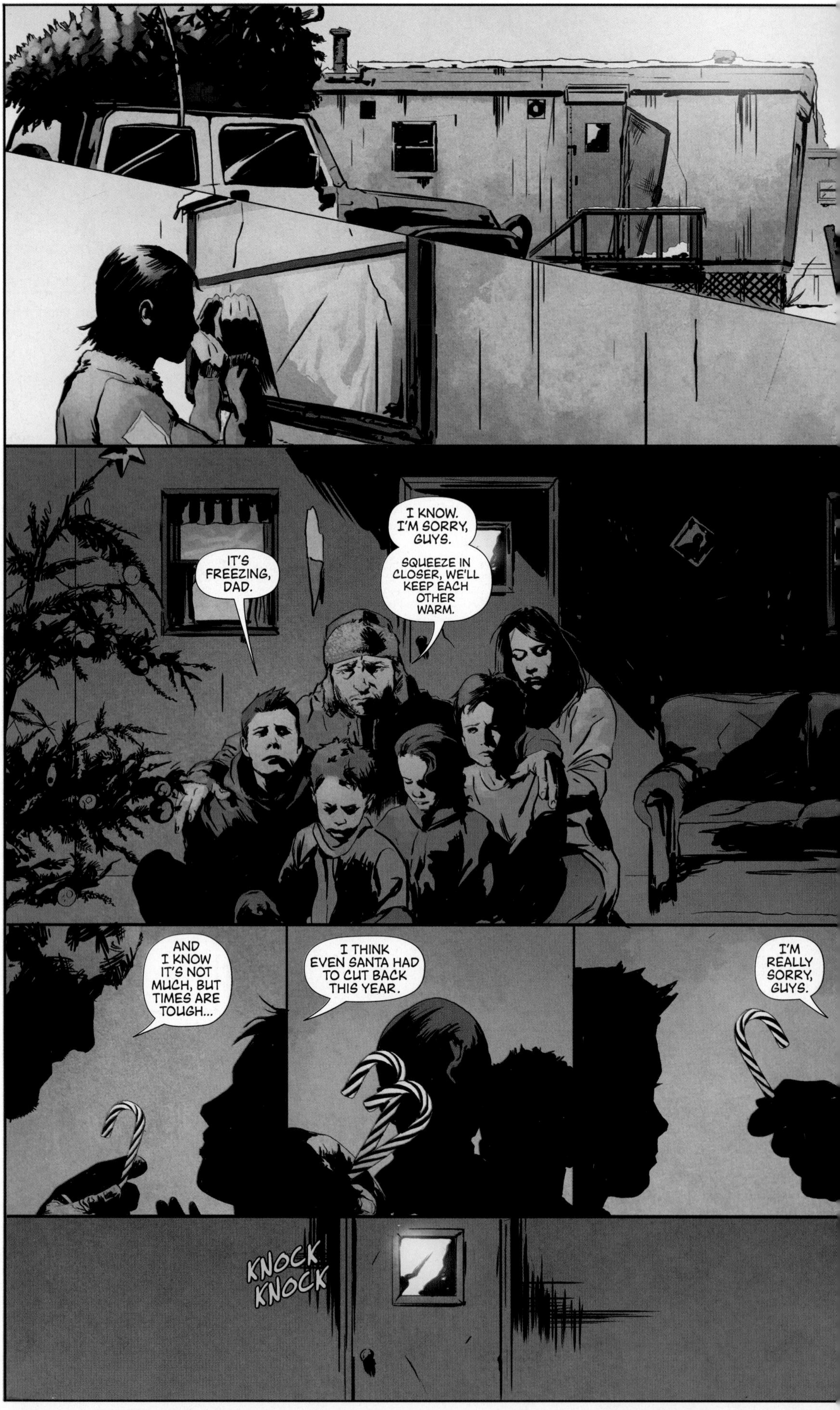
IT'S FREEZING, DAD.
I KNOW. I'M SORRY, GUYS.
SQUEEZE IN CLOSER, WE'LL KEEP EACH OTHER WARM.
AND I KNOW IT'S NOT MUCH, BUT TIMES ARE TOUGH...
I THINK EVEN SANTA HAD TO CUT BACK THIS YEAR.
I'M REALLY SORRY, GUYS.
KNOCK KNOCK

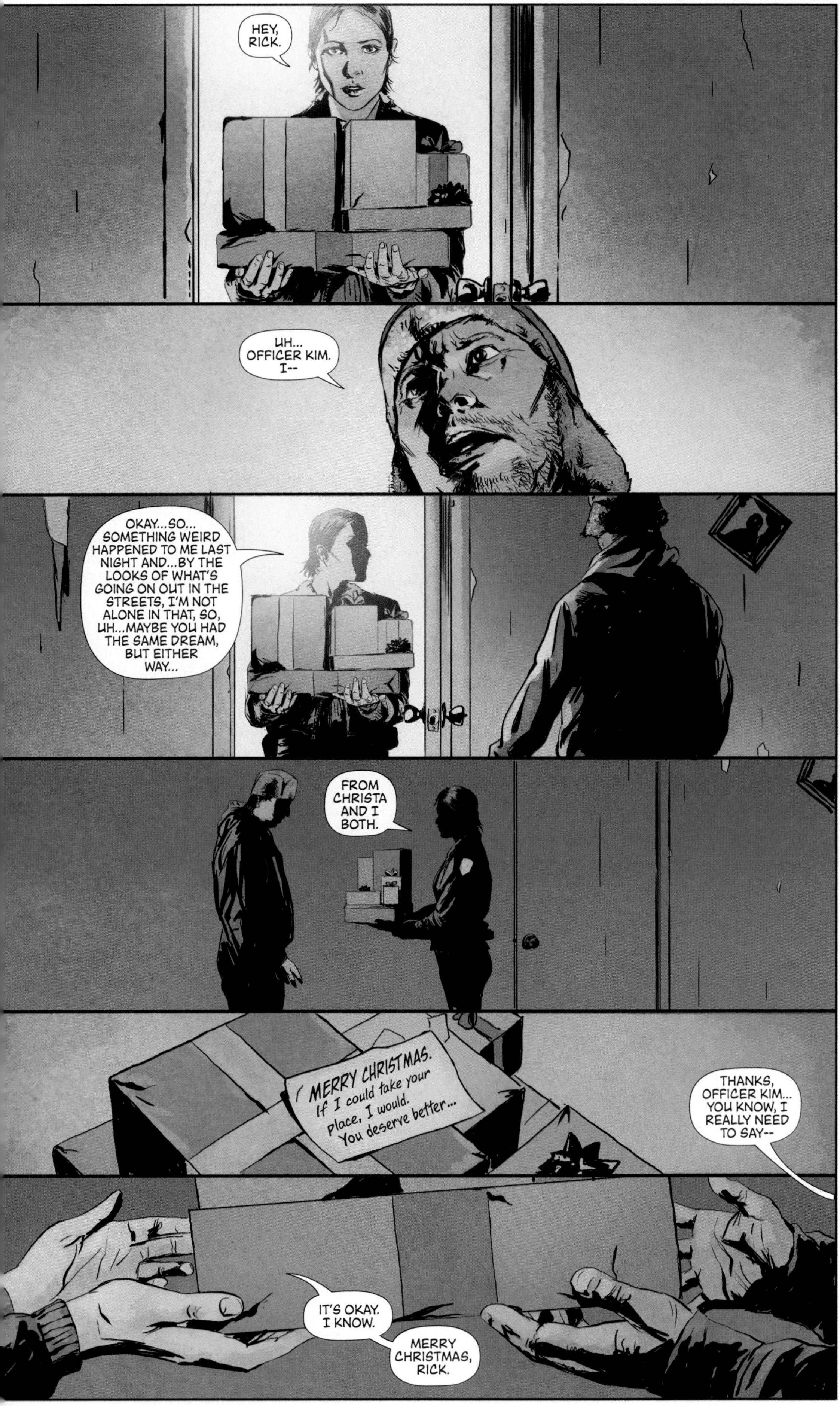
HEY, RICK.
UH... OFFICER KIM. I--
OKAY...SO... SOMETHING WEIRD HAPPENED TO ME LAST NIGHT AND...BY THE LOOKS OF WHAT'S GOING ON OUT IN THE STREETS, I'M NOT ALONE IN THAT, SO, UH...MAYBE YOU HAD THE SAME DREAM, BUT EITHER WAY...
FROM CHRISTA AND I BOTH.
MERRY CHRISTMAS. If I could take your place, I would. You deserve better...
THANKS, OFFICER KIM... YOU KNOW, I REALLY NEED TO SAY--
IT'S OKAY. I KNOW.
MERRY CHRISTMAS, RICK.

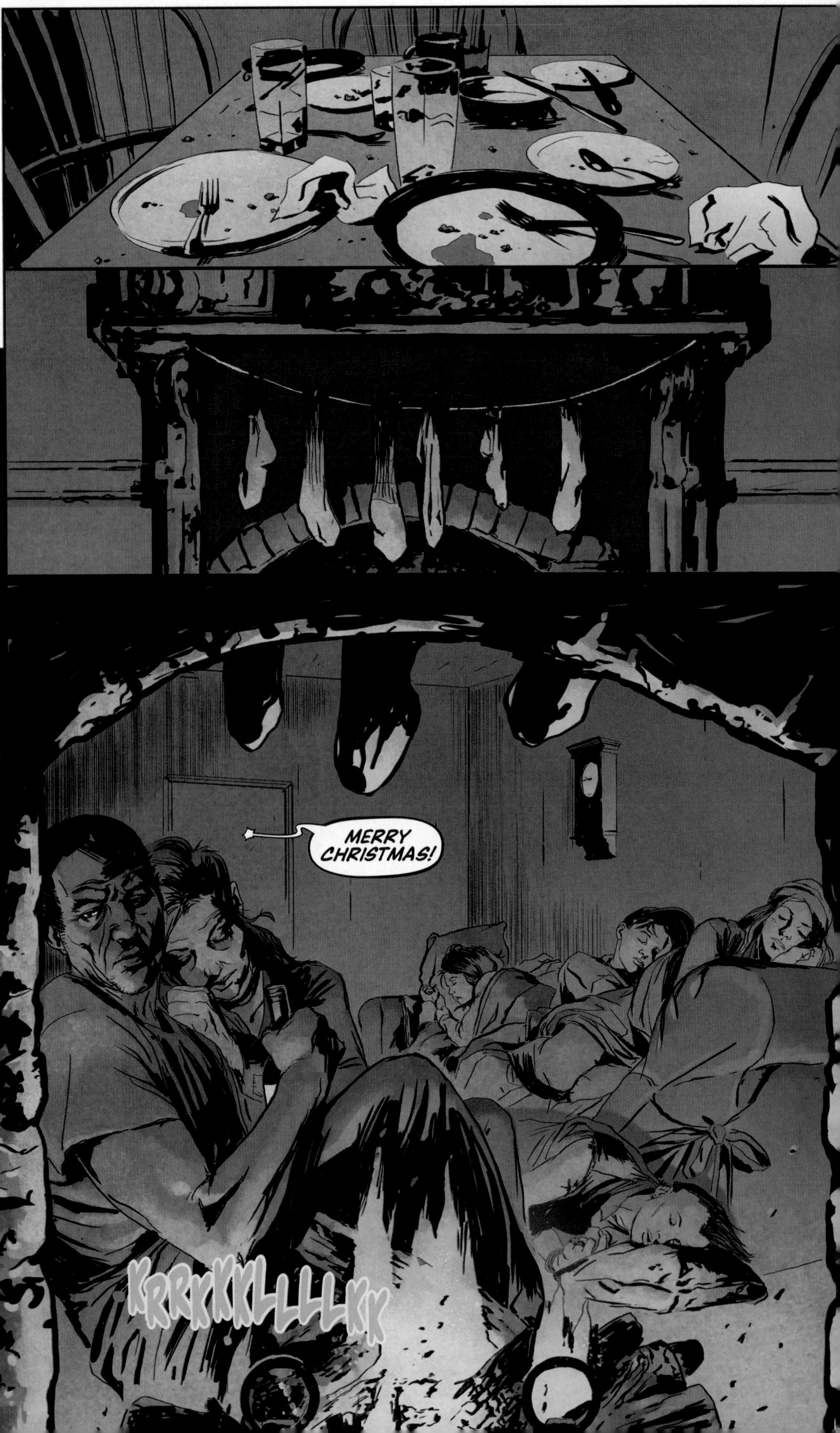
MERRY CHRISTMAS!
KRRKKKLLLLKK

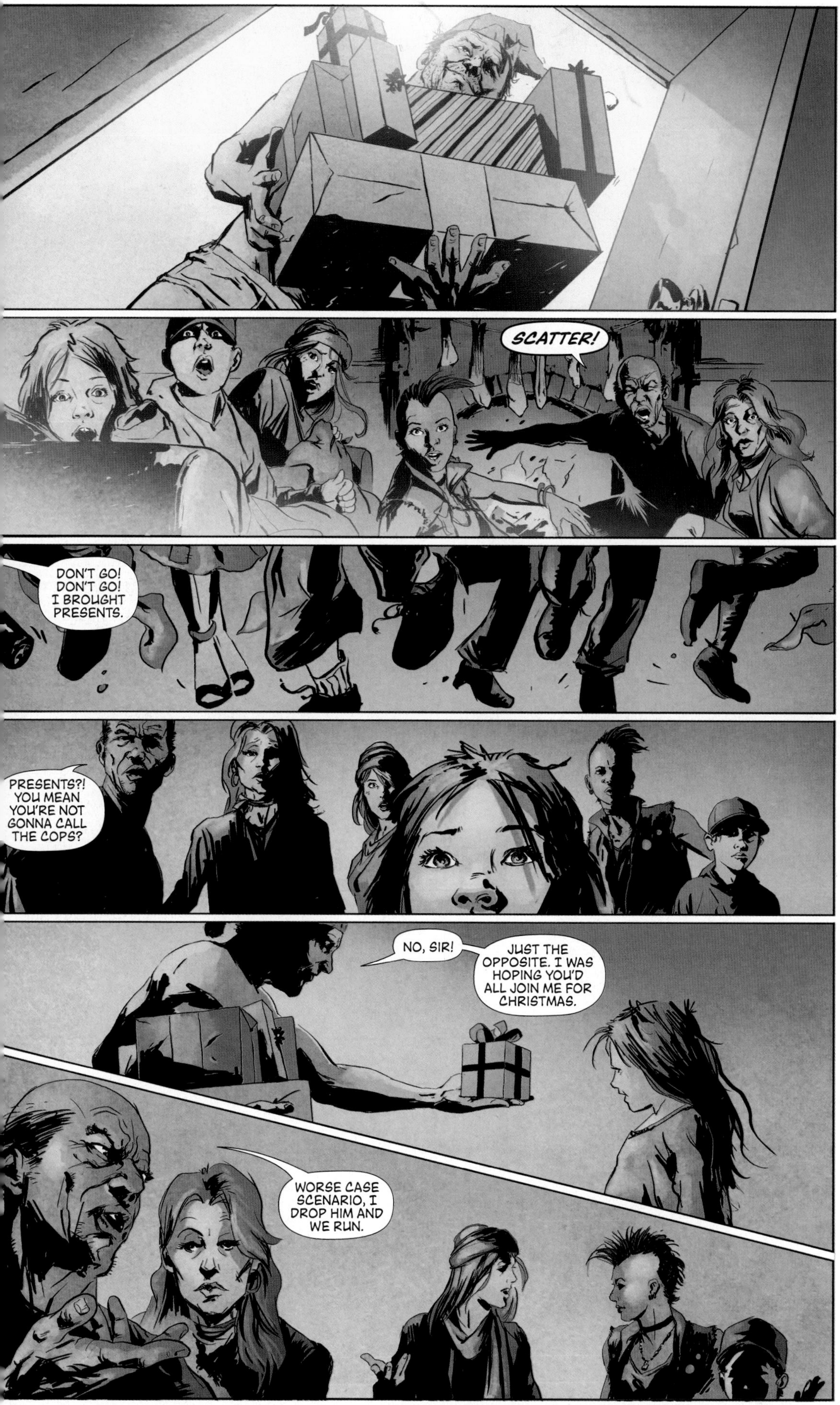
SCATTER!
DON'T GO! DON'T GO! I BROUGHT PRESENTS.
PRESENTS?! YOU MEAN YOU'RE NOT GONNA CALL THE COPS?
NO, SIR!
JUST THE OPPOSITE. I WAS HOPING YOU'D ALL JOIN ME FOR CHRISTMAS.
WORSE CASE SCENARIO, I DROP HIM AND WE RUN.

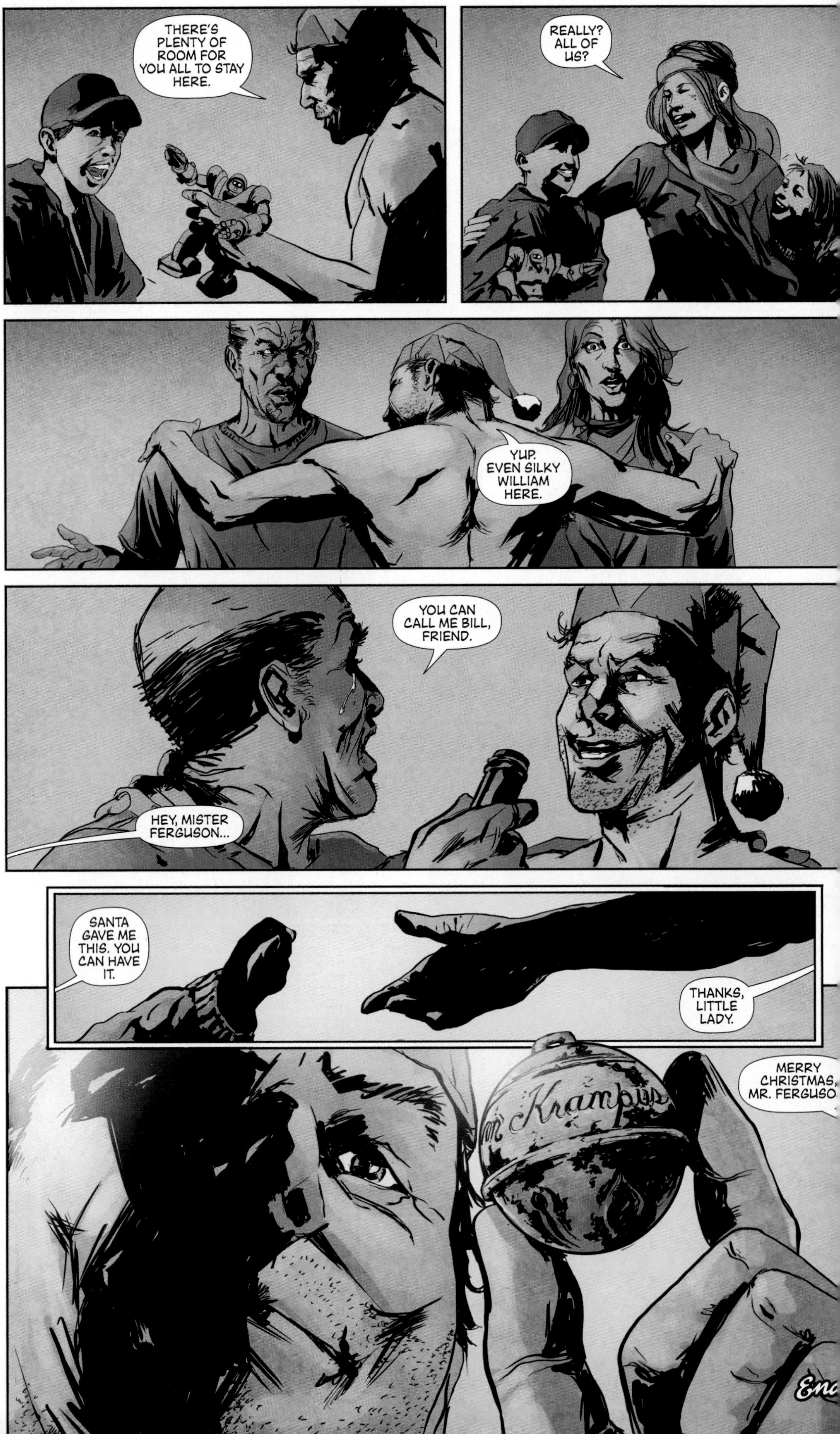
THERE'S PLENTY OF ROOM FOR YOU ALL TO STAY HERE.
REALLY? ALL OF US?
YUP. EVEN SILKY WILLIAM HERE.
YOU CAN CALL ME BILL, FRIEND.
HEY, MISTER FERGUSON...
SANTA GAVE ME THIS. YOU CAN HAVE IT.
THANKS, LITTLE LADY.
Krampus
MERRY CHRISTMAS, MR. FERGUSO

STOCKING STUFFERS

One of the great pleasures of creating comic books is seeing an artist bring a story to life. From the first sketch, to the penciled page, to inks and colors, every step of the process is a little gift for the creative team.

With *Krampus: Shadow of Saint Nicholas* we were able to assemble some amazing artistic talent, many of whom are well known for their work in the genre of horror comics. One of those individuals is Maan House, who in addition to having a very cool name, was the perfect artist to visualize the twisted tale of Sandy and Rick because of his unique blend of stark blacks, eastern influences, and quality character renderings.

Like many of the artists, Maan, in addition to making original characters, was tasked with coming up with his interpretation of the creature designs from the movie. Over the next few pages you'll get a look at Maan's sketches as he brought the movie world of Krampus into the world of comic books.

Robert Napton, *editor*

SKETCHBOOK

CHARACTER DESIGNS BY
MAAN HOUSE

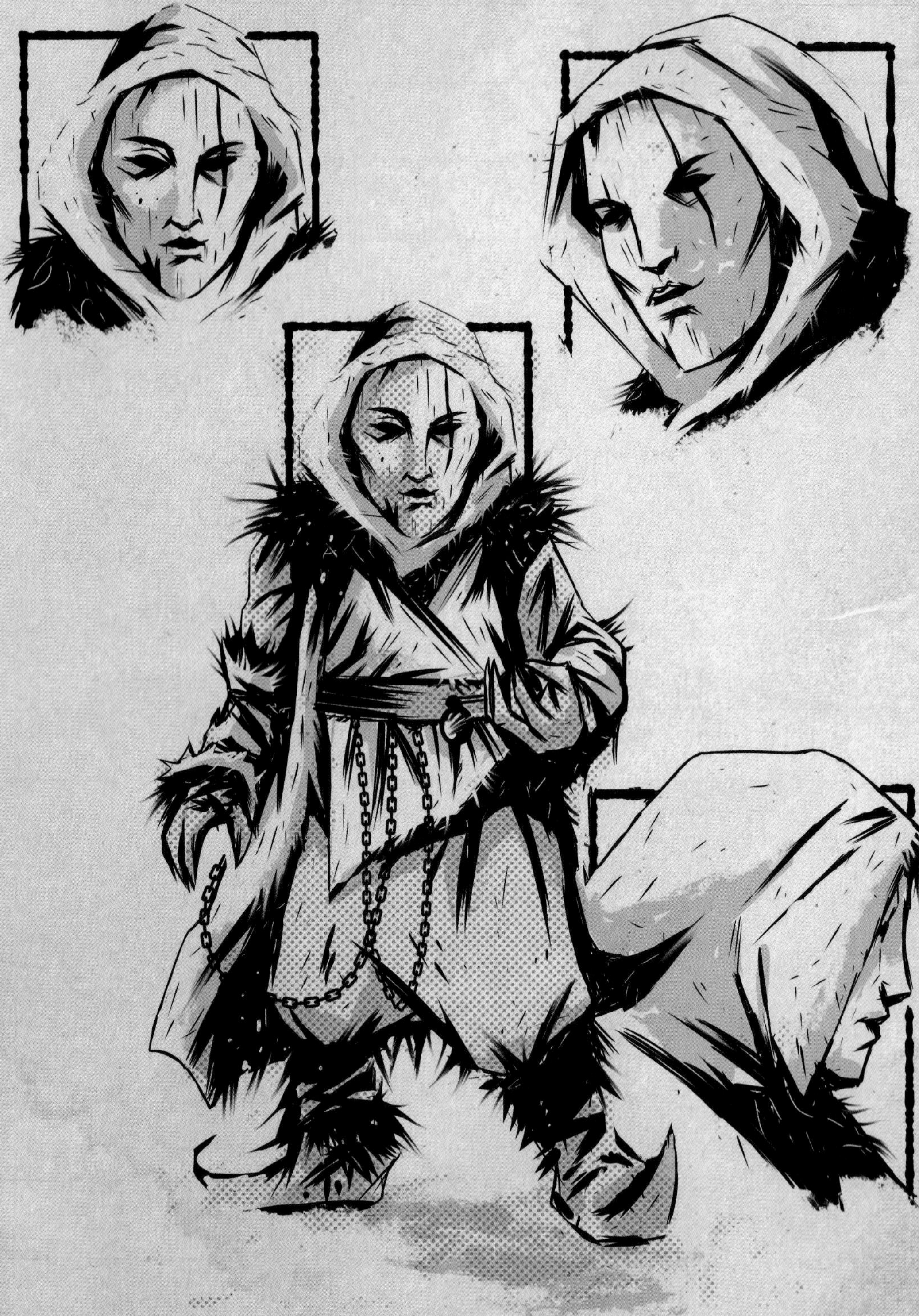

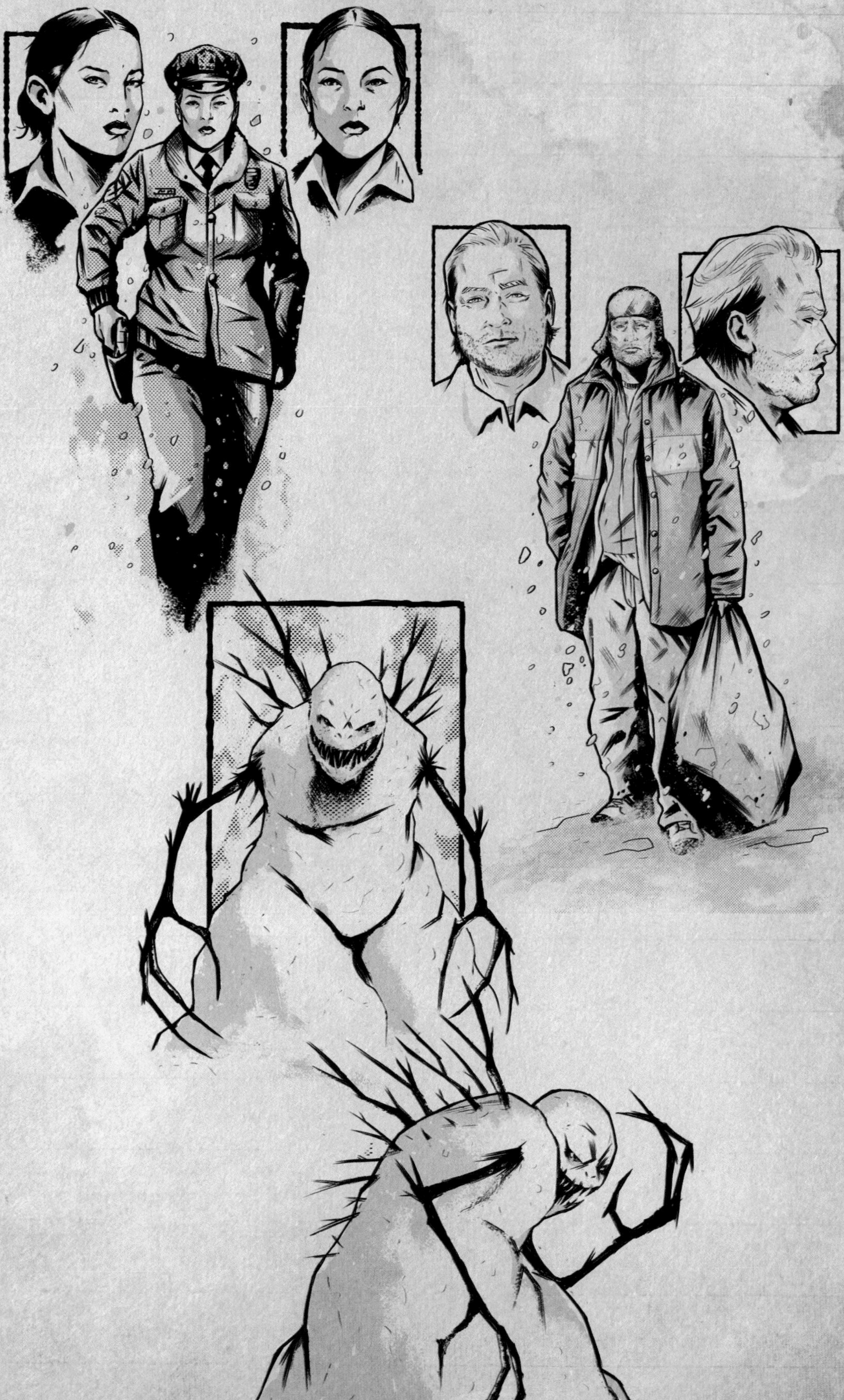

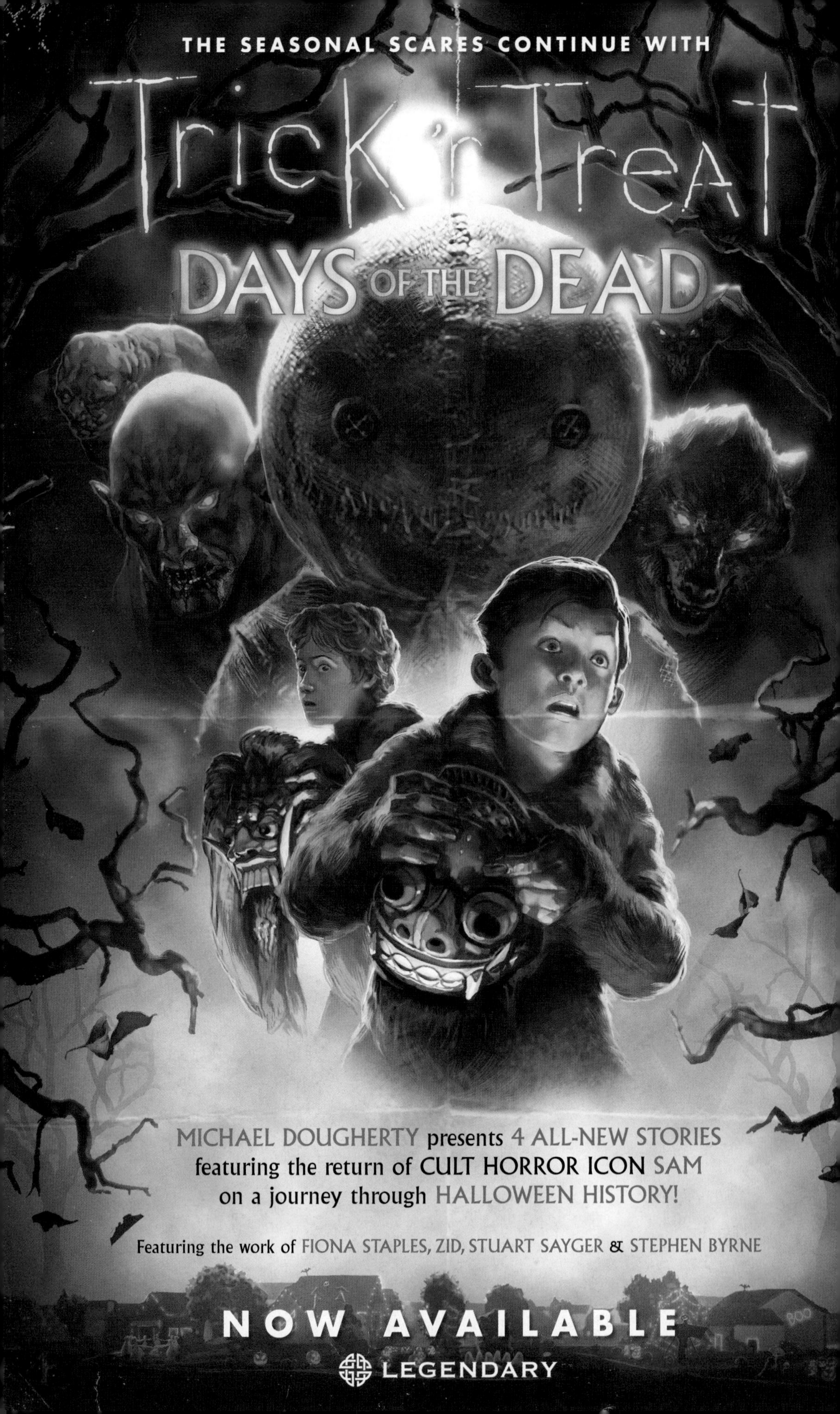
THE SEASONAL SCARES CONTINUE WITH
Trick 'r Treat
DAYS OF THE DEAD
MICHAEL DOUGHERTY presents 4 ALL-NEW STORIES
featuring the return of CULT HORROR ICON SAM
on a journey through HALLOWEEN HISTORY!
Featuring the work of FIONA STAPLES, ZID, STUART SAYGER & STEPHEN BYRNE
NOW AVAILABLE
LEGENDARY